K for Köchel

The Life and Work of Ludwig Ritter von Köchel, Cataloguer of Mozart

Thomas Edmund Konrad

The Scarecrow Press, Inc.
Lanham, Maryland, and London
2001

SCARECROW PRESS, INC.

Published in the United States of America
by Scarecrow Press, Inc.
4720 Boston Way, Lanham, Maryland 20706
www.scarecrowpress.com

4 Pleydell Gardens, Folkestone
Kent CT20 2DN, England

British Cataloguing-in-Publication Information Available

Library of Congress Cataloging-in-Publication Data

Konrad, Thomas Edmund, 1928–
    [Weltberühmt, doch unbekannt. English]
    K for Köchel : the life and work of Ludwig Ritter von Köchel, cataloguer of Mozart / Thomas Edmund Konrad.
        p. cm.
    Includes bibliographical references (p.) and index.
    ISBN 0-8108-3939-3 (alk. paper)
    1. Kèchel, Ludwig, Ritter von, 1800–1877. 2. Musicologists—Austria—Biography. I. Title.
ML423.K725 K6613 2001
780'.92—dc21
    [B]   00-061949

♾™ The paper used in this publication meets the minimum requirements of American National Standard for Information Sciences—Permanence of Paper for Printed Library Materials, ANSI/NISO Z39.48-1992.
Manufactured in the United States of America.

Contents

Acknowledgments   vii

Part I: His Life

1   Köchel's Destiny   3

2   The Day of Decision   8

3   Köchel's Ancestry   13

4   The Three Stages of Köchel's Life   17

5   Learning and Teaching   20

6   Köchel's Romance   24

7   In the Service of Archduke Karl   33

8   Reward for Services Rendered   41

9   Köchel in Great Britain   47

10 Scientific Activities   57

11 Final Journey   66

12 Last Will and Testament   71

13 The Memorial Plaque on the Wrong House   79

14 Köchel and Mozart   87

15 Köchel as Others Saw Him   94

16   Nineteenth-Century Man   104

17   Remaining Mysteries Surrounding
     Köchel's Life   109

Part II: His Work

18   The Writer   117

19   The Poet   126

20   The Composer   143

21   The Botanist   149

22   The Mineralogist   154

23   Köchel and the Beethoven Letters   159

24   Johann Joseph Fux: The Second
     "Köchel Register"   166

25   Music at the Imperial Court   176

Part III: The *Köchelverzeichnis*

26   The Starting Point   183

27   Köchel's Detective Work in Tracing and
     Authenticating Mozart's Compositions   193

28   The Thematic Order of Mozart's Works   199

29   The Chronological Order of Mozart's Works   204

30   The "Wiegenlied" and Other "Spurious"
     Compositions   216

31   The Appendix   223

32   The Mystery Surrounding Mozart's Requiem   228

33   Köchel as Motivator of the First "Complete
     Mozart Edition"   236

34   The *Köchelverzeichnis* after Köchel's Death   241

Appendix A: Chronological List of Books and
          Articles by Ludwig Ritter von Köchel   257

Appendix B: Mozart's Compositions as
          First Published in Köchel's
          Register in 1862   259

Bibliography   275

Index   281

About the Author   291

Acknowledgments

It would have been impossible to write this book without the assistance of a number of institutions and individuals, who provided old papers, documents, books, articles, anecdotes, and much more. I wish to thank all of them for their generous help and to acknowledge the great importance of this in aiding my endeavor.

Of libraries, first mention must go to the British Library in its old setting in the British Museum, and in particular to Robert Parker and his colleagues in the Music Reading Area. Other libraries that assisted me were the Central Music Library in Westminster; the Swiss Cottage Library in Camden Town; the library of the Austrian Cultural Institute, all in London; the Library of the Mozarteum in Salzburg and in particular Dr. Johanna Senigl; the Austrian National Library in Vienna; and the University Library in Salzburg.

Archive material was provided by, among others, the Royal Archives in Windsor Castle, England; the Konsistorialarchiv, the Landesregierung, and the Mozarteum archives, all in Salzburg; the Austrian State Archives; the Austrian Adelsarchiv; the archives of the University; the Stadt- and Landesarchiv; and, foremost, the Gesellschaft der Musikfreunde (archive director, Dr. Otto Biba), all in Vienna; the state archives of the former East Germany in Leipzig; and the Hungarian State Archives (Országos Levéltár) in Budapest.

Great help was provided by two abbeys in Austria: the Benediktiner-Stift Göttweig and particularly Dr. Friedrich W. Riedel, director of its archives, and custodian Dr. Gregor Lechner OSB; and the Stift Kremsmünster and particularly Dr. P. Alfons Mandorfer, who is in charge of its music department.

The publishing firm Breitkopf & Härtel in Wiesbaden, Germany; the Botanics section of the Biology center of the OÖ Landesmuseum in Linz and its departmental leader, Dozent F. Speta; and Neal Zaslaw, Herbert Gussman Professor at Cornell University, Ithaca, New York, who is now in charge of the latest revision of the *Köchelverzeichnis*, all furnished invaluable material and advice for the book.

In Krems and Stein, Austria, where much of my research took place, I must first mention Dr. Ernst Englisch, director of archives of the magistrate, who gave much of his time to help locate old papers and illustrations and other concealed facts, coupled with most helpful advice, without which much of what follows here would not have emerged. He was the most able and willing helper of my project, and my very special thanks go to him.

Other persons who helped in Krems were the grammar school (Gymnasium) professors Dr. Engelbrecht, Schlichtinger, Sohm, and Musiol-Sollinger as well as Suzanne Bruckner and local historian Dr. Gerd Maroli.

Elsewhere I received assistance from Sir Hugh Wontner, GBE, CVO, Claridges, London; the Austrian Steamship Company (Erste Donau Dampfschiffahrts-Gesellschaft); Charlotte Marshall in Wilton, Connecticut; George Szirtes; Robert Burford Judge; Ruth Waterman; Leslie Howard; Richard White; and many, many others.

Finally, it is a pleasure to thank all my personal friends and my family, especially my wife, Jutka, who for the past six years has "köchelled" with me, morning till night, who accompanied me on all my journeys, and who gave my project her diligent and loving support even when, at times, I was downhearted and frustrated and must have been bad company.

Again, thanks to you all!

I
HIS LIFE

1
Köchel's Destiny

Every day in thousands of concert halls and opera houses throughout the world and over the airwaves of radio stations, some of the 626 listed works by Mozart are performed. And every time such a performance is announced the letter K will appear, followed by a number, to identify the work in question. Yet if you ask any music lover, as I have been doing for some time, what the letter K stands for, at best you get the name behind it: Köchel. In my experience, perhaps seven out of ten regular concertgoers or opera fans are familiar with this name.

Ask the next question: Why Köchel? The chances are you get no worthwhile response at all. Who was Köchel? What was his full name? Where and when did he live? In what way is his name connected with those Mozart compositions? Has he done anything else? None of the people I asked knew the answer to any of these questions, and, indeed, to be frank, until my own curiosity was aroused some time ago, I would have done equally poorly if anyone had asked me. Even if someone took the trouble to check in general and specialized textbooks, the entries are brief and sometimes contradictory. Moreover, it became obvious to me that they just copied from one another because the same mistakes in one encyclopedia were repeated in another.

When I started to look into this man's life and work, I found to my amazement that while no biography had ever appeared on Ludwig von Köchel, a handful of articles were printed in various musical publications, usually in connection with a Mozart anniversary date or sometimes on a Köchel anniversary.

The main achievement for which Köchel is known is the *Register* in thematic and chronological order of all Mozart's compositions, completed and published in 1862. Some twelve years were spent on this task, and it must be stated right here that no one commissioned Köchel to undertake this work, and no one paid him for doing it. On the contrary, he spent a considerable fortune in pursuance of the task, and he had to travel widely to trace original manuscripts and to follow up any lead that presented itself. The question is, why did he do it?

The more I looked at the background leading to this labor of love, the more I became convinced that Köchel was almost predestined to undertake this task. There appears to have been a link between Mozart and Köchel in spite of the fact that Köchel was born more than eight years after Mozart's death. Recent research by the Austrian historian Dr. Gerd Maroli shows that Mozart's maternal grandmother, Eva Rosin (Barbara) Pertl, née Altmann, lived in Stein, the town of Köchel's birth. Her second marriage was to Wolfgang (!) Nikolaus Pertl, who came from St. Gilgen on the Wolfgangsee. Out of this wedlock a daughter, Maria Anna Pertl, was born, and she married Leopold Mozart, Wolfgang's father. Although this was at a time when Köchel's ancestors had not yet moved to Stein, it is most likely that the fact of Mozart's grandmother having lived there must have been known to Köchel's father who, as will be seen, was an ardent Mozart fan.

It is also known that Leopold Mozart was "Vizekapellmeister"— that is, assistant conductor of the Court Orchestra in Salzburg at the same time when Köchel's maternal grandfather Johann Franz Stain (1687–1743) was garrison commander of Burg Hohensalzburg, the castle of Salzburg. Given the limited scope of social contact in this period, the two men most likely knew each other, a theory expressed by Heinz Schöny, who devoted considerable time to researching the genealogy of Köchel.

The house in which the Köchel family lived in Stein and which for a long time was wrongly supposed to be the house in which Ludwig Köchel was born (and which, therefore, wrongly carries a memorial plaque to this effect) was known for its musical activity. Young Ludwig had ample opportunity to listen to good music from an early age and in particular to his father's favorite composer, Mozart; it is indeed likely that Ludwig on the cello joined in when string quartets and other chamber works were played at the house.

Köchel's ability as a performing musician has been questioned by some musicologists who criticized his work. It has even been questioned by some whether he played any instrument at all. Dr. Anton Kerschbaumer tells us in an article written in 1906 that he attended a musical "soirée" in the house of Baron Eduard von Sacken in 1860, where Köchel played the cello part in a string quartet. The adjective used for his playing is *meisterhaft*, meaning "masterly" or "brilliant."

Eduard Melly, a nineteenth-century Austrian historian, reports that Köchel's father, in conjunction with District Commander Baron Stiebar, organized the first ever Mozart Festival. The likely date of this event was 1816. No accurate records remain, but it is thought that the timing of the festival must have been a notable anniversary year, and experts rule out 1806 (fiftieth birthday year) as at that time Stein/Krems was still under (Napoleonic) French occupation. The next likely date therefore is 1816, the sixtieth birthday and twenty-fifth death anniversary. Also, because Köchel's father died in 1820, a date later than 1816 is not feasible.

Ludwig would have been sixteen at the time, a most impressionable age. Parallel to his general studies at the Kremser Piaristengymnasium (grammar school), he frequently visited nearby Stift Göttweig. This abbey was well known then, as it is now, for its musical activity, for its devotion to all types of music that were practiced and taught there. I am privileged to have visited the music archives of this Stift where thousands and thousands of original manuscripts and first editions are stored, a veritable Aladdin's cave for anyone interested in music. Young Ludwig must have been most impressed by what he saw there, and again, we must assume that he became even more familiar with the music of Mozart, which was held in great esteem at the Abbey.

It will be seen that Köchel in mature years returns to Göttweig to catalog, as part of his musicological activity, the many manuscripts by the Austrian baroque composer and principal Court Conductor Johann Joseph (or Josef) Fux (1660–1741) that were in the abbey.

The idea of the "Mozart Register" probably existed in Köchel's mind long before he found the time to undertake the work. His training and discipline made him unquestionably and eminently suitable for the task. The actual trigger to commence the work was a study by his friend Franz Lorenz entitled "In Sachen Mozarts" (Matters Concerning Mozart), published in 1851, which highlighted the chaos surrounding Mozart's compositions. Just then Köchel found himself with time on his hands, having been appointed regional school inspector in Salzburg in 1850, a job he held for only two years. Salzburg was the scene for many years of Mozart's musical activity, particularly in his younger years, and it is this period that is the most chaotic regarding the listing of his works. The compositions after 1784 were cataloged by Mozart himself, thus making Köchel's task of listing the later works much easier, but the early compositions caused major problems.

If it was Mozart's destiny to die young and to be buried in a pauper's grave, if it took many years following his death for his true genius to be recognized again, Köchel's destiny was that although his work gave us the basis to understand Mozart's musical activity, he himself remained a stranger, an unknown person, a name without personality. Let me prove this by the following two examples.

A few years ago I visited the present school inspector in Salzburg in quest of material relating to Köchel's activity in the same position. I put my questions to Herr Magister Gerhard Schäffer and found not only that he was ignorant of the fact that Ludwig von Köchel had been a predecessor of his in the job but also that he was not at all sure who this man Köchel was!

The other incident took place in an elegant bookshop in Salzburg where I made inquiries about a first edition of the *Köchelverzeichnis*. The young assistant said, "You mean the cookery book?" (*Koch* means "chef" in German!) I suggested to him that he must be joking, and he produced a glossy little book entitled *Köchel Verzeichnis* that summarizes recipes of local dishes from the eighteenth century. And this was the only *Köchel Register* this bookseller had ever heard of!

When I began to collect material for this book, I could not know how much I would find. I was also unsure as to how to tackle the subject. On the one hand, I had the intention of producing a "serious" textbook from which the student of Mozart could for the first time learn all he needed to know about the man who "organized" his work. But I also wanted to provide a "readable" book for the music lover, for the people who fill the auditoria of opera houses and concert halls nightly or listen to recordings, tapes, and CDs at home and who may have been wondering at times about the identity of the mysterious *K* or the grossly mispronounced name, Köchel.

I cannot do better in seeking a compromise between these two extreme aims than to adopt a quotation of Mozart's about some new piano concertos he had written. In a letter to his father he described them as "an in-between of 'too difficult' and 'too easy' . . . here and there to afford satisfaction to the connoisseur, but in such a way that the dilettanti must be satisfied without knowing why!"

2

The Day of Decision

There are a few great days in history, days that most people have learned about in their schooldays or remembered in later life because of the effect the particular event had on them. Such days are, for instance, Christmas Day, the Ides of March, the day on which World War II commenced, or the one on which President John F. Kennedy was assassinated.

Musical history has its own great days. I am thinking of the birth date of noted composers or of the creation or first performances of major works. But there is one such day that, in spite of its significance to the world of music, cannot be accurately defined. We know the year: it was 1851. Detailed research might take us nearer to the actual date, and maybe this is something that ought to be done. For the moment let me try to describe the events of the day, as I see them.

Fifty-one-year-old Ludwig Köchel received an unexpected package. The sender was his friend, medical doctor Franz Lorenz of Wienerneustadt. Köchel lived in Salzburg at the time, staying with his friend Scharschmid, president of the local law court, and his family.

When opened, the package revealed a small pamphlet, privately printed (probably at the author's own expense), and circulated among his friends and others whom he thought might be interested in what he had to say. The title of the booklet, which consisted of twenty-six printed pages, was "In Sachen Mozarts" (i.e., Regarding Matters of Mozart).

Köchel started reading, and almost from the first page, he was in a state of thrill and excitement that did not abate, not while he was reading his friend's message, nor afterward, when he started to think about the contents of the booklet. In the event, the excitement was to carry him through the next eleven years of his life, and the end result is known to us all, the creation of the Mozart Register, the *Köchelverzeichnis*, one of the cornerstones of musical history.

Lorenz set out to prove that, unless something was done almost immediately, the vast treasure of Mozart's compositions could be lost to posterity. Manuscripts were scattered all over the world, many already lost, others no longer securely identifiable, and their numbers shrinking each day. (All this will be explained in a later chapter.) The final aim, explained Lorenz, should be the creation of a Mozart "Gesamtausgabe"—that is, a complete edition of all compositions—but the present state of affairs gave him no hope that this was a feasible project. He pointed out that barely a third of Mozart's compositions had appeared in print, the most secure method of saving them for posterity, whereas roughly one-sixth of them were in a warehouse, concealed from the music-loving public and endangered by the possibility of fire. He concluded by challenging a "younger man," any young man, to come forward and devote himself to the task of finding what is now so nearly lost, to assemble what is still available and to search for what is known to have existed, but what already belongs to the growing list of lost compositions.

Who was this Lorenz? Why should a medical doctor be so concerned about a matter belonging more to the domain of musicologists or musicians? I have looked at what is known about this man and found that he was born in the same town as Köchel (Stein an der Donau), on 4 April 1805, five years after Köchel; he was a student at the Piaristengymnasium in Krems, the same school as Köchel. Their friendship is thus likely to have commenced at this early time when they were both students, yet another piece in the jigsaw of Köchel's destiny. And if this coincidence of a shared birthplace and of studies in the same institute is not sufficient, it must also be taken into account that the place where Köchel received this extraordinary pamphlet was Salzburg, Mozart's birthplace and a city where the very air exuded the spirit of the composer. No wonder that the pamphlet had such a compelling effect on Köchel!

Lorenz moved to Vienna in 1822, and his studies were first in the field of old literature and art. Although for practical reasons he later switched to medicine, he never abandoned his love for the arts. He gained his medical degree in 1831 and started practicing in Wienerneustadt. Later, he held an appointment as house doctor at the "Stift" (abbey) Lilienfeld; then, for a few years, he earned his living as translator and traveling doctor in Italy and other countries, but in 1847 he returned to Wienerneustadt. Throughout his life he devoted much time to writing, and many of his studies and articles appeared in private editions, newspapers, and periodicals. Most of these were on musical subjects. Here are a few titles:

"Haydn, Mozart und Beethoven's Kirchenmusik und ihre katholischen und protestantischen Gegner" (1866) (The Church Music by Haydn, Mozart and Beethoven and Their Catholic and Protestant Opponents)
"Mozart's Requiem" (1861, Deutsche Musikzeitung) (Concerning Mozart's Requiem)
"Mozart's zweihändige Klaviersonaten" (1862) (Mozart's Piano Sonatas for Two Hands)
"Geheimgeschichte des Mozart'schen Requiems" (1862) (The Secret History of the Mozart Requiem)
"Mozart's Messen" (Mozart's Masses)
"Mozart's Tod" (1850, Wiener Zeitung) (Mozart's Death)

Köchel's thrill and excitement in reading the pages of the pamphlet were unbounded. An admirer of Mozart's music since earliest childhood, he had often tossed similar ideas around his head, without coming to any conclusion. He knew that every word he was reading here was true, and this fact almost burned a fiery path in his brain.

He was reading passage after passage again and again; he was reading them aloud, although he was alone in his room. "A younger man. . . . Someone with sufficient musical knowledge . . . an organized mind . . . someone with time, sufficient funds and total devotion. . . ."

"Is there such a one?" he wondered.

He knew that he himself was capable of the work, that he had the time and the money; he knew that he possessed all other attributes needed for a successful conclusion of the task; all, except one: youth. At over fifty in the middle of the nineteenth century, a man was well past his prime, or, to put it more directly, he was "old."

Here was a dilemma. He was bursting to undertake the task yet unwilling to start on something that he might not be able to complete. He went to his mirror and stared at the image this revealed. The face that looked back at him was not exactly young, but it was keen; the eyes still retained their penetrating quality, and intelligence radiated from every feature of the smooth-shaven face. His health was good: he had always been an active man, a lover of nature. His studies in botany and mineralogy had taken him up mountains and into valleys, and he often camped out during such excursions. He was tough for his age. Even so, he found it difficult to make a decision that would commit him to a task of such magnitude.

He needed help and advice. In the evening, he put the matter in front of friend Scharschmid, who must have been encouraging in his reply. He talked to others he knew in Salzburg, but in the end the decision rested with himself.

Suddenly he made up his mind: there was no time to lose. There may be another person somewhere, better equipped than himself, younger in years. If so, he did not know him and had no time to look for him. He was quite prepared to yield the ground to such a better man, should he appear at a later date; however, once he started on his colossal task, all such thoughts were buried. In any event, no other individual came to the fore to wrest the work away from him.

The feverish activity commenced at once. It is known that he was appointed schools superintendent of Salzburg in 1850, a job from which he was to "resign" in 1852, quite possibly because his time was now better spent, in his opinion, on the new undertaking that was much more to his liking. (Other reasons for his "sacking" are described later.)

Letters had to be written; the one to Professor Otto Jahn (written considerably later) proved to be of the utmost importance. This German professor was then working on a three-volume biography of Mozart that came to be regarded as the most authoritative one published to date. The work contained numerous references to Mozart's compositions, stating the circumstances of their origination and many "stories" surrounding them. There was a great deal of additional material that never found its way into the book and that was vital to Köchel's work. Fortunately, Jahn, who had also toyed with the idea of preparing a Mozart register, was only too willing to cooperate with Köchel. As a result, the greatest number of source references in the Köchel Register comes from Jahn, to whom he felt obliged to dedicate his work; moreover, in later editions of Jahn's book, every reference to a Mozart composition is accompanied by the number allotted by Köchel, and Köchel's work receives the highest accolade in the new edition.

The importance of Köchel's decision cannot be overemphasized. Without this work, at least one-third, possibly even half, of Mozart's compositions known today would have disappeared, lost to posterity. It is not enough to know that a work exists: if no trace of it can be found, it may as well not have been created. The world of music is full of feverish excitement whenever the manuscript of a single composition by one of the "great ones" is found that was hitherto unknown. Measure this against the huge number of works located by Köchel as a result of his work, and the significance of his achievement becomes obvious.

This book takes full account of the work performed by Köchel in furtherance of Mozart's compositions. But this is the only fact known to the world about this man. All his other achievements remain obscure, and the very man is not known to us. It will be seen that his other activities were equally important. I maintain that had he done nothing else, he would richly deserve his fame, but equally, had he not compiled the Köchelverzeichnis, his entitlement to recognition should also be assured.

3

Köchel's Ancestry

Ludwig Alois Friedrich Köchel was born 14 January 1800, in Stein, a small town in Niederösterreich, Austria, on the banks of the Danube River, today about an hour's drive from Vienna.

His father was Johann Georg Köchl (note the different spelling), who on 6 November 1797 had married Maria Aloisia Maximiliana Susanna Stain (or Stein, Steiner). Ludwig had two younger brothers and a sister: Heinrich Gottlieb, born in 1801; Alexander Franz, born in 1806; and Karoline Susanne Aloisia, born in 1808—all reported to have died in infancy. Fuller details are available of elder brother Johann Friedrich Wenzeslaus Wilhelm Köchel (at birth spelled as Köchl), born on 28 September 1798 in the same house as Ludwig. This brother, known as Friedrich or Fritz, became engineer of the k.k. Waterworks Directorate. The date of his death is given as 3 November 1836. A poem written by Ludwig Köchel entitled "Mein Fritz" (My Fritz), published in his book of poetry in 1872, starts with the line "Fünfzehn Winter stürmten an deinem Grabe vorüber" (fifteen winters have rushed past your grave). This poem bears the date 1841, which would put Fritz's death into 1826. It seems that the date printed in the book is wrong because the date of Fritz's death is verified in Köchel's testament and in the documents dealing with Fritz's estate in the town hall archives in Vienna. The various biographical notes that agree in saying that by the time Köchel completed his studies in 1827 all his brothers and sisters had died are therefore wrong.

Fritz was buried in Vienna's St. Marxer Friedhof (cemetery), and his remains were transferred from there to the Zentralfriedhof (central cemetery) in 1874 when part of St. Marxer was closed for the redevelopment of the area. When Ludwig died in 1877, he was buried in the same grave, as prophetically forecast in his poem to Fritz and as decreed in his testament of 1868. Köchel's father lived until 10 March 1820, his mother until 26 March 1824, and when Fritz died in 1836, Ludwig was left without any living close relations.

Köchel's father, whose name at birth was registered as Georg Sebastian Fidelis Köchl and who later changed his forenames to Johann Georg, was head of the local tax collection office for the Episcopy of Passau. His job definition of "Kastenamtverwalter" needs some explanation.

Kasten, which today means "wardrobe, chest, or box," had an earlier meaning of "barn." This was in fact the "tithe barn" where farmers had to deliver one-tenth of their produce in kind. The "Verwalter," or supervisor of the barn, was in effect the manager of the tax collector's office (Amt), a prestigious occupation. (The house in which the office was located, the "Grosser Passauer Hof," still stands and is very near to the Mazzetti Haus on Schürer Platz, Stein. It is now thought to be the house in which Köchel was born.)

Interestingly, the father of Köchel's mother, Johann Teophil (Gottlieb) Stain (1720 or 1730–1799), held the same appointment immediately before Köchel's father, and we may assume that this is how Köchel's parents first met.

Köchel's father lost the job of tax collector for the Bishopric in 1803. By this time, the family lived at No. 8 Schürerplatz, today's Mazzetti Haus, which erroneously has long been regarded as Köchel's birth house. There is no record of the date when the family moved from the Passauerhof, but by 1803 the house on Schürerplatz belonged to the bishopric of Passau, Johann Georg Köchl's employers, and although the office for the tax collection was closed upon the secularization of church properties in 1803, or rather taken under different supervision, he was permitted to stay on with his family.

As his occupation in later records is stated as "k.k. Kameral-Oberbeamter," which is something like senior civil servant of finance, and as the office of tax collection became a function of the local authorities throughout Austria, we may assume that he more or less carried on in the same job, but for different employers, and that there was no material change in the financial circumstances of the family, contrary to the belief of some biographical notes about

Köchel indicating that the family was under financial strain during his childhood. During this period, Köchel's father also obtained the title of Court Councilor (Hofrat).

I obtained a copy of a study prepared and signed by Johann Georg Köchel in 1810, entitled "Historische Beschreibung des KK Kasten- und Kelleramts zu Stein (Historic Description of the K.K. Tithe and Cellar Office in Stein), which throughout its twenty-nine pages examines the background, the facilities, and the activities of the office of which he had been in charge for many years. This is written in a systematic way, foreshadowing the disciplined methods his son was to employ some fifty years later.

In fact, this study, which he signed as "Verwalter" (manager), was written seven years after the secularization, thus confirming that the family's material circumstances did not change as a result of this. Another interesting point is that Johann Georg by this time signs his name as "Köchel" with the *e*.

Looking into Köchel's ancestry is very rewarding. Each of his four grandparents has important connections that in combination go a long way toward explaining the versatility, intellect, confidence, and amiability of the man. There are painters, soldiers, musicians, ecclesiastical dignitaries, self-made businessmen—altogether a collection of interesting personalities, many of whom were well known throughout the land.

Taking first the paternal grandfather, we find representatives of the Niederösterreich middle class: shopkeepers, calico printers, self-made men who had started out as servants. The origins of this branch of the family can be traced back to Michael Kögl, born in 1662 in the small town of Langenlois, Niederösterreich, and whose father's name is given as Valentin Kögl. As to the grandfather, Georg Gerhard Köchl (1735–1808) was a cloth merchant and calico printer in Krems, having come from Vienna in 1761 after completing an apprenticeship in the printing trade. He became mayor of Krems and Stein first in 1781 and again in 1791, and in 1784 Emperor Joseph II honored him with the gold medal of merit (Ehrenmedaille). A little-known fact about him is that he was best man at the marriage ceremony of Matthias Laager, Franz Liszt's grandfather. He was also the godfather of Ludwig Köchel. Strangely, some biographers refer to him as Köchel's uncle, but there is no evidence to support this and, as he was born twenty-eight years before Köchel's father, this is indeed most unlikely.

The paternal grandmother, born Maria Theresia Giegl (1732–1780), was related to many notable families, particularly in the field of art. Most famous of these is the landscape painter Michael Wutky (born in 1739 in Krems, died in 1822 in Vienna), whose son Emanuel was an amateur violinist and played in the Orchestra of the Vienna Gesellschaft der Musikfreunde. Others include Wutky's half brother and the numismatist Franz Neumann (1744–1816); most likely a family connection also exists to the Alt family of painters and their most famous member Jakob Alt (1789–1872) via Alt's mother-in-law Cäcilie Schaller, born Schleicher. The Schleichers descended from the Giegls of Herzogenburg, where Köchel's grandmother was born.

In the third quarter represented by the maternal grandfather, we find military connections and contacts to the administration of the Passau Bishopric. The Stains, Steins, or Steiners came from Salzburg, and the oldest-known ancestor was Johann Franz Stain, military commander of Hohensalzburg (1687–1743), who, as already mentioned, was acquainted with Leopold Mozart.

In the fourth quarter, the maternal grandmother, born Maria Ursula Hyacintha Fixlmillner (1728–1805), we find a close connection to the famous art-loving abbot of the abbey of Kremsmünster, Alexander III Fixlmillner, who was responsible for the present format of this famous "Stift." He was in fact the brother of Maria Ursula's father Erasmus Anton Fixlmillner (1681–1731), administrator of an important estate in Oberösterreich. We are left to wonder whether Köchel's later work in the Stift of Kremsmünster where he "organized" the manuscripts of the baroque composer Johann Joseph (or Josef) Fux leading to his "Thematisches Verzeichnis der im Stifte Kremsmünster vorhandenen Compositionen von Johann Josef Fux" (Thematic Register of the Compositions of Johann Josef Fux in the Kremsmünster Abbey), is a result of this family connection.

It will thus be seen that with ancestry in so many different spheres of public and artistic life, with discipline inherited from military forebears and diligence from self-made merchants and artisans, all the requisites were in place for a brilliant career.

4

The Three Stages of Köchel's Life

Before looking in detail at Köchel's life and work, it is worthwhile examining a broad outline so as to perceive how this man born in a small provincial town of parents remote from the world of science came to have such a brilliant career and to accomplish at least one task for which he will always be remembered.

Köchel's life can be divided into three entirely different sections. The first of these covers his childhood, schooling, and university days and is little different from that of any other young middle-class person of the period. His father was in a job that may be described as slightly above average, and the family home was upper middle-class.

Today it takes little more than an hour to drive to Vienna from Stein where Köchel was born and where he spent his early years. In the early part of the nineteenth century such a trip to the capital where the "action" was would have taken the best part of a day in a horse-drawn carriage. This meant that Köchel spent most of the time in the town of his birth, a fact that was equally true for most of his contemporaries. A day trip was out of the question; the enjoyment of theatre, opera, or concert necessitated careful planning and several overnight stays.

An impressionable young man finding himself in this situation would have done a great deal of reading, participated in musical evenings organized in the family home, and taken part in the many discussions that took place in the parental home and in the houses where friends lived. This, plus the education received at the local Gymnasium (grammar school), controlled by the order of the Piarists, would have prepared him for the life of an intellectual, ready to move into a position of teaching after completing the initial learning process.

Thus Köchel, after moving to Vienna and during his university studies, was ready for the second phase of his life, which lasted until he was forty-two and saw him move from a modest teaching post to the highest level of tutoring in a house close to the imperial throne of Austria. As he was now in Vienna, he was able to indulge in visits to the theatre and the opera and to go to concerts, mostly in the company of the young archdukes in his care. Doubtless his knowledge of music (he had learned to play the cello while still at school in Krems) and of plays and poems he had read became most useful, as did his great interest in natural sciences—rather more so, I imagine, than the degree of law he had obtained at the University of Vienna.

That he was keenly interested in poetry is evident from the fact that throughout his life he tried his hand at writing poems himself, and some have compared his style to that of Goethe, whom he much admired. In later life when he was able to afford to do so, he had a collection of these poems privately published in a volume of some 150 pages, and he sent dedicated copies of this book to his numerous friends.

The many signs of recognition shown to him during this period, culminating in his elevation to the titled aristocracy of the land, created the basis for the third—and for us, most interesting—part of his life.

When his tutoring days in the archducal house were over and he found himself in a financially secure position with no need to look for another job, Köchel was able to devote his time and energy, his knowledge and ability, to the things that mattered most to him: natural sciences, literature, and, particularly, music. His admiration of Mozart's music instilled in him by his father, a contemporary and an ardent admirer of the composer, was combined with the frustration of realizing that much of what this genius had written was likely to be lost unless someone stepped forward and took upon himself the task of "organizing" what was in a state of utter chaos. His scientific mind was equipped to see through the maze of hundreds of manuscripts scattered all over Europe, sometimes unique in being originals in Mozart's hand, at other times duplicates—copies of the original but genuine works—but in many instances spurious imitations by lesser composers eager to bask in the glory of Mozart's fame.

Köchel spent some eleven years of his mature life on the preparation of what we now call the *Köchelverzeichnis* (Köchel Register), and he had the satisfaction of seeing this published at the age of sixty-two.

Thus he had created a base that all later musicologists specializing in Mozart used as their starting point. This is as true today as it was in the period immediately following its first appearance. Because the *Register*, beyond listing 626 compositions Köchel recognized as being by Mozart, also includes as an appendix a list of those works that seemed dubious to him or of which only a fragment remained, it must be obvious that his work was a fundament on which to build rather than a completed structure where everything was in place, where no stone ever needed to be moved again. He himself knew this only too well, as evidenced by the fact that after the book appeared in print, he continued to make corrections to his notes, which were then sometimes published in musical publications and which were later incorporated in the second edition of the *Register*, published nearly thirty years after his death.

Although best remembered for the *Register*, Köchel had additional achievements during these years. There were other major literary activities in the field of music, such as a history of Austrian Court music stretching over a period of more than three centuries and a very detailed work on the compositions of the Austrian baroque composer Johann Joseph Fux (1698–1740). There was also his continuing work in natural sciences, particularly in botany and mineralogy with major collections compiled by him, articles written and published, and very active memberships of prestigious societies in the field leading to executive positions and honorary life memberships. He was highly regarded by fellow scientists in spite of the fact that he had no official qualifications; his own studies more than made up for the lack of degrees.

Perhaps he was fortunate to reach the goals of his early imagination—this is something not granted to the majority of us. I believe, however, that it was not a question of luck but a well-conceived and -executed plan that took him through his life. The first and second phases thus prepared him for the productive tasks of the final one, in which he excelled and for which he is now remembered best by the music-loving public of the world, by the grateful admirers of Mozart.

5

Learning and Teaching

Ludwig Alois Friedrich Köchel was christened on the day he was born, 14 January 1800, in Stein, Niederösterreich, his grandfather officiating as godfather. There may have been fears for his survival, because it was usually under such circumstances that a christening took place in such a hurry. No records confirm this assumption, but we do know that his sister and younger brothers were to die in infancy.

Some time after his birth in the house Passauerhof, the family moved to the nearby square now known as Schürerplatz, to the attractive house built in the baroque style now carrying the number 8, then registered as Stein No. 26. This elegant house was built in the first half of the eighteenth century for Imperial Councilor (Kaiserlicher Rat) Oswald Jakob Mayreckh. It was here that Köchel was to spend his childhood shared with elder brother Fritz, to whom he must have been devoted throughout Fritz's short life as evidenced by the poem written fifteen years after his brother's death and by the fact that he chose to be buried in the same grave.

Ludwig attended elementary school at Stein, probably in the house now known as 62 Landstrasse, until recently wrongly believed to be the house of his birth, and at the age of ten became a pupil at the Piaristen Gymnasium (grammar school of the order of the Piarists) in Krems, the twin town of Stein. At the time this school had four grades, but students who wanted to go on to college had to do a further two years of so-called Philosophikum (translated as philosophical studies but also including other sciences in the curriculum) until age of sixteen.

This Gymnasium still stands; its premises are today occupied by boarders of the Piarist convent school. It is connected by an enclosed bridge with the more modern State Grammar School of Krems, which inherited the teaching traditions and archives of the Piarist institution.

The main entrance that used to be in steep Piaristengasse is now from Hoher Markt square. When I visited, I found a bustle of activity on my way to the Sekretäriat (registrar's office), and from there I was guided to the Department for Natural Sciences, which now houses the valuable collection Köchel bequeathed to his former school. Herr Professor Schlichtinger, the custodian of these valued treasures at the time of my first visit (now retired, his post having since been taken by Herr Professor Sohm), was glad to interrupt his dinner break to show me around. On the main landing in a glass case, a small permanent exhibition has been set up to commemorate Köchel. This contains a framed photograph of him; a picture of No. 8 Schürerplatz; some of the minerals from the collection; an example of the eighty-seven scientific books, all donated by Köchel to the school; and a volume of the school register from the period when he was a student there. Most of the books left by Köchel have disappeared, and the librarian of the school, Frau Dr. Musiol-Sollinger, told me on my second visit that no list survived the ravages of war. I found two books on botanical matters, one by Köchel's friend August Neilreich; these may well have come from the collection.

On the opposite wall, engraved in stone and with gold lettering, the notable former pupils of the school are honored, including, of course, "Ludwig Köchel 1800–1877." The earliest recorded notability is Thomas Resch (1460–1520), humanist and professor at the University of Vienna. From the school records, we learn that Köchel entered the Gymnasium in the same year, 1810, as his brother Fritz, although the latter was more than fifteen months his senior. They attended the same class for one and a half years, but in the second half of 1811, Fritz is not mentioned in the register. Presumably he was ill, which may also have been the reason he started a year later than normal. In 1812 he voluntarily repeated the second class with younger brother Ludwig now one year ahead.

Ludwig's initial progress at the school was exemplary, although, strangely, his poorest marks in the first year were in natural history, in which he was to achieve such remarkable results in later life. At the end of his first year, he received second prize for overall progress and consequently for the following year is entered as "Sekundus" in the register. He continued to make good progress, but without any awards of distinction, until 1813. This year shows a sudden reverse: at midterm he is failed in four subjects. Such grades must have badly shaken the ambitious boy and given him the impetus to show what he was capable of doing, because by the end of the same school year we see him as the only prize winner of his form, occupying the coveted "Primus" place for the following year.

Next year he maintained this excellent form while his only real competitor, a boy called Josef Werner, seemed to suffer a setback, leaving Ludwig unchallenged in claiming top honors again. He completed the four grades of the Gymnasium and in 1815 entered the two-year philosophy course held at the same premises.

At the end of the first year Ludwig took public examinations in philosophy and mathematics and the following year a similar exam in physics, all with excellent results. Brother Fritz, although not as distinguished in his progress as Ludwig, finished his studies a year later with good results and moved on to study engineering, in which he later obtained a degree.

Ludwig entered the University of Vienna to continue his studies, which eventually led to a law degree in 1827. This seemingly long time of study is partly explained by the information received from the University archives. Köchel first enrolled in the faculty of philosophy for the school year 1816–1817. He then transferred to the juridical faculty, which he attended for the next four years until 1820–1821. He took the required *examina rigorosa* on 3 August 1822, 13 January 1823, and 26 May 1823. The "Disputation" (i.e., the academic debate on his thesis) was held on 8 June 1827.

The long gap between his exams and the debate, after which he was awarded his degree, is perhaps best explained by the fact that by 1823 Köchel had commenced his tutorial activities. He may have been unable to devote sufficient time to preparing his thesis as a result.

Another possible reason for the delay is that he may have interrupted his studies to take up some temporary employment. Later we will learn that he was accused of "loafing around the world taking jobs where chance presents them"; indeed, he probably needed the money to see him through his university days. His father having died in 1820 (when Ludwig was twenty), it is likely that he lacked sufficient family funds for his continuing studies. He was a gifted man and may have received an offer as a companion traveler; he could also have undertaken to organize some private library or may have started on his career as tutor earlier than generally reported. In effect, unfortunately, no firm information is available for these years. When he first enrolled, Köchel gave his father's address as Vienna, Bauernmarkt 623. By 1827, his own address is stated as Vienna, Untere Bräunerstrasse 1129, second floor, and there are no clues as to the in-between years.

In 1823 Köchel became a private tutor in the house of Anton von Wittman, who was bailiff (Güterverwalter) of the estates belonging to the Archduke Karl. Soon he was to continue in a similar capacity at the house of Count P. F. W. Grünne-Pinchard, who served as head steward (Obersthofmeister) of the same estates.

On Count Grünne's recommendation, Köchel, with his friend and fellow tutor Dr. Franz Scharschmid von Adlertreu, was later engaged as a private tutor to the children of the Archduke Karl. However, before we consider this new position, which was to be of paramount importance for his future, we must pause to look at an episode that is well documented and that—in a different way—may also have played a significant part in his life.

6

Köchel's Romance

Very little is known about Köchel's personal life and, in particular, about his love life. He never married, and, as far as can be ascertained, he never had a permanent relationship. For most of his adult life, he was to stay in the house of his friend Scharschmid and his family. Whether this was just a friendly arrangement or something more between the two men cannot be established. The episode to be described here is therefore of special interest as it introduces us to the world of Köchel's youth and as it may well be the only time in his life when he was emotionally involved with a girl.

The girl in question is Sophie Kleyle, the fifteen-year-old daughter of Regierungsrat (Government Councilor) Franz Joachim Ritter von Kleyle (1775–1854), who was ennobled in 1828 and who was from 1810 personal secretary to Archduke Karl, a position he was to hold until the archduke's death in 1847. He was also head of administration of the estates of Count Grünne-Pinchard, whose family lived in the palace at No. 3 Hofgartengasse, Vienna. As mentioned earlier, Köchel was private tutor to the Grünne children parallel to studying law at the University of Vienna, and he lived in this building that belonged to Archduke Karl. Interestingly, this was also the palace in which his later pupil, Archduke Albrecht, was to grant him a "grace and favor" apartment in 1863 and where Köchel was to die in 1877. It is also worth noting that one of Count Grünne's sons, who was thus Köchel's pupil (Count Karl Grünne), was later to become chief adjutant to emperor Franz Joseph.

Sophie, like many girls of her age and time, kept a regular diary, and the volume covering the years 1826 and 1827 has been preserved. Its contents are quoted in their entirety in two books to which I shall refer here.

The Kleyles first lived in an apartment in central Vienna, on the corner of Annagasse and Seilerstätte, in a house that still stands. In the course of the period described in the diary, Herr Kleyle bought a villa with a huge garden in elegant Penzing (today No. 14 Beckmanngasse), near the Palace of Schönbrunn.

There were six girls and two boys in the Kleyle family. One of the boys, Karl Kleyle (1812–1859), made a distinguished career in the service of the empire, receiving numerous signs of recognition and many decorations. The girls, like their mother, are described as beautiful, and when young Köchel, through the connection between his employer and father Kleyle, first entered the apartment, he must have been bedazzled by all this beauty. He was twenty-five at the time. He first targeted his attentions on the eldest daughter, Charlotte, who later was to marry Dr. Philipp Mayer, a friend of Köchel's who subsequently shared tutorial duties with him to Archduke Karl's children.

Mayer, who was born in 1798 in Prague, probably befriended the younger Köchel while they both studied law at the University of Vienna. He obtained his degree in 1824 and accepted a tutorial position in the house of Landgraf (Landgrave) Joseph Egon von Fürstenberg. From 1825 he was tutor to Archduke Friedrich in the service of Archduke Karl. Tragically, both Charlotte and Mayer died of typhus fever, one year after they were married, in 1828. The close friendship between Köchel and Mayer is also evidenced by the fact that several of Mayer's poems were set to music by Köchel, as will be seen in the chapter dealing with Köchel's musical compositions. After Mayer's death, his friend and brother-in-law Max Löwenthal arranged to publish his poems privately under the title *Dichtungen*. He was buried in Penzing, near the Kleyle home.

Sophie was the second daughter; the third, Rosalie, was later married to Schubert singer Baron Karl von Schönstein. Johanna was first engaged to Emanuel Mikschik, an amateur pianist who later was to become accompanist to Johann Michael Vogl, the well-known singer, who in 1795 had participated in a Benefit Gala Concert organized by Mozart's widow, Konstanze. Emanuel died in 1838, and Johanna eventually married his brother, Dr. Eduard Mikschik. Emanuel Mikschik is referred to in Köchel's testament as "mein unvergesslicher Freund" (my unforgettable friend), and bequests were left for his two sisters in Köchel's will.

This background highlights the social circumstances of young Köchel's life in this distinguished circle of intellectuals, surrounded by people interested in music and literature. Schubert was an occasional caller at the Kleyles, and three of his close friends, including Ferdinand Walcher (of whom more will be said later), were regular visitors. Another one of these friends was the portrait artist Josef Teltscher, who painted Schubert and Beethoven as well as the ladies of the Kleyle family.

Sophie's diary commences on Sunday, 1 January 1826, with frequent entries throughout the month. Köchel is almost always mentioned in these, and the comments about him include "he is so good and amiable" and "Köchel was here, our faithful friend, who never deserts us in sorrow or happiness."

On 12 January Sophie accompanied her mother on a visit to the Countess Zoe Grünne, Köchel's employer. "I sat on a chair. Köchel sat down by my side. Thus came about what I had both wished and dreaded: to meet him in that house; it was pleasant and dreadful at the same time. . . . Fortunately the Countess neglected us. This gave me time to recover my composure and Köchel's pleasant company, his informal manner, allowed me to completely regain my poise. We were chatting quietly and unobserved and I was glad to find that Köchel was no more reserved toward me in this company than at our home."

The next day Köchel again visited in Annagasse, and Sophie again found herself sitting to him. She noticed a burn on his hand, perhaps the result of some scientific experiment in his tutorial work. "I drew his attention to my horny hands and pressing them gently he said that he did not care for soft, idle hands. I am unable to describe the many thoughts and feelings that crossed my mind as I looked at him and as I saw how he returned my gaze with those radiant eyes of his. . . . Köchel had pressed my hands—and I was floating on air in an incredible dream; I never thought that I might be pleasing, interesting, worthy to him. I did not even dare to hope."

On Sunday, 15 January, during a visit to the theatre, Köchel politely visited the Kleyles' box during the interval and stayed there until the end of the performance. "He was so cheerful, so amiable, that the evening passed in the most pleasant way. When the play ended and we hurried to our carriages he was by my side and behaved in such an exuberant manner that I said he must have had a very agreeable experience. He replied: I spent the evening in your company; what could be more agreeable?"

There followed a serious discussion between Sophie and her mother. This concerned Charlotte. Mother had noticed that Köchel no longer seemed to take an interest in the eldest daughter, who was still in love with him. Could it be that she had noticed nothing of Köchel's attentions toward Sophie? Sophie writes in her diary, "If only I knew that Köchel loves me, that I am of interest to him. . . . True, a few times he has gently pressed my hand and has looked at me with those shining eyes of his, but he has never said anything."

During February and March, other thoughts seemed to occupy the diary writer's attention, as there are very few entries and none of these mention Köchel, who must also have been busy with his dual activity of studying and teaching. The Kleyles were preparing to move, and it is in this context that Köchel, who helped pack their belongings, is next mentioned. On Thursday, 13 April, Sophie writes, "Köchel, my dear Köchel, comes to us again for the past eight days or so; it is easy to imagine that this is not unpleasant for me." When he reappears, unannounced and unexpected, she writes, "I am not superstitious, am not scared of ghosts or goblins, never try to interpret my dreams, but I believe in presentiments." Somehow she knew that he had come; her heart told her so although her common sense said:

> He could not be there. And behold: the heart was right! Here stood Herr Ludwig Köchel [the first time his first name appears in the narrative!] in all his charm and amiability and he glanced at me with his kind and smiling face as I stood frozen in the door. He is the same good and lovable man he was before we were parted for such a long time and I totally lost my calm and composure; in their place came the restlessness already described; but, to be candid, this is indeed more pleasant than to drift without my heart. I would be most miserable could I not hope to be of some consequence to him.
>
> He composed two charming poems about me which is the more strange as I really cannot fathom what anyone can want to say about me, let alone in verse. . . . My hero brought these to me yesterday with the request that they should on no account be shown or mentioned to anyone, a request I found easy to promise and easier to comply with. When I unfolded the papers in the evening I found a description of myself in verse; so he must have been thinking about me when I assumed I had been forgotten! Good, kind man!

These verses and all others mentioned in Sophie's diary are lost. None of them are included in the book of poems privately published by Köchel in 1872 and mentioned elsewhere in greater detail.

Nor does the small volume contain any other love poems. And Köchel's musical compositions are generally also not of a romantic nature, although they all date from 1822 to 1828, which therefore includes the years of Sophie's "romance." In particular, there is no song composed by Köchel to a poem of his own, whereas there are several attempts to set to music those written by his friend Philipp Mayer.

The next episode described in the diary is an unexpected visit at the Kleyles by Köchel's employer, Count Grünne-Pinchard. Köchel apparently had asked for a leave of absence, pretending to go to the university; when the count finds him instead flirting with the beautiful Kleyle girls, he says sarcastically, "Is this where the University is?" to which Köchel replies, "This is even better!" Nonetheless, he must have been in an embarrassing situation. Sophie proves how faithful she is in her belief of the unimpeachable Köchel by writing, "Köchel is unable to utter a lie. If he said at home that he was visiting the University he must have been there before he came to us or have intended to call there before returning home." Nevertheless, she tried to tease him afterward, but Köchel could not see the funny side of the situation, and after uttering a bitter remark to Sophie, he marched out of the room.

As if this reaction were not enough to upset the young girl's feelings, in the afternoon of the following day, Köchel's fellow tutor and friend Philipp Mayer called on the Kleyles and read out some letters Köchel had written to him in which the girls were mentioned but, to use Sophie's words, "as you might talk about a pair of old boots." It becomes obvious from the way Köchel refers to her in one of the letters, calling her "la jolie maligne" (the pretty imp), that "he considered me a charming doll, a plaything, of entertainment value for a while but then to be remorselessly crushed." "Had he come yesterday," she continues, "I would have been full of rueful apologies for what I had said, but should he come tomorrow he might just see my face reddened from the shame I feel for believing that he could lovingly embrace me or anyone else. Deceived!" But even after this outburst Sophie concluded the entry of 23 April by saying, "Even though he scorns me, he is a good man . . . and I often wrong him through my wounded self-love."

Two things are obvious from this sequence of events. It marks some sort of a breaking point in the developing relationship, and it demonstrates that young Köchel, a serious man of learning, had no sense of humor.

Later Sophie tried to apologize for having mocked him. This happened a fortnight after the events described when the two of them were again walking in the gardens of the Penzing villa. Köchel's reply to the apology was "What you have done to me is not the kind of thing for which you need to apologize. . . . There are matters that exercise a miraculous power over our lives and for which we have no explanation."

Sophie is thus reassured in her love and concludes, "From all he said there shone his high intellect, his remarkable heart and his firm fundamental views. His courage and fortitude are truly wonderful to behold; as I walked by his side my feet seemed not to touch the ground, he lifted me above the dust, above the circumstances of our bourgeois life, I floated with him into a radiant distance."

The next episode, reported a day later, tells of a secret exchange of rings between Köchel and Sophie that had been effected the previous autumn. Köchel showed her the ring, saying, "This is my constant escort, my dame's violet, because only at night can I invigorate myself from its shine."

But in spite of these promising incidents, a cooling of their relationship is obvious ever since the day when Count Grünne unexpectedly called finding Köchel in the Kleyle house when he should have been at the university. One more positive event occurred when Köchel gave Sophie a small package—"a sort of diary . . . consisting of poems addressed to me . . . full of love and tenderness." In her naiveté she showed these to her mother (perhaps on this occasion there was no request from Köchel not to do so?), who questioned her daughter closely about her conduct with Köchel. Later, through her sister Charlotte, Sophie learned to her dismay that her mother had told her that Sophie "deserved someone better" and stated her preference for Mayer or Walcher.

Sophie's diary makes no further reports of visits to the house by Köchel. Perhaps by handing over the poems written to her in happier days, he wanted to rid himself of any mementos of their acquaintance. If they met at the house of mutual friends, there is no mention of such meetings, but an entry on Monday, 20 January 1827, demonstrates that Köchel is never far from Sophie's thoughts. "I can safely declare that since I started to be in love with Köchel I have at most had ten happy nights. . . . He is such a splendid, educated, witty man, but he is not affectionate. The inner cordiality so apparent in Mayer and Walcher is missing in him. . . . When we are alone together he is full of love; as soon as another person is near us he is all frigidity and disdain. It is as if he were ashamed of me, as if he were afraid people might notice that he was close to me."

In May Sophie decided to end what never really was a relationship. She composed a letter to Köchel and showed it to Walcher, her sister Charlotte, and Philipp Mayer. They all found it terrible and begged her not to send it. It is not clear from her diary whether the letter was ever dispatched.

Walcher left Vienna for Venice, and Sophie sent regular letters to him, some of which are attached to the diary. We do not know what Walcher wrote to her in reply, but he must have been asking questions about Köchel because in one of her letters, written some time between 1 June and 15 July and bearing no date, she writes, "I am now quite content, Ludwig [!] and I are reconciled, I have recognized his true and faithful love and he has realized his errors. I am very happy. Lotte [Charlotte] is engaged to Mayer, this also contributes to my satisfaction. If only you were here, all would be so very jolly."

In the context of events, I think this account was a figment of Sophie's imagination or possibly just a way to stop Walcher from further inquisitiveness. At any rate, no further mention of Köchel is made in letters or diary entries, until quite abruptly we come to the undated "Scheidebrief" (letter of parting) to Köchel. In this she quotes verbatim what her father had said to her. The full text of the letter is as follows:

> Because you are requesting this of me and as I also consider it essential, I want to reiterate to you, verbatim as far as possible, my father's speech. If you feel hurt, as I cannot doubt, if it sounds strange and hard, perhaps even peculiar to you, please consider that what I write here has been said by the most gentle, wise and just father to his beloved daughter in the hour of sincerest confidence. He said: "About the matters that have passed and cannot be altered I do not want to waste any words; I want to accuse neither you nor Köchel, but both of you have entered into this relationship most imprudently and as to Köchel's delicacy, so often praised to me. . . . I would have expected more consideration for my house. However, all this is past history; but has he taken even a single step these last two years to come nearer to his target, namely to possess you? I know of nothing.
>
> That he loafs around the world taking jobs where chance presents them I cannot condemn: I acted the same way in the past. But to tie the

fate of another being to his own and still behave in this way I must censure severely. He is sufficiently clever and practical to make a living at all times, therefore he needs to have little concern for himself; but if he has no other plan than to be governed by chance and to wait for something to turn up, if he has no wish to possess you, it was very wrong of him to disturb the tranquillity of a respectable family for the sake of a mere flirtation!"

This is as far as the diary goes. It was the end of the year, and there might have been a sequel, lost to us. A footnote by Sophie reads, "After 58 years I read this with lively interest. This diary of mine was returned to me after Köchel's death by the Scharschmids. They now have from me Köchel's diary." From this it seems that Köchel and Sophie exchanged their diaries at some stage, perhaps many years later, and that her original came back after Köchel and, presumably, Scharschmid had died. Unfortunately, Köchel's diary is lost.

Apart from the insight we gain through Sophie's diary into Köchel's intellect and behavior, I feel it is important in demonstrating how easily Köchel moved among these highly placed families even as a young student. Having come from a humble provincial background, he must have been full of confidence in his abilities, and his poise and charm enabled him to reach his goal.

As to whether he was truly in love with Sophie or simply treated her as a much younger friend, almost a child, "a pretty imp," we cannot know. There was a considerable age gap between them, about ten years. Köchel was twenty-five, Sophie just fifteen, at the start of the events recorded by her, and she was even younger when she first fell in love with Köchel. There is no real evidence in the events described that her love was at any time reciprocated; as she says, beyond pressing her hand gently a few times and gazing at her with shining eyes, nothing happened between them, and at no stage did Köchel "say" anything from which his "love" would have been apparent. On the one hand, therefore, it is quite possible that this frustrated affair, terminated by a letter that must have deeply wounded his vanity, was the cause of Köchel remaining a bachelor throughout his life. On the other, it leaves open the possibility that his sexual desires took another direction.

The story would not be complete without disclosing the source of the diary and what became of Sophie. The diary is quoted in full in a book published in Leipzig in 1906, written by Eduard

Castle with the title *Lenau und die Familie Löwenthal* (Lenau and the Löwenthal family). Nikolaus Lenau (1802–1850), whose real name was Edler (nobleman) von Strehlenau Niembsch, was an Austrian poet of Hungarian birth. He was most famous for his religious epics, including one entitled *Savonarola*. (By the way, there is a memorial plaque of Lenau on the walls of what was the Kleyle villa in Penzing.)

His close friend was Max Löwenthal (1799–1872), an official of the Austrian Civil Service who later was to become the equivalent of postmaster general and who in 1863 was ennobled. He was also a writer. In May 1829 he married Sophie Kleyle, the heroine of the Köchel "romance." This was a marriage of convenience based on mutual respect rather than love. Thus it comes as no surprise that Sophie soon fell hopelessly in love with the poet Lenau, a frequent caller at the house.

For ten years, from 1834 to 1844 (when Lenau went mad), Sophie suffered from this second unfulfilled love in her life because she refused to be unfaithful to the father of her children, whereas Lenau respected his friendship with Max Löwenthal. His poems and letters to Sophie, which are part of Austria's literary heritage, are a monument of his passionate love.

An almost identical version of the events described here also appears in a book entitled *Mesalliiert* (Misallied), based on the literary heritage of Sophie Löwenthal and also published in 1906 with an introduction by Dr. Eduard Castle, the author of the other book mentioned. In addition, a revived account of the story came in 1963 in Friedrich Mickwitz's book, *Nikolaus Lenau and Sophie Löwenthal.*

7

In the Service of
Archduke Karl

When Köchel was engaged as private tutor to the young archdukes, the sons of Archduke Karl, in 1827, this appointment was, according to several biographical articles, on the recommendation of Count Grünne-Pinchard, whose children were then under his tuition. I believe that in spite of the incidents described in the previous chapter, it was Hofrat Kleyle who made the main recommendation. He had been in Archduke Karl's service since 1804 and his private secretary since 1809, and it is inconceivable that his opinion would not have been sought in such an important matter, particularly as Köchel had been such a frequent caller at the Kleyle house, a fact that cannot have escaped the archduke's notice.

Whatever opinion Hofrat Kleyle may have nursed regarding Köchel's uninvited flirtations with his daughters, he knew what the man's abilities were, he respected them, and even at the time of his stern refusal of him as a suitor with no declared intentions, he complimented Köchel on his skill and knowledge. Perhaps Kleyle even thought that if Köchel were introduced into a tutorial position in the imperial household, thus lending stability to his existence, he would make a good husband to Sophie, if only he could be made to declare his serious intentions.

Let us now take a look at the man in whose service Köchel was to spend the next fifteen years of his life and who was so vitally important in shaping his future well-being.

Karl (Carl) Ludwig Johann Joseph Laurenz, archduke of Austria (1771–1847), was born in Florence, where his father, the future emperor Leopold II, Maria Theresia's second son, was grand duke of Tuscany at the time. Leopold II was to reign from 1790 to 1792 after the death of his brother Joseph II, and he was to be followed on the throne by his eldest son, Karl's brother Franz II, who reigned until 1835.

Karl was brought up in Tuscany, then part of the Austrian Empire. He showed an early interest in military history, mathematics, and Roman history and devoted much time from his earliest youth to the study of these subjects.

After his father's death in 1792, Karl, who was then twenty-one, and his brothers moved to Vienna. A year later a legal form of adoption was signed between his father and Archduchess Maria Christine, Empress Maria Theresia's "favorite daughter" who was unable to bear children and who, with her husband Albert von Sachsen-Teschen, wanted to accept the responsibility for Karl's future well-being. Albert was governor of the Austrian Netherlands, and it was planned that Karl should be "heir presumptive" (Erbsouverän) to this title.

This project had been on Maria Christine's mind for a number of years. After a trip to Tuscany in 1776, she expressed the following thoughts about Karl:

> The third son, Karl, is the most charming of the family. He is small, but strong and beautiful. His fine features tell of good fortune, kindness and frankness, his eyes display a somewhat languishing and subdued look, his nose is well-formed, his hands pretty, he is vivacious and nimble and shows a spirit which at his age of four can only cause amazement. He knows no fear, has a cheerful disposition and, without being burdensome, is the most confiding of the children. . . . He has a kind heart. . . . For his age he appears to be remarkably well educated and knowledgeable. In short, he is one of the most amiable children I have ever encountered.

This description comes from a book by H. von Zeissberg, published in 1883.

The same source also tells us that after the adoption Maria Christine became "a second mother" to the twenty-one-year-old archduke. She declared, "The idea to possess Karl had been my wish for fifteen years." (On the journey to Belgium, by the way, Graf Grünne was one of the escorts of the young archduke.)

There is a connection to Mozart here. Some years before the aforementioned events took place, in 1786, Maria Christine, who was also described as Joseph II's "favorite sister," visited Vienna with her husband, Albert. Joseph was keen to provide some interesting entertainment for them and so summoned Mozart. Within a few days a newly composed work was committed to paper, based on a libretto by Gottlieb Stephanie the younger, a one-act "Singspiel" (perhaps best translated as operetta), called "Der Schauspiel Direktor" (The Theatre Director), now known under K. 486. This was duly performed in the theatre of Schloss Schönbrunn on 3 February 1786 to unanimous acclaim.

This musical parody was partly prose, partly music, hence the description of "Singspiel" instead of opera, and to add spice to the proceedings, the leading straight part was played by Joseph Lange, the actor-husband of Mozart's erstwhile love Aloysia Weber (sister of Konstanze), who in turn was cast in the most unsympathetic soprano part. Lange had the reputation of being able to do anything on stage except sing—so Mozart forced him to do so in this performance! It also deserves mention that the second part of the evening consisted of a work by Mozart's adversary Salieri: "Prima la musica, poi le parole" (first the music, then the words). There must have been a joker in the pack.

Reverting to the plans surrounding Karl's future, these were frustrated by a sequence of political, military, and family matters that need not be mentioned here in greater detail. The outcome was that Karl entered the army and launched himself on a military career that soon saw him rise to the rank of general and then to Reichs-Feldmarschall by the age of twenty-five. His victorious exploits secured Belgium for the monarchy.

His greatest victory securing his lasting fame in Austrian history came in May 1809 at Aspern against Napoleon's all-conquering army, until then hailed as invincible. His imperial brother Franz, in a letter congratulating him on this great victory, expressed his thanks by saying, "You are the savior of the Fatherland which thanks you and blesses you eternally, as do I, its monarch."

The losing battle of Wagram followed on 5 and 6 July 1809. Soon after, on 31 July, plagued by constant intrigues and tired of continuing in his role as overall army commander when his better judgment was on the side of peace, Karl requested to be relieved of his command and withdrew into private life.

In 1815 he married eighteen-year-old Henriette, princess of Nassau-Weilburg. This was a true love match in spite of the great age difference: Karl was forty-three at the time. There had been several prior plans of "political" marriage, all of which came to naught; there was also a much-reported early romance with a Hungarian baroness, Clemence Vay. When Henriette and Karl met, however, it was love at first sight for both of them, and all that remained was to secure permission for the marriage from Karl's imperial brother.

Five boys and two girls were born of this marriage, but one of the boys, Rudolf Franz, died just sixteen days after his birth in 1822. The others were Albrecht, Karl Ferdinand, Friedrich, and Wilhelm and the two girls, Maria Theresia and Maria Karolina. The family first lived in Karl's small palace in Vienna's Annagasse (the same street on which the Kleyles resided), but in 1823, after the death of Karl's adoptive father, Albert, they moved into his grand palace in the Augustinerbastei.

Albert's death, as intended, brought great wealth and financial security to his adopted son. Apart from a large estate, the seat of which was at Dobersberg, some 120 kilometers northwest of Vienna (today close to the Czech border), there was castle Halbthurm in the village of Féltorony (*fél torony* means "half tower"; i.e., *Halbturm* in Hungarian), not far from Magyaróvár (known as Ungarisch-Altenburg then and later combined with another town to become today's Mosonmagyaróvár) and further possessions at Béllye in Hungary. (Most of the archive material relating to Archduke Karl was found at Halbthurm and is now in the Országos Levéltár, the State Archives of Hungary where I was able to obtain some of these details and documents.) There was also a huge art collection, which elevated Karl to the highest echelons of Austrian culture.

One more event important to mention that took place well before Köchel was engaged was the purchase of a large tract of land near Baden, a favored spa then and now, not very far from Vienna but far enough "to escape the dust and boredom" during the summer months in Vienna, to use Karl's own words. On this land, in Helenental, a summer residence was built for Karl by the architect Kornhäusel; this was to be called "Weilburg" as a reminder of the archduchess's origin. The apartments designated for Henrietta's use were an exact replica of those of the original Weilburg near Mainz, Germany, where she had lived before she was married—down to their internal furnishings and contents.

When the archduchess first entered these new/old premises on 4 June 1823, she found her old piano with her favorite music on its stand, her embroidery frame, and her canary in its cage. And at a sign given by Karl, the servants appeared—none other than her own faithful ones from the original Weilburg. At this, Henrietta burst into tears and embraced her husband.

This, then, was the background of the imperial family to which Köchel was introduced in 1827. The winters were mostly spent in the palace in the Augustinerbastei, the summers (usually starting in May) at the new Weilburg. We know from the archives of the St. Stephan parish church in Baden that Köchel spent these summers with the family. We even know the rooms he occupied in the Weilburg on each occasion: in the first year there, 1828, he was in room 121 from 29 May; in the last year of his employment, in room 140 from 15 May 1842. The Weilburg, by the way, was totally destroyed during World War II. Later in his life Köchel undertook an important study of the flora of this region. The foundations for this work were most likely laid during these annual visits, when perhaps also the first specimens were collected for his herbarium.

In 1829 tragedy was to befall this happy household. The archducal family was preparing for the Christmas festivities and, as each year since 1823, a decorated fir tree was to be the main attraction. This custom was introduced to the Habsburg household and throughout Austria by Henriette, who was accustomed to the Christmas tree from her childhood in Germany. The family had only just returned from an extended stay at the Weilburg, and the archduchess had to do some last-minute Christmas shopping. Her eldest daughter, Maria Theresia, then thirteen, accompanied her. Private Secretary Kleyle, in his biographical notes on Archduke Karl, writes:

Before Christmas 1829 the archduchess, accompanied by her eldest daughter, visited a woodturner's shop to buy some toys as Christmas presents for the younger children. In her sympathetic and friendly way she asked the sales lady how her own children were. In tears she responded that she had just lost one of her children who had died of scarlet fever. Firmly convinced that the contagious nature of the disease would affect anyone in a wide circle of the patient's environment, the archduchess was so forcefully affected in her concern for her daughter, that she frantically gripped her hand and hastily fled. But after arriving at home, it was the archduchess who immediately felt unwell and soon became feverish, a condition instantly recognized as dangerous. In the short space of four days she succumbed to the illness at the age of 32; during the night of 28th to 29th December, she died of scarlet fever. Her daughter and all other members of the family were spared. Throughout the archduke remained with his most anxious concern at the sickbed and only after she passed away did he part with great difficulty and in bitter grief from the deceased.

The archduke was disconsolate. Apart from his personal grief, which he could never overcome and which prevented him from marrying again, he had the children to consider. The eldest, Maria Theresia, was thirteen, and the youngest not yet three. From this day on Archduke Karl, who had always taken a keen interest in the upbringing of his children, devoted even more time to this task. Oskar Criste writes, "The education which he himself had received, with all its advantages, shortcomings and consequences, stood clearly in front of his eyes. . . . His firm decision, which he explained to all concerned, was to spare no means or pains in the upbringing and education [of his children]." We know that a team of tutors was simultaneously engaged in the household. Köchel was assisted by his friend Scharschmid, employed shortly after him; Dr. Johann Bihler, who was to retire soon afterward, had been in charge of all educational matters since 1823. There was also a Dr. Flury since 1824. Scharschmid's responsibilities were confined to the tutoring of the two archduchesses. Also employed was Dr. Philipp Mayer, who was engaged before Köchel and stayed until his sudden death in 1828.

After Bihler's retirement in November 1828, Colonel von Cerrini, a fifty-one-year-old disciplinarian, was taken on to supervise the military tuition of the eldest two archdukes. He was assisted in this by First Lieutenant Felix Freysauff von Neudegg, who stayed with the archdukes until 1837; later Major Wilhelm Ritter von Lebzeltern, Colonel Anton Freiherr (baron) von Schön, Colonel Camillo Ritter Vacani von Fort Olivo, and Major Franz von Hauslab joined the military teaching staff of Cerrini.

On the nonmilitary side, Josef Freiherr von Kalchberg was put in charge of teaching politics and political science. He may have been assisted by Joseph Bergmann, whose specialty was history and who became a close friend of Köchel. In one of his books about Erzherzog Friedrich, Bergmann expresses his thanks to "my loyal friend of long standing who gave many details about the archduke's personality as a result of his fatherly guidance when acting as travelling companion to the archduke." These remarks refer, of course, to Köchel.

Additional tutors were Johann Bingler, followed after his death in

1835 by Friedrich Gallina and Baron Andreas von Baumgartner, who later became minister of finance. Köchel, ably assisted by his friend Scharschmid, appears to have had overall responsibility apart from military matters for all subjects except religious education, which was in the hands of Wilhelm Sedlaczek, canon of Klosterneuburg.

A new stewardess/foster mother was installed as well: Countess Antonia Eltz-Lodron. She was assisted by governess Clara Hauser. The countess carried out her functions as foster mother until 1835 but was to be reengaged in 1851 as Obersthofmeisterin (chief stewardess) by Archduchess Hildegard, the wife of Archduke Albrecht, and she continued in this position until her death in 1874.

The visits to the Weilburg continued, and from here many small excursions were made by the children accompanied by their tutors. These trips were well prepared by readings from geographic manuals and local travel guides, and the pupils were expected to give account of their discoveries made during each excursion. One such excursion was a visit in September 1834 to the model farm "Brandhof" in the Styrian Highlands, which belonged to their Uncle Johann Baptist, Karl's brother, who had established the farm in 1818. Another excursion took them to Mariazell, a famous place of pilgrimage then and now.

Archduke Albrecht accompanied his father to the coronation of cousin Ferdinand in Prague in September 1836. We do not know whether Köchel was included in the traveling party.

In 1837 Albrecht and Karl Ferdinand left the parental home to complete their military training in the army, and from that time Köchel's responsibilities were for the younger children only. Of the teaching routine we know the following:

At age six, each child commenced studies of the three "R's"; at seven, religious training began (before the engagement of Sedlaczek, the archbishop of Vienna, Leopold Maximilian Count Firmian, provided this education). Later a dancing instructor was also engaged. The language of instruction was German, but French and Italian were also taught, and from the age of ten, Latin, geography, and history became part of the curriculum. Köchel was fluent in modern languages such as French and English, and his translations from Latin and ancient Greek poetry witness his knowledge of the classic languages as well.

A typical day for the young archdukes went like this: Up at 5:30, they had breakfast with their father, then tuition from Köchel and the other tutors, followed by tests until 11 A.M., then riding and walking (often with Köchel, who instructed them in the botany of the area), at 12 noon lunch with their father, followed by recapitulation, and then fencing and music lessons until 7 P.M.

As mentioned, in the summer this routine would be interrupted by day trips; in the winter, when they were staying in the archducal palace, officially known as "Vienna No. 1160," they would sometimes go skating in the park of the Belvedere Palace. Entertainment consisted of visits to the theatre and participation at carnival time in children's balls at the Imperial Palace (the Hofburg).

The eldest daughter, Maria Theresia, was later to marry Ferdinand II of Naples, but the youngest, Maria Karolina, stayed with her father until his death in 1847.

Köchel's departure from this employment after nearly fifteen years of continuous service did not mark the end of his association with the imperial family. He remained on friendly terms with the archdukes he had tutored, all of whom went on to have military careers. The eldest, Albrecht, showed his appreciation later by making available to Köchel an apartment in the palace known today as No. 3 Hanuschgasse in the I district of Vienna, where Köchel was to spend the last fourteen years of his life. This later association with Archduke Albrecht is surprising inasmuch as his tutoring was less in Köchel's hands than in those of Colonel von Cerrini, who, as mentioned, was engaged in 1828, soon after Köchel, to take charge of the military education of the two eldest sons, Albrecht and Karl Ferdinand.

Albrecht proceeded to have a glorious military career, following in his father's footsteps. At the age of thirteen, remarkably, he became titular colonel of the Forty-fourth Infantry regiment and was made "Knight of the Golden Fleece." By the time he had command of the Vienna garrison during the revolution in 1848, he had faced enemy fire on no fewer than fourteen occasions, yet contemporary military reports misunderstood his reluctance to fire into the people of Vienna by ascribing it to "inexperience." It is much more likely that Albrecht followed his father's liberal thinking and that the civil war was distasteful to him. Köchel shared in these liberal sentiments, as is shown by later events.

8

Reward for Services Rendered

As Köchel's employer was the younger brother of Emperor Franz II of Austria, the most convenient way for him to show his appreciation for his employee's good work was to bestow on him those honors and titles that were customary in the monarchy. Thus, after five years in the archducal household and at a very young age for this distinction, Köchel was made a Kaiserlicher Rath (imperial councilor) in 1832 when he was thirty-two. Needless to say, the title did not involve him in any advisory duties, but it was the first step of elevation for the ambitious young man.

Upon completion of his services, on 30 April 1842, Köchel was awarded the Ritterkreuz des Leopold Ordens (Knight Cross of the Order of Leopold), for which the diploma was issued to him on 24 June of the same year. This decoration carries with it the statutory right to a hereditary title of Ritter (chevalier), and application for this was duly made by Köchel a few days before he received the aforementioned document, on 19 June. By this time the emperor was Ferdinand I, a nephew of Köchel's employer, Archduke Karl Ludwig.

As will be seen, by 30 June Köchel was on the high seas en route for the African coast and eventually Great Britain, and the lengthy preparation for this journey necessitated the early application in which he made provision for the official document to be received on his behalf by Herr Franz Lingölf, who was then Official (deputy) in the service of his erstwhile employer.

A copy of the formal request by Köchel for the statutory award of the diploma has been made available to me by courtesy of the Austrian State Archives, together with copies and drafts of all relevant documents, some of which are reproduced here. This is the translation of the text of Köchel's application:

Your Majesty,

His K.K. apostolic majesty has deigned to bestow upon me per "A" the small cross of the Austrian Imperial Order of Leopold. In consequence I request obediently, in accordance with the statutes exempt of tax, the bestowal of the "Ritterstand" and attach hereto under "B" a short description of the services rendered by me, under "C" a design and description of the coat of arms. For the event of my absence I authorize Herr Franz Lingölf, Deputy, in the service of His Imp. Highness Archduke Karl Ludwig (Wien City No. 1160) to receive the diploma against payment of the taxes.

Wien, 19th June 1842.

A contradiction in this application is obvious. On the one hand, Köchel points out (correctly, as it turned out) that the letters patent should be granted in accordance with existing statutes, on a tax-exempt basis; but on the other hand, he authorizes his representative to discharge these (nonexistent) dues. It seems to me he was playing it safe, wanting to ensure the handing over of the document and prepared to argue over the tax-exempt status after the event, if necessary. Strangely, some of the other documents I have seen indicate that he did in fact pay these dues and that they were later refunded to him, but all this occurred in September 1842 while he was in Great Britain and must therefore have been handled by his appointee.

Referring to the services rendered, mentioned in the application under "B," Köchel writes:

The services rendered which His Majesty may have taken into consideration in conferring upon me the Order of Leopold consist in my employment as a tutor and educator of the young archdukes, their K.K. Highnesses Albrecht, Karl Ferdinand, Friedrich and Wilhelm, sons of His Imp. Highness the serene Archduke Karl Ludwig, from the year 1827 till 1842 for almost fifteen years. The satisfaction of my gracious lord regarding my achievements is attested in the document attached to my application for the diploma of the Order.

As to the coat of arms, it is subsequently described as follows:

A blue shield in which there are three silver cubes arranged in rows of one and two, of which the one can be seen above the two. On the outer edge of the shield rest two open tournament helmets, facing each other, each of which is decorated with golden buckles and jewels, from which blue and silver tinted helmet covers hang on both sides. Each of the helmets is adorned with a golden crown, from the one on the right grow two eagle wings, diagonally divided in alternate silver and blue colors, from the crown of the helmet on the left five ostrich feathers rise of which the second and fourth is silver, the others blue in color.

This was not Köchel's original description, which was much simpler and related only to the basic design of the three silver cubes in a blue shield. The "experts" came up with a more elaborate design, and what is quoted here is the final text of the approved coat of arms.

Many have speculated about the meaning of the central design of three cubes, and in the absence of firm evidence, this significance must obviously remain a matter of opinion. At first I assumed it could represent a connection with Freemasonry and even with the lodge "Zur Wohltätigkeit" (to charity), to which Mozart had belonged and which had three squares arranged in a similar way as its symbol. The Viennese Grand Lodge of Freemasons advises me that freemasons were forbidden in Austria during Köchel's lifetime and that there is no record of membership of a clandestine lodge. Even so, this is still a distinct possibility of motivation as another example of Köchel's homage to Mozart.

Another theory expressed by several researchers is that each of the three cubes represents one of the fundamental spheres of interest in Köchel's life: music, mineralogy, and botany, with the sky-blue background symbolizing his great love for the outdoors.

Tournament helmets were customary for "nonaristocratic" coats of arms since the beginning of the fifteenth century. Ostrich feathers were frequently included in the designs, one example being that of the coat of arms of Field Marshal Radetzky, one of the foremost military commanders of Austria, immortalized by the famous Radetzky March by Johann Strauss's father, traditionally the final "encore" item of Vienna New Year's Day concerts. There is also a poem "Radetzky" in the small volume of poetry by Köchel.

After receipt of the application, a lengthy document was prepared and signed on 28 July 1842 by the Emperor Ferdinand I, from which the following details are quoted in translation:

> We Ferdinand, k.k.k., following the examples of Austrian regents, our most serene forefathers, have always regarded it as one of the most

significant obligations and at the same time as one of the most beautiful privileges of our sovereignty, to confer public tokens of our favor upon those individuals who have distinguished themselves by their loyalty and devotion toward the state, our person and our family and who gloriously excelled by their conformity with good manners in military service, in offices of civil administration, in the sciences, or who contributed in other ways to the furtherance of universal welfare; and to reward such persons specifically through their honorable elevation of rank whereby others will be spurred to praiseworthy eagerness in serving the general community, and in particular to always remind the descendants who inherit the honorable reward merited by their ancestors, of their duty to show themselves worthy of their noble descent by emulating this duty.

Our personal attention is therefore unceasingly conscious not to overlook distinctive merits and we have made it the duty of all our authorities and their principals to bring to our knowledge those persons who are worthy of our rewarding favor, and we shall then be no less inclined to listen to the representations reaching us from those persons who support their applications for these honorable distinctions with conclusive proof of their merits.

Now it has come to our knowledge that Ludwig Köchel, doctor of law, k.k. councilor, former tutor and educator of the most serene sons of our uncle, the Imp. Highness Archduke Karl Ludwig, and knight of our Imp. Austrian Order of Leopold, has requested his elevation to the Austrian Ritterstand (the noble rank of chevaliers). Dr. Ludwig Köchel has obtained our special satisfaction by his important and successful participation in the upbringing and teaching of their Imp. Highnesses, the Archdukes Albrecht, Karl Ferdinand, Friedrich and Wilhelm and as Dr. Köchel always proved his loyalty and devotion to us and to our most serene imperial house we have decreed to make him, as proof of our sovereign grace, on the 30th April 1842, knight of our Austrian Imperial Order of Leopold for which the diploma was prepared on the 24th June 1842.

As by virtue of having been granted this order there is a right to apply for an elevation into the "Ritterstand" of our Empire and as Ludwig Köchel has applied for this elevation in rank, we have in accordance with the statutes elevated him, Ludwig Köchel, together with his legitimate descendants of both sexes for all future times to the Ritterstand of our Austrian Empire and have given permission for the use of this title in conjunction with his previous surname from now on and henceforth by him and his legitimate descendants.

We wish hereby and decree accordingly that Ludwig Ritter von Köchel and his legitimate descendants of both sexes now and henceforth be regarded as Ritterstand persons of our Austrian Empire and that they partake of all rights and privileges appropriate to the Ritterstand. As lasting proof of our grace and of the elevation to the Ritterstand we have bestowed upon him, Ludwig Ritter von Köchel, the following knightly coat of arms as depicted in its true colors in the center of this Ritterstands Diploma, that is a blue shield in which three silver cubes . . . [etc., as already described].

We therefore authorize him, Ludwig Ritter von Köchel, and his legitimate descendants of both sexes to carry and use unimpeded the coat of arms described above from now on and for all times, but without affecting the rights of others who may possess a similar coat of arms. In particular we command all authorities of church and secularity of our Empire to regard him, Ludwig Ritter von Köchel and his legitimate descendants as real Ritterstand persons and as such to allow their undisturbed use of the Ritterstand and neither themselves hinder this use nor permit other citizens to do so, whereby we intend to impose our sovereign disfavor and appropriate penalty unto those who act against this our decree.

This document we have confirmed by adding our signature in our own hand and by attaching to this diploma our secret great seal of majesty, the use of which serves us in our capacity of Emperor of Austria and have commanded this to be handed to Doctor of law, k.k. councilor Ludwig Ritter von Köchel and his legitimate descendants.

Granted this eight and twentieth day of the month of July in the year of the Lord One Thousand Eight Hundred and Forty-two.

From this excerpt, it appears that the date on which Köchel rose to the rank of nobility was 28 July 1842, but the official document is dated 5 September, and the date of handing this over to Köchel's nominated representative was 24 December 1842—at least that is the date on the "receipt" issued, the text of which is as follows:

Acknowledgment of Receipt for the Ritterstands diploma signed in his own hand by His Imp. Royal Apost. Majesty for him, doctor of law, k.k. councilor, former tutor of the most serene sons of His Imp. Highness the most serene Archduke Karl, knight of the Imp. Austrian Order of Leopold, Ludwig Ritter von Köchel.

Wien, 24th December 1842
Franz Lingölf
Archducal Deputy

Between the time of the application by Köchel and the final acknowledgment of receipt of the letters patent, a number of other official papers passed among the various departments dealing with minor aspects of the matter, such as the exact description of the coat of arms, the question of the tax exempt status, announcements for the official paper, and so forth. On one of the papers is a footnote to indicate that Köchel was not available to receive the letters patent "as he is absent in England."

As we will see in the next chapter, Köchel was consistently referred to by the title "chevalier" during his stay in Great Britain. Whether this reference was technically correct—the official document not having been handed to his representative until December, whereas the title was used by him in September—would be a matter for experts in this field to decide.

When Köchel applied for his elevation to a hereditary title, he was a bachelor, and he remained a single man for the rest of his life. If he had any desire at that time, at the age of forty-two, to marry and start a family, no trace can be found about any such plan.

As to the effect of the title on his future, he made good use of it by moving in the elevated circles to which he was now readily admitted. His financial situation had become stable, as he had probably saved most of his considerable salary during the fifteen years of his employment by the archduke when he had little opportunity to spend what he had earned. He was also to receive a substantial pension from the day he gave up his tutoring position.

All this is in stark contrast to the precarious state of his financial affairs when he first came to Vienna. His newfound "financial independence" allowed him to devote his time to the scientific subjects of interest to him. But first, one more service was requested of Köchel.

9

Köchel in Great Britain

Almost immediately after leaving the imperial household of Archduke Karl, having accomplished the task of educating the young archdukes (the youngest now being fifteen), Köchel was invited by his former pupil Archduke Friedrich to accompany him on a most important journey. As part of his military training, Friedrich was to visit the leading naval power, Great Britain, and to meet the men who commanded its navy. The recently launched frigate *Bellona*, armed with fifty-two cannons and fully manned, awaited its archducal commander at Pirano (now Piran in Slovenia).

This was by no means the first sea journey for Friedrich; he had visited Venice, Gibraltar, Algeria, Corfu, Piraeus, Smyrna (today Izmir, Turkey), Constantinople (today Istanbul), where he had stayed for two months, Athens, and Syria, where he had been in command of 150 Austrian troops who participated on the side of the British in the campaign commanded by Sir Robert Stopford. His bravery in almost single-handedly seizing the citadel of St. Jean d'Acre earned the praise of Foreign Secretary Lord Palmerston (in a letter to Lord Beauvale) and in Admiral Stopford's letter to Baron Bandiera "detailing the circumstances under which His Imperial and Royal Highness, the most serene Archduke Frederic entered the town of Acre and took possession of the citadel early on the morning of the 4th inst. . . . I am not surprised that he should take advantage of any circumstances to continue the fame he has always acquired." This of a man nineteen years old at the time! All this happened in 1840–1841.

The date of *Bellona*'s departure was 30 June 1842, and the importance of the enterprise is accentuated by the fact that Friedrich's father, Archduke Karl, accompanied by his sons the archdukes Albrecht and Wilhelm and by his daughter Archduchess Maria Theresia, came to Pirano to see off the party on a trip that was to take almost seven months.

Archduke Friedrich was being prepared to take command of the Austrian naval forces; now, at twenty-one, he was still learning, and his principal military tutor, Major Wilhelm von Lebzeltern, was to accompany him on the voyage, as was Lieutenant Commander von Marinovich, his naval instructor. They had both been on his earlier voyages as well. Captain B. du Mont was also part of the official contingent, as was Count Ladislaus Károlyi. Köchel had been specifically invited by the archduke as a mark of courtesy toward his former tutor and doubtless because of Köchel's knowledge of languages, which was bound to be useful and which may have been missed on the earlier trips, although, as we shall see from a letter written by Köchel to Archduke Karl, Friedrich had at least some basic knowledge of English.

The first port of call was Algiers, where they anchored on 21 July 1842, having been plagued by adverse sailing conditions that were to be encountered throughout the voyage. Here they were met by Governor-General Thomas-Robert Bugeaud de la Piconnerie of Algeria. During their six-day stay, they visited the casbah, the Plain of Metijah, traveling through Duera and Blida.

The party left Algiers on 27 July, and on 7 August the frigate anchored at Gibraltar. Here visits were exchanged with the retired British general Sir Charles Smith, who had his residence in San Rocco on the Spanish mainland. Departing the Rock on 14 August, they reached Lisbon four days later; here they stayed for a fortnight, meeting the king and queen at Cintra.

Two letters by Köchel survive in Archduke Karl's archives, now in the Országos Levéltár (State Archives) in Budapest, Hungary. The first of these was sent from Lisbon and is dated 22 August 1842. This is what Köchel wrote:

Most Serene Archduke!
Most Gracious Sir!

With my most respectful warmest congratulatory wishes on occasion of Your Highness's birthday, for which heaven may grant its richest blessings, may Your Imperial Highness permit me to express my deeply felt thanks for all favors which Y.I.H. have bestowed upon me over a number of years in a way which was as pleasing as it was meaningful. Even beyond the duration of my limited activity has Your Highness through the most gracious offer of one of the most interesting voyages, under conditions which could not be planned to be more pleasant, given me unforgettable proof of the continuation of Your highest goodwill, and it will be my most diligent endeavor to be worthy at least to some extent. Providence has so far averted from our journey all significant adversity: Since our departure from Gibraltar Archduke Friedrich has shown no trace of the insignificant influenza-like attacks which he had shared with the greatest part of our company. Through the most caring attention both toward His closer and more distant associates, through the unconstrained behavior and gay dignity of His conduct toward his friends, He wins all hearts, not to lose them again. Just now when we are returning from a stay of several days at Cintra, He most decidedly aroused the participation of the royal family causing thereby that the festivities arranged in honor of the archduke were completely devoid of the customary stiltedness and that everyone felt very much at ease. I have absolutely no doubt as to the most favorable impressions to be created by Archduke Friedrich in England, particularly as he has also made some headway with the language.—From the botanic point of view, so far I can mention only a camellia tree near Cintra which thrives in the open air and the abundant head of which could barely be encircled by the complete company of 10 men. Full of beautiful memories and expectations and humbly offering again his gratitude and felicitations Your Imperial Highness's most obedient servant Ludwig Köchel

Lisbon harbor, 22nd August 1842.

Ten days after leaving the Portuguese port, the frigate arrived on 9 September at its destination in the Bay of Plymouth. The archduke's party was welcomed with due naval honors by Fleet Admiral David Milm, Rear Admiral Sir Samuel Pym, and General Murray. The next few days were spent viewing the naval establishments of Plymouth. On 19 September they took the Southampton train from Gosport to London—this may well have been the first time any of the visitors had traveled by steam train, as the first passenger service in Austria was not fully operational until 1843. The ambassador of Austria, Prince Paul Esterházy, welcomed and joined the party. They stayed in the Mivarts Hotel (today known as Claridges) in London, before leaving on the 21st for Windsor Castle, where they were most cordially received by Queen Victoria and Prince Albert.

The identity of Mivarts Hotel came from an old Baedeker guide of London, where its address is given as 42 Brook Street and it is described as follows: "Der erste Gasthof Londons, in jeder Beziehung empfehlenswert, aber nicht gerade billig, das gewöhnliche Absteigequartier fürstlicher Personen" (The foremost hotel in London, in every respect worthy of recommendation, if not exactly inexpensive, the customary quarters of titled persons). I tried to find out more about the imperial party's stay, but on behalf of the present owner, the Savoy Group of Hotels, Sir Hugh Wontner advised me as follows: "We do have very ancient records, but I regret nothing as old as 1842, and consequently, with regret, we cannot help you."

According to information received from the Royal Archives, Archduke Friedrich's party stayed at Windsor until 28 September. Of the five men in the archduke's suite, one is described as "Le Chevalier de Köechel" in Queen Victoria's journal. The Windsor Castle dinner list also refers to him by that name, as does a contemporary newspaper cutting that was attached to the journal entry and lists the persons who attended a royal dinner party in the Waterloo Gallery on 23 September 1842. During the archduke's stay at Windsor, Köchel also had the opportunity to meet other guests there. These included the Lords Liverpool, Lincoln, Sydney and Exeter, Lord and Lady Jersey, the Duke of Wellington, and Prince Castelcicula. Queen Victoria herself had returned a few days earlier from her historic first visit to Scotland.

Earlier the same year, in June and July, two visits were paid by Felix Mendelssohn-Bartholdy to Buckingham Palace. The composer wrote to his mother after the first of these, "The pretty and most charming Queen Victoria, who looks so youthful and is so gently courteous and gracious; who speaks such good German, and who knows all my music so well. . . . Yesterday evening I was sent for by the Queen, who was almost alone with Prince Albert and who seated herself near the piano and made me play to her—first, seven of the 'Songs without words' . . . then two impromptus on 'Rule Britannia' and 'Gaudeamus Igitur' . . . [in] the splendid grand gallery in Buckingham Palace where we took tea." After the second visit, he wrote as follows:

Prince Albert had asked me to go to him on Saturday at 2 o'clock, so that I might try his organ before I left England. I found him alone . . . the Queen came in, also alone . . . the wind had littered the whole room

. . . with sheets of music from a large portfolio. . . . She knelt down and began picking up the music. Prince Albert helped and I, too, was not idle. . . .

I begged the Prince to play me something . . . and he played a chorale, by heart, with the pedals, so charmingly, and clearly, and correctly, that it would have done credit to any professional . . . and the Queen . . . looked pleased. . . . [When later I played,] before I got to the end of the first verse [of "How lovely are the Messengers" from "St. Paul"] they both joined in the chorus.

The archive records indicate that the archduke's party returned to Windsor on 6 December, leaving again on 9 December 1842. When the delegation left Windsor Castle, they visited Hampton Court Palace before returning to London across the new and much-admired Hammersmith Bridge.

A few more days were spent in and around London to allow for visits to St. Paul's Cathedral, Kensington Palace, Marlborough House, Westminster Abbey and Cathedral, the Houses of Parliament, and the Blackwall Tunnel, proudly shown to the group by the engineer Sir Marc Brunel. On 1 October they visited Greenwich, where they were shown around the famous observatory by its director, Sir George Biddell Airy. They also saw the naval school for seven hundred cadets before returning to their London quarters.

There followed an overland tour of thirty-seven days through England and Scotland (and a bit of Wales), which started with a railway journey on the Birmingham line to Tamworth. Two miles south of here was Drayton Manor, the country residence of the prime minister, Sir Robert Peel, where they visited on 5 and 6 October. Then they traveled via Derby and Chesterfield to Chatsworth, home of the duke of Devonshire. This palace in its present form (which is virtually unchanged since the time described here) dates from 1687. In the gardens they admired the twenty-four groups of steps of the "tumbling waters" of the cascade, designed in 1696 by the Frenchman Grillet. The design of the uneven spacing of the steps is such that it varies the sound to be heard from each point.

A day later they were at York, where they visited the Minster with its one hundred beautiful stained glass windows and richly carved altar. From here they proceeded to the port of Seaham near Sunderland. On 11 October, their schedule took them via Durham to Newcastle upon Tyne, an important industrial center even then. They were the guests of the duke and duchess of Northumberland at Alnwick Castle; their hostess proudly showed them around the Egyptian Museum.

On the way to Scotland through Berwick-on-Tweed, the party visited the residence of Lord Haddington, first lord of the admiralty, and on 16 October they got to Edinburgh. Here they saw Holyroodhouse Castle and particularly the rooms that had been occupied by Mary, Queen of Scots. High Mass was attended at the Catholic church to the strains of Mozart's music. In nearby Dalkeith they called on the lord privy seal, the duke of Buccleuch, before departing on the Glasgow railway line for Stirling, Perth, and Dunkeld on the River Tay. They then crossed the Grampians to reach Inverness, the northernmost point of the tour, and continued along the Caledonian Canal via Loch Ness first to Fort Augustus, then to Fort William by the side of Ben Nevis, Scotland's highest peak—alas, a long way short of the heights of the Alps, well known to the travelers and particularly to Köchel, who was a pioneer in popularizing the High Alps of Austria to the extent that some observers have suggested that the Austrian tourist industry is greatly indebted to Köchel for his contribution.

After visiting the ruins of the old Inverlochy castle (not to be confused with today's hotel/restaurant of that name, not yet built at that time), the visitors went to Inverary and from there to Loch Lomond and on to Glasgow, which was the final point of the Scottish sojourn. Here they inspected several factories of the fast-developing industrial center and were introduced to Sir Robert Napier, who owned the steam engine manufactory and who was described by the archduke as "one of the cleverest and most obliging men of England."

It was from Glasgow that Köchel's second surviving letter from this trip to Archduke Karl was sent. This is its text:

Your Imperial Highness!

Whilst I take the liberty to lay humbly before Your Imperial Highness my most respectful felicitations on your most esteemed name day, I do so with the uplifting sentiment of joyful gratefulness.

May providence, through the abundant prosperity of your children allow Your Imperial Highness to enjoy for long the fruits of your noble activity to which end your Highness has so richly sown the seeds in all directions.

It would be difficult to imagine a journey of several months of such scope and with a similar number of participants, which would produce so much of what is pleasant and so little of what is not, as the present one of our Archduke Friedrich with his retinue. A sea voyage of several thousand miles, an expedition into the interior of Africa, now again an overland trip of several hundred miles—and all of this without a significant accident, must be a rare thing. And Archduke Friedrich is healthy throughout and cheerful, always of a good disposition to appreciate the changing impressions, everywhere congenial through his unpretentiousness, giving all of us sincere happiness.

We had the opportunity by now to be able to observe, if only in its outlines, but under the most propitious circumstances, life at Court and on the estates of the greats of England together with the beautiful natural scenery of Scotland: there still remains for us the industrial section and part of the naval life, whereby we shall have collected sufficient material to assimilate on the return journey in the winter.—It must obviously be the heavens that guide the steps of our beloved archduke, because in the land of fog and rain, at such an advanced time of the year, on a northbound journey, to have 3 weeks, where with the exception of only 2 days we had cheerful weather, we recognized as a special and unmistakable favor from above. But we ascribe it a little to our own account if so much fortune has not made us arrogant and we look forward confidently to the ultimate success of our enterprise.

My very special thanks must be expressed for the letter graciously addressed to me by Y.I.H.: I would be most happy if I could satisfy at least to some extent the expectations of Y.I.H. The commission by H.I.H. Archduke Ludwig to the gardener Loddiges I shall discharge favorably. In repeating my most sincere felicitations, I humble myself as

Your Imperial Highness's most obedient servant
Köchel
Glasgow, 24th October 1842

In reading (and translating) this letter, I am led to wonder whether the reference to "the fruits of noble activity . . . [as a result of] seeds so richly sown in all directions" can be restricted to mean the imperial children of Archduke Karl. The normal meaning of such words would be a reference to wild oats. When the two Köchel letters written from this trip are read together, it becomes obvious that although the occasion of each was a celebration of his erstwhile employer's birthday and name day, respectively, the comments in the letters indicate that Köchel was here not only by special invitation of Archduke Friedrich but very much on behalf of Friedrich's father, Karl, who obviously wanted Köchel's reports on his son's health and behavior during the journey.

On 28 October the group was back in England, having traveled on the steam packet from Greenock to Liverpool. On the 29th they made an excursion to Manchester, described in the archduke's diary as being "full of very unclean and ugly houses." The train took them back to Liverpool; then came Chester and Bangor in North Wales, where they admired the suspension bridge built by Thomas Telford in 1826 over the Menai Straits to Anglesey.

On 1 November the journey continued via Shrewsbury to Birmingham, then to Bristol and Oxford (which they described as a "dull city enlivened only by its colleges"). From here they visited Blenheim Palace, the duke of Marlborough's country residence at Woodstock, then Lord Jersey's home at Middleton Park, and took their return journey through Stow and the Cotswolds, reaching London on 9 November.

In London they became part of the social activities attending numerous receptions, among these most memorably the one at Apsley House, the Duke of Wellington's London residence, on 16 November, when "many excellent personalities were present," to quote the archduke. There was surely no shortage of conversational subjects between the son of the first victor over Napoleon and the last conqueror of the French emperor!

On the same day they also visited the British Museum, where they inspected the coin collection, the minerals, and the zoological specimens. Again, Köchel's scientific knowledge must have been useful, at least in regards to the minerals.

On the 15th and 17th the party visited Woolwich with its arsenal and on the 18th Buckingham Palace and St. James's Palace. The 19th was spent viewing the Tower of London; the 21st was spent at Chatham and the 22nd at Sheerness, in both places to see the naval facilities. There were also visits to Trinity House, the printing works of the *Quarterly Review* and *The Times,* the prisons of Newgate and Tothill, the Guildhall, the Bank of England, and East India House.

On the 26th came a visit to the Royal Mint, where the principal engraver, William Wyon, R. A., designed and struck a memorial silver coin bearing on the reverse side the inscription "H[is] I[mperial] H[ighness] Archduke Frederick of Austria visited the Royal Mint Nov 26," with the year 1842 underneath. The archduke wrote in his diary that he found the machinery "very antiquated and not up to the standard of ours." Memorial coins were handed to all members of the visiting imperial party.

The whirl of social activities during these four weeks in London included four dinner engagements at the welcoming and cheerful house of the duke of Cambridge at Kew. There was also a visit on the 30th to Strathfield Saye House, the duke of Wellington's country residence near Basingstoke, now a museum to commemorate the soldier who freed Europe from the menace of Napoleon. Here they took part in a hunt led by the seventy-three-year-old duke, along with no fewer than seven hundred others.

As mentioned earlier, on 6 December they revisited Windsor Castle on the queen's invitation, staying until the 9th and taking part in a pheasant shoot. The archduke was decorated with the Grand Cross of the Order of Bath. The return journey to London was by train.

After spending a few more days in the capital city, they traveled to Gosport on 13 December; from here they made a brief visit to the Isle of Wight on the 17th, going to Ryde, Shanklin, and Cowes. This was followed by an inspection of the embankments of Portsmouth and Portsea. They were now back on board their frigate, the *Bellona*, having sailed from Plymouth to Spithead.

Naval exercises were held on 20 December under Colonel Jones. On the 21st farewell calls took place, including a visit to the Naval College. Bad weather forced the party back on shore, where they stayed in the George Hotel until finally, on New Year's Day 1843, they were able to rejoin the *Bellona* and commence the homeward journey. With more favorable winds, they arrived at Trieste on 22 January 1843. Tragically, the young archduke was to die less than five years later on 5 October 1847 in Venice, surviving his father, Archduke Karl, by only a few months.

Köchel liked England. In fact, he liked the English so much that he said, half in jest, perhaps, after this long visit, "If I were not an Austrian I would quite like to be an Englishman!" The acquaintances he made at Windsor and throughout the visit stood him in good stead in his later life and work. He came back to England in the 1850s in the course of tracing Mozart's compositions. The exact time of his visit then is not known. A further visit took place between 1862 and 1864.

Among the Mozart manuscripts Köchel found and listed in the *Register* were several he had traced to London proprietors: The Andantino for Piano K. 236 (Mr. J. B. Cramer); Introduction and Fugue K. 291 (Mr. Ella); Twelve Variations for Piano and Violin K. 359 and Six Variations for Piano and Violin K. 360, Adagio for Piano K. 540

and Adagio and Fugue K. 546 (Mr. Caulfield); the Six String Quartets dedicated to Joseph Hayden K. 387, 421, 428, 458, 464, and 465; a further String Quartet K. 499 (Mr. Plowden); two String Quintets K. 406 and K. 593 ("bought in March 1847 for £2 in London from J. A. Stumpf's estate"); a Concerto for Piano K. 488 ("sold to London by J. B. André in Berlin"); three String Quartets K. 575, 589, and 590, dedicated to the king of Prussia (Mr. Hamilton); and the String Quintet K. 614 (Mr. Schmidt "from the estate of J. A. Stumpf for £3.10"). Any or all of these may have been traced by Köchel during his London visit, but in the absence of more detail about the proprietors of the manuscripts, I found it impossible to determine the exact time of Köchel's visit.

He may also have looked at the *only* Mozart manuscript owned at the time by the British Museum (which he had also visited in 1842), the Setting of Psalm 46 "God Is Our Refuge" for four voices, K. 20, but having searched through the Reading Room records of the British Museum for the relevant period, I found no evidence of Köchel's presence there. Further research may have to be carried out by persons who find a link with some of the aforementioned names. Cramer was of course the music publisher and piano manufacturer whose business was later acquired by Chappells, and John Ella (1802–1888) was violinist/conductor/critic, a friend of Meyerbeer and Wagner.

As a result of various bequests and purchases, the collection of Mozart manuscripts now housed in the British Museum is a very different proposition. From Stefan Zweig's estate comes the original manuscript of Mozart's own register of compositions from February 1784 to his death (Ref. Zweig MS. 63). Also available is the manuscript copy of Johann Anton André's Catalogue of Mozart's "precatalog" compositions (Ref. Add MS. 32412).

10

Scientific Activities

When Ludwig, now at age forty-two known as Ritter von Köchel, found himself in a position of financial independence and with no obligations toward a family, he started to construct for himself a new life that was to take him into various branches of science and filled more and more by his love for music.

During his years as tutor to the imperial archdukes, Köchel made several journeys at home and abroad, as described in prior chapters. In the course of these trips, Köchel's interest in natural sciences and, in particular, in botany and mineralogy was much in evidence, and the foundations were laid for the very substantial collection of minerals and the herbarium that eventually consisted of more than thirteen thousand plants.

For the first time in his life Köchel was in the fortunate position to have time on his hands and funds available to indulge in these matters. The work for which he was to become famous and which has preserved his name to this day, the compilation of the register of Mozart's compositions, was still a long time away, however. Thus it was not this work that lent prestige to his other activities. Köchel had already "outlived" Mozart by some six years, yet he felt that the first part of his adult life was but a stepping stone toward his real aims.

Between 1842 and 1847 Köchel's residence was in Vienna, but he spent long periods of this time on foreign travels. In 1845, for instance, he undertook a journey to Italy and Sicily for botanical studies; 1847 sees him traveling to France, the Pyrenees, and Switzerland. Each of these journeys must have taken many months in view of the means of transportation then available and the scientific work to be done at each point of destination. Regrettably, no additional details are available about these trips.

In 1848 he followed his friend Scharschmid to Teschen in Bohemia (known as Cesky Tesin in Czech, Cieszyn in Polish). Scharschmid had been appointed president of the district court and governor (Landeshauptmann) of the region in 1843, immediately upon leaving Archduke Karl's service. Köchel stayed with him there until 1850, when his friend received a similar law court appointment in Salzburg. This development led to Köchel packing his bags again and moving to Salzburg.

Let us take out some time here to look at the friend who was of such evident importance to Köchel and whose name appears again and again throughout his life, in whose home he was able to enjoy a degree of family life in the absence of a family of his own.

Franz Scharschmid von Adlertreu was born in Aussig, Bohemia (now Usti nad Labem in the Czech Republic), on 25 August 1800 (i.e., the same year as Köchel). One of his ancestors was nobleman Cajetan Scharschmid von Adlertreu. He studied law first in Prague, then in Vienna, where he obtained his Juris Doctor degree and first came in contact with Köchel.

Parallel to his studies, just like Köchel, Scharschmid started on a career of private tutorship, first in the household of Landgraf (Landgrave) Joseph Egon von Fürstenberg, where he took over tutorial duties from Philipp Mayer (who became one of Köchel's closest friends), and later in the imperial household of Archduke Karl. This latter appointment commenced in 1828; he followed Philipp Mayer in this job as well, after Mayer died that year.

Scharschmid was in charge of the tuition of the archduchesses, but he also participated in Köchel's work of teaching the four young archdukes. Their careers ran a parallel course throughout this period; Scharschmid was made Kaiserlicher Rath (imperial councilor) in 1832, the same year as Köchel, and his elevation to the hereditary Ritterstand came a year after that of Köchel, on 29 April 1843.

In 1843, upon termination of his tutorial work and appointed to his new post by Archduke Karl, he set out on a legal career, becoming court president and Landeshauptmann of Teschen. He also became the archduke's official deputy at the lawmaking Silesian Convention in Troppau (today Tropov). From 1848 to 1850 he was acting ministerial commissar for the organization of the judicial authorities in Silesia. In 1850 he was promoted to be president of the

District Court of Salzburg, and in 1852 a further promotion saw him in his final post of president of the Vienna District Court. With this appointment he also became a member of the State Court of Austria. In 1854 he received for services rendered in the field of justice the Comthurkreuz of the Franz Joseph Order, and on 16 June 1872 he became Freiherr (baron). He married in 1830 and had two children.

The friendship with Köchel started in the men's early twenties when they were both law students in Vienna and continued throughout their lives. It is likely that when Scharschmid joined the household of Archduke Karl as a tutor, the engagement was on the recommendation of Köchel, who had been active in this capacity for the last year.

In 1848, when Köchel returned from his latest scientific journey, he joined the Scharschmid household in Teschen. He followed him to Salzburg in 1850 and again to Vienna in 1863, although soon after arriving there, he moved into the apartment granted him by his former pupil, Archduke Albrecht. The newspaper notice announcing Köchel's death in 1877 was to be placed by Scharschmid, and his daughter, Baronin (Baroness) Paula Baltazzi-Scharschmid was to be the prominent family representative at the unveiling of Köchel's memorial plaque in Stein in 1906.

Two of Köchel's published poems refer to the men's friendship. A short one, probably written in 1841, is called "Scharschmid"; in 1855 under the title "Festgabe" (Festive Gift) and dedicated to Franz and Marie von Scharschmid, he commemorated their silver wedding anniversary in a moving testimony to this happy marriage. Scharschmid wrote a treatise entitled "Von der Alimentation der geschiedenen Ehegatten" (Concerning the Alimony Payments by Divorced Husbands)—a subject in which Scharschmid must have lacked all personal experience!

In the earliest known biographical notes on Köchel, those by Professor Carl Victor Reusch from Cannstatt (which are included in the foreword of the 1905 second and in subsequent editions of the *Köchelverzeichnis*), a sentence appears that is later reproduced in the entries of various encyclopedias and other biographical articles on Köchel. This states that when Köchel moved to Vienna in 1863, "In dessen [i.e., Scharschmid's] Hause verbrachte er, der unverehelicht gebliebene, wie früher seine Mussestunden und teilte dessen Tisch" (As before, he, who remained unmarried, spent his hours of leisure and shared the table in the hospitable house). For an unmarried man, it was obviously of tremendous value to have a friend, happily married, with a pleasant family, in whose house he could reside when he had no home of his own and where he could regularly visit after taking up residence in the archducal palace; whose family could serve as a substitute for not having one of his own; and with whom he could share reminiscences of their joint past. Whether there was more to this than pure friendship cannot be judged.

On 18 June 1850, soon after moving to Salzburg, Köchel was appointed "provisional imperial and royal school councilor" (Schulrat) of Salzburg and grammar school inspector (Gymnasialinspektor) of Oberösterreich. Being of independent means throughout this period, it is likely that he accepted the appointments without having in mind a new career in teaching, this time in a supervisory capacity, but merely to have an occupation for his very active mind. The Landesarchiv (state archives) in Salzburg contains stacks of reports made by the directors of the various schools to Köchel; these were shown to me by Dr. Schopf, the director of the archives. I found Köchel's handwritten comments on many of these reports, and reading his notes and comments, it is obvious that he took a serious interest in his work. This prestigious but temporary appointment could have led to a career in the educational establishment of Austria, but he resigned from the job after only two and a half years at the end of 1852. The reason given for his resignation is that "his enlightened views differed from the prevailing tendency" of the authorities.

Let us stop and consider. A man spends fifteen years of his adult life in the service of an archduke who is third in line to the imperial throne. For services rendered he is richly rewarded and raised to a hereditary title. In other words, he is very much part of the "establishment." This is in 1842. Yet, barely ten years later, he resigns or, more likely, is made to resign for his "enlightened views." What happened in those ten years to change the direction of this educated man, to turn him from being a trusted supporter of the imperial cause into a "libertine," someone who could not be trusted to exert his potentially "harmful" influence over the grammar school students under his supervision?

The answer is likely to be in the history of the period, for 1848 was a year of revolutions throughout Europe. In Austria this led to the resignation of Kaiser Ferdinand I, who had reigned since 1835 and who was replaced on the throne by his eighteen-year-old nephew Franz Joseph I, who was to reign until his death in 1916.

The year 1849 brought the total victory of the conservative monarchist powers in Austria. It also saw the defeat of the Hungarian revolution that had started on 15 March 1848, with the object of separating that country from the monarchy and turning it into a republic. The revolutionary forces were also broken in the Italian provinces that were under Austrian jurisdiction, the final capitulation being that of Venice on 22 August 1849.

All this signaled the start of a period of draconian measures, court-martials, death sentences, executions, and banishments. No wonder if an educated man like Köchel found it difficult to reconcile himself with the atrocities that became only too common. Whether he took an active part in the events of 1848–1849 cannot be established; his name does not appear in history books about the period. He may have sympathized with his enlightened contemporaries, but his title and his involvement with the imperial family would have prevented him from openly exposing himself in this way.

Köchel's views must have been clear, however, to those who knew him, and a word whispered here or there into the right ear would have meant that he was considered unsuitable for the job of school inspector. The man who had been his patron for a long time, his former employer Archduke Karl, a man well known for his progressive views, had died in 1847, so no support could be expected from this direction.

Köchel was to stay in Salzburg, apart from his travels and occasional brief visits to Vienna, until 1863. This was the period of his life that must be described as the most productive of his career. In 1853 he undertook another journey in furtherance of his studies in natural science. This took him via Berlin and Stettin (now Szeczin in Poland) to St. Petersburg and Moscow, then to Copenhagen and via Christiana (now Oslo, Norway) to the North Cape. He became a member of the newly formed Salzburg Society of Geography and of the Austrian Society for Zoology and Botany in Vienna.

As part of his musicological activities he became a member of the Dom Music Society and the Mozarteum of Salzburg in 1854. The Consistory-Archives in Salzburg advise me that from 11 June 1854 he was an elected member of the Dom Society's Committee, a position he held until 1867, when he continued as an honorary member. In conjunction with the archivist Jellinek, he was prominent in his care for the Mozart heritage and was strongly opposed to lending Mozart autographs to various world expositions. Numerous references to his activity are to be found in the minutes of meetings of the Committee of Representatives. His main contribution to the 1856 Mozart centenary celebrations was his lengthy poem "Mozart Canzone," which I will discuss in a later chapter when reviewing Köchel's poetry.

Foremost during this whole period, however, were Köchel's attempts to prepare the first complete register of Mozart's compositions. This necessitated a number of further journeys, including foreign destinations such as Germany, France, and England, as he was always prepared to follow up any lead, however slender, to trace some of the many missing manuscripts. The costs of this research were born entirely by himself, and in all, half his fortune was spent on the furtherance of this work.

This activity culminated in the publication by the leading music publishing house, Breitkopf & Härtel of Leipzig, in 1862 of the work that has become known as the *Köchelverzeichnis* (Köchel Register), although it would have been more apt to refer to it as the "Mozartverzeichnis" as it is not the only register compiled by Köchel. This, together with the events leading to Köchel's dedication to the task, will be discussed in a separate section.

A summary of Köchel's classification of Mozart's opus also formed part of a lecture he gave in May 1862 about Mozart's music to the members of the Society for Geography in Salzburg; this is reprinted in the society's bulletin, to which I shall also return later.

The *Register* itself is dedicated to his friend and fellow Mozart researcher Otto Jahn, whose definitive four-volume Mozart biography began to appear in 1856 and who made his research material available to Köchel. Moreover, Jahn dropped his own plans to prepare a register of Mozart's compositions when he heard that his friend was engaged in the same pursuit.

It could have been an anticlimax to see in print the work whose compilation had taken some ten to twelve years. But Köchel did not rest on his laurels; instead, he continued the research as if the register were still in preparation. New material, new information, came into his possession. In 1864 he published his findings into the origin and completion of Mozart's Requiem in an article totally ignored subsequently by musicologists for some eighty years but verified in every respect in recent times. He also prepared handwritten notes for a second edition of the *Köchelverzeichnis* to incorporate the results of his further research. Indeed, great use was made of these notes when the second edition appeared in 1905 under the revision of Count P. Waldersee.

The years following were devoted to further scientific and literary activities. The year 1865 saw the publication in Vienna of eighty-three newly discovered letters from Ludwig van Beethoven to Arch-duke Rudolph; these were followed by the publication of four Beethoven letters to Count Brunswick in 1867. In 1866 a privately published work appeared, entitled "Die Pflege der Musik am öster-reichischen Hofe vom Schluss des XV. bis zur Mitte des XVIII. Jahrhunderts" (The Cultivation of Music at the Austrian Court from the End of the Fifteenth until the Middle of the Eighteenth Century), a reprint of a lecture he held to members of a scientific association, to be followed by another comprehensive work in 1869: "Die Kaiser-liche Hof- und Musikkapelle in Wien von 1543–1867" (The Imperial Court Orchestra in Vienna 1543–1867) and in 1872 by the definitive work on the life and work of Austria's great baroque composer and conductor Johann Joseph Fux (1660–1741), under the title: "Johann Joseph Fux, Hofcompositor und Hofkapellmeister der Kaiser Leopold I., Joseph I. und Karl VI. von 1698–1740" (J. J. Fux, Court Composer and Court Conductor of Emperors Leopold I, Joseph I, and Karl VI from 1698–1740).

During this period Köchel also published several long articles and studies in the fields of natural science, in which he was actively in-terested. These are dealt with in greater detail later in this book.

In 1867 Köchel became an honorary member of the Mozarteum in Salzburg, having continuously supported this institute in its cultivation of Mozart's memory. In 1871 he became vice president of the Imperial and Royal Zoological and Botanical Society in Vi-enna, but from the musical point of view, most important is the honorary life membership he received on 29 December of the same year to the Gesellschaft der Musikfreunde (Society of the Friends of Music) in Vienna, having previously served as vice president there.

In proposing Köchel for honorary membership at a meeting where the same honor was bestowed on Richard Wagner, Leopold Sonnlei-thner, the famous Austrian musicologist, told the assembly, "Köchel's activity for the Society and the significance of his book about Johann Joseph Fux which constituted a detailed presentation of the art of mu-sic of a complete century, drew the attention of the whole world upon him." (It is perhaps typical that Sonnleithner, who was an early and vehement critic of Köchel's pioneering Mozart *Register,* mentioned his work on Fux rather than his more famous opus.)

Information on Köchel's activity in the society is verified from two sources. A book by C. F. Pohl published in 1871, *Die Gesellschaft der Musikfreunde des Österreichischen Kaiserstaates* (The Society of the Friends of Music of the Austrian Empire), lists his name on page 120 among those regarded to be "supporters and motivators" of the society. The other work is the centenary edition of the society published in 1912 and compiled by Richard von Perger and Dr. Robert Hirschfeld. The title is *Geschichte der K.K. Gesellschaft der Musikfreunde in Wien* (History of the Society of the Friends of Music in Vienna). Page 279 shows Ludwig Ritter von Köchel as vice president from 1843 to 1849 (although previously published biographical notes always referred to a "brief" vice presidency in 1847!); on page 283 he is listed as one of its honorary members, a distinction shared with such notables as Beethoven, Berlioz, Brahms, Bruckner, Cherubini, Dvořák, Donizetti, Grieg, Massenet, Mendelssohn, Rossini, Johann Strauss, Verdi, Wagner, and Weber. Also honored were some persons less well known today but important in the field of music of their time and mentioned in other parts of this book, such as von Eybler (one of the composers who participated in the completion of the unfinished Mozart Requiem), the music critic Dr. Eduard Hanslick, and Leopold von Sonnleithner.

Köchel's portrait is reproduced on page vii of the introduction to the second volume (Zusatzband), which lists the "Sammlungen und Statuten" (collections and statutes) of the society and which was compiled by Dr. Eusebius Mandyczewski, the society's archivist. After comments on the Witteczek/Spaun collection of Schubert manuscripts, the text continues:

> In a similar way the much-traveled scientist, Ludwig Ritter von Köchel, collected for decades the works of Mozart, eliminating after thorough examination the spurious ones from those that are genuine. He published, as a result of his studies, in 1862 his famous Mozart Catalogue which will prove to be authoritative for all times. His collection was bequeathed to the Society in 1877. This proved to be in many ways indispensable for the Complete Edition of Mozart's Compositions published at a later date.

Köchel's name also appears on the list of donors to the society, and all references in the book to Mozart compositions are followed by the appropriate Köchel number.

Köchel's own compositions, which are preserved in manuscript form in the archives of the society, are mentioned on page 104 as part of an alphabetical listing of "Musik Autographe" (musical autographs): "Köchel, Ludwig von: Lieder, Chöre, Tänze und verschiedene andere Hausmusik.—Abschriften unvollendeter Kompositionen Mozarts" (songs, choruses, dances and various other pieces of "Hausmusik"—[i.e., works to be performed in the home] copies of unfinished compositions by Mozart). This is the first mention anywhere that Köchel, apart from his Mozart expertise, was a composer in his own right.

Finally, it is interesting to read the definition in the society's statutes that its main aim is "the development of music in all its branches," whereas the role of "supporting members" is described as those who, without being performers of the art, nevertheless support the aims of the society through their contribution and other participation. And honorable members are "invited by the Society itself to become members and who in consideration of their knowledge are required as councilors." A good way of summing up what Köchel did for the society!

11

Final Journey

Köchel undertook one more scientific journey, to Italy and Sicily in 1874. He returned a sick man, but in spite of his failing health and great age, he continued to strive toward fulfilling his life ambition: the publication of the collected works of Mozart in a single edition. This was to be undertaken by Breitkopf & Härtel, the famous Leipzig music- and book-publishing house that had brought out in 1862 the *Köchel Register* of Mozart's compositions. As will be seen, apart from making the suggestion in the first place—indeed, as early as 1862 when in the foreword to the *Köchelverzeichni*s he gave as one of the many reasons for it "the influence of the idea that this register may serve as a preliminary exercise for a future collected edition of Mozart's works"—Köchel was instrumental in persuading many of his influential friends to become actively involved in the venture.

Köchel made one more journey before his death. This trip took him over the Alps to Bozen (now Bolsano, Italy), in the middle of the winter 1876–1877 to attend the funeral of a friend (whose identity I was unable to establish). He was not in good health when he set out on this trip, and he never fully recovered after his return home; from this time, in fact, he did poorly right up to his death on 3 June 1877. Köchel died peacefully in his sleep in the apartment granted him rent-free by his former pupil, Field Marshal Archduke Albrecht, in his palace in No. 3 Hofgartengasse, today known as Hanuschgasse. Due to rearrangements of the interior of this building, which has recently accommodated the Graphics Collection "Albertina," the box office of the Bundestheater, and various university institutes, it is no longer possible to identify the exact location of Köchel's apartment. From here the cortège set out in the afternoon of 6th June 1877 to take his coffin first to the Court Parish Church of St. Augustin for the consecration of his earthly remains and then to the Zentralfried-hof (central cemetery) of Vienna.

The cortège was headed by Köchel's "catafalque shield," a slightly modified version of the coat of arms earlier described. The middle section again consists of three silver cubes on a pale blue back-ground; the rococo-style surround in gold is surmounted by a coro-net with five pearls. The Leopoldsorder (i.e., the cross of his knight-hood, Ritterkreuz) is suspended underneath. The whole design is on a pale gray background in the shape of the inner shield and carries the name "Ludwig Ritter von Köchel" on the top and the year of his death, "1877," on the bottom. (The original has been acquired at an auction by the Gesellschaft der Musikfreunde in Vienna, whereas the municipal authorities of Krems/Stein possess two copies.)

Upon his own request, Köchel was laid to rest next to the remains of his brother Fritz, sharing his grave with him. This is number 23 (not 24, as is sometimes mistakenly reported) in group 16A, row 7, in the Zentralfriedhof. The epitaph on the beautifully engraved stone proclaims, "Mein lieber Bruder Fritz. Mit dir bis zum Grabe treu, dein Bruder Ludwig Ritter von Köchel, geboren am 14. Jänner 1800, gestorben am 3. Juni 1877" (My dear brother Fritz. True to you unto the grave, your brother Ludwig Ritter von Köchel, born on the 14th January 1800, died on 3rd June 1877).

The grave, which for many years was totally neglected, is today cared for by the municipal authorities of Vienna. This arrangement is a result of an agreement reached between Freiherr Maximilian Scharschmid, son of Köchel's friend, and the authorities, signed on 23 March 1887, whereby a capital sum specified in Köchel's testament and intended for this purpose is bestowed on the municipal authority. It is a mystery to me why this provision was overlooked for decades.

The memorial service was held on 8 June 1877 in the same church in which the consecration had taken place. The elite of Austria's cul-tural life participated, and the imperial court was well represented. On Köchel's own request, Mozart's Requiem was performed by the leading soloists of the day.

The Vienna daily *Neue Freie Presse* carried the customary notice of death in its advertisement columns on 5 June 1877. This was placed by his friend Scharschmid and reads as follows:

> The undersigned announces with deep sorrow the death of his friend for many years, Ludwig Ritter von Köchel Esquire, Juris Doctor, k & k coun-cilor, knight of the Imperial Austrian Leopoldsorder, former tutor of the

most gracious sons of the late imperial and royal highness Archduke
Carl Ludwig. He passed away after lengthy suffering, having received
the last rites, on 3rd June 1877 at 5 a.m. in his seventy-eighth year.

The earthly remains of our dear departed will be consecrated in the
k & k Court Parish Church of St. Augustin on Tuesday, 5th June, at 2
p.m. and will then be buried in his own grave in the Central Cemetery.

Friday, 8th June, at 10 a.m. there will be a solemn memorial service
at the above Court Parish Church.

Vienna, 3rd June 1877.
In the name of the relatives and friends of the deceased:
Franz Freiherr Scharschmid von Adlertreu
k & k District Court President (retired)

This advertisement, surrounded with the customary black border,
was on page 14. The same paper, on page 5, published the following
brief obituary:

(†Dr. Köchel) On 3rd June k & k Councilor Dr. Ludwig Ritter von
Köchel, a personality of highest regard in the widest circles, passed
away here. Formerly tutor of the sons of Archduke Karl (victor of Aspern), since 1842 after completing this task, he was tirelessly engaged
upon scientific studies and activities, particularly in the fields of nature
and music. He is the author of the chronological thematical register of
Mozart's compositions (1862), a work well known by the world of music, also of various writings on musicians and musical conditions in
Austria, in particular of a detailed biography of J. J. Fux, Court Conductor at the Austrian Court from 1698 till 1740. In his final years his
activity and enthusiastic reverence were devoted mainly to the memory and compositions of Mozart. The Complete Edition of the works of
Mozart which is now being undertaken by Breitkopf & Härtel was
above all suggested by Köchel and was made possible through the significant sacrifices made by him. The funeral service will take place on
5th June at 2 p.m. in the Court Parish Church of St. Augustin where on
the 8th of June at 10 a.m. a memorial service will be held which will
consist of Mozart's Requiem Mass.

Another Viennese newspaper, the *Neues Wiener Tagblatt*, in its 6
June 1877 edition, reports: "5th June 1877. The day before yesterday
the imperial councilor Ludwig Ritter von Köchel died here. He was
formerly tutor of the archdukes Albrecht, Karl Ferdinand, Friedrich,
and Wilhelm and he continued to enjoy their intimate friendship
and particularly that of Archduke Albrecht in whose palace he

resided. He was 77 and has made a name for himself as musicologist and as nature researcher. Generally known is his 'Chronological-Thematical Catalogue of Mozart's Works.'" The same paper, in its issue of 7 June 1877, reports as follows:

> (Funeral) Yesterday afternoon, at 2 p.m., took place the funeral of k & k Councilor Dr. Ludwig Ritter von Köchel who died here on 3rd of June. In the Court Parish Church of St. Augustin the consecration of the remains took place in the presence of the archdukes Albrecht, Wilhelm and Rainer, chief stewards FML Baron von Piret, FML Baron von Schloissing and FML Count Messen, chamberlain G. M. Ritter von Koblitz, Baron Schwarz-Sennborn, Prof. Braun, Court Councilor Neumann, furthermore a significant number of writers and scientists. After the church ceremony the coffin, decorated with numerous magnificent wreaths, was lifted to the hearse drawn by four horses, of the undertakers "Pietät" [piety] and transported to the Central Cemetery where the interment in his own grave took place. The servants of Archduke Albrecht accompanied the cortège as far as the Schwarzenberg bridge.

An obituary of sorts also appeared in the *Neue Freie Presse* on 21 July 1877 from the pen of Eduard Hanslick as part of an article reporting on a series of festival concerts held between 17 and 19 July in Salzburg. (Hanslick was a Czech-born Austrian music critic steeped in classical tradition, an ardent supporter of Brahms, and fierce opponent of Wagner, who based on him, without reference to the man's gentle nature, the Beckmesser of his "Meistersingers" opera. The fragment quoted here is also repeated in Hanslick's 1911 autobiographical book *Aus meinem Leben* [From My Life], a very readable account of much that happened in nineteenth-century Vienna.) After reminding his readers of the Mozart festivities held in Salzburg in 1856 (the centenary of Mozart's birth), Hanslick continues: "It will not be taken amiss if I conclude my report with remembrances of two Austrians who, much revered at the time, occupied places of honor in the Salzburg assembly hall and who no longer move among the living: Karl Mozart, son of the great composer, and Ludwig von Köchel, author of the thematic Mozart catalogue." There follows an appreciation of Karl Mozart, and then comes this "obituary" of Köchel:

> Ludwig von Köchel, the musicologist who died but a few weeks ago, belonged to the old guard of the Mozart cult and was closely connected with Salzburg, at least whilst his friend (court) president von Scharschmid resided there with his art loving family. There has hardly

ever existed a more eager and active admirer of Mozart. Half his life and half his fortune were devoted by Köchel to assemble a complete "Catalogue raisonné," the enormous compendium of the Mozart compositions; to sort and sift these and to combine them into the colossal volume that is now an indispensable aid to the musician. Not satisfied with this herculean task fulfilled in honor of Mozart, this lively old man tirelessly moved everything in his power toward the production of a complete edition of Mozart's compositions. The idea to publish the collected works of Mozart in a "critically revised" engraved edition, as a counterpart to the new Beethoven edition, has often been suggested with eloquent words to appeal to the German hearts, in particular by Ferdinand Hiller who intended thus to raise a worthy edifice to Mozart. The untold toil and enormous costs of such an edition, however, always acted as a deterrent to executing this project. Now Breitkopf & Härtel of Leipzig, this highest authority of culture as regards German music, has undertaken the job in great style and Köchel lived to enjoy the happiness of opening the first volume of this Mozart edition to which he had contributed the sum of 20,000 Marks.

12

Last Will and Testament

On 1 July 1868, Köchel prepared his testament. Whether earlier versions existed is not known, nor whether his action was initiated by a particular event, perhaps an illness. Thoughts of death are not unusual at the age of sixty-eight and must have been uppermost in his mind, as the opening paragraphs read as follows:

> My funeral should be respectable but without pomp. At the funeral service I wish, if I die in Vienna, that the Requiem by Mozart be well performed. If I die in my homeland my body should be interred in the grave of my brother Friedrich Köchel (who died on 3rd Nov 1836) in the cemetery of St. Marx in Vienna. The inscription on the tombstone "My dear brother Fritz" should have this addition: "With you faithful unto the grave, your brother, Ludwig Ritter von Köchel, born 14th January 1800, died."

As mentioned elsewhere, by the time Köchel died his brother's grave had been transferred to the Zentralfriedhof of Vienna, complete with the tombstone. The altered position of the grave is acknowledged in the third codicil to the will (dated 30 June 1875), which changes the instructions accordingly.

The will proceeds as follows:

> After my death my estate should be disposed of in the following manner: 1. As my heirs I nominate the three sons of ret. KK major Eduard von Zerboni, namely Max, Franz and Julius von Zerboni in equal parts and with mutual substitution.

It is necessary to stop at this point and ask the obvious question: who is Major Zerboni, and what is the connection between him and

Köchel? One of the many documents attached to the Verlassen-schaftsakt (the file of the estate) in the Vienna Rathaus is the Tauf-schein (certificate of baptism) of Franz Josef von Zerboni di Sposetti, one of the beneficiaries named, from which it appears that he was the legitimate son of Eduard von Zerboni di Sposetti and his spouse, Johanna, née Scharschmid von Adlertreu—legitimate daughter of Dr. Franz Scharschmid Ritter von Adlertreu, Köchel's lifelong friend.

Why Köchel should single out Johanna and leave the main part of his estate to her three sons, whereas small bequests only are made to other members of the Scharschmid family, is one of the mysteries I was unable to resolve; perhaps he felt that they were more deserving or more in need than the other offspring of the Scharschmids. There may of course have been a closer link between Köchel and Johanna, as hinted elsewhere.

As to the Zerboni name, I was able to trace this back to Joseph Zerboni di Spinossi (1726–1807). In spite of the Italian sound, the family appears to have originated from Zerbo, a village in the Sternberg district of Prussia. Joseph had five sons: the first of these, also named Joseph (1766–1831), was accused of high treason in the latter part of the eighteenth century and caused a "defense document" under the title "Aktenstücke zur Beurtheilung der Staatsverbrechen des süd-preussischen Kriegs- und Domainenrathes Zerboni und seiner Freunde" (Documents for the Judgment of the Act of Treason by the South Prussian War- and Domain Councilor Zerboni and His Friends) to be published in 1800. His brother Karl (1772–1836) was the fourth son of Joseph senior, and it was one of his sons, Eduard (1809–1878) who married Johanna Scharschmid and whose three sons, Max (born 1856), Franz (born 1857), and Julius (born 1859), were to inherit the bulk of Köchel's considerable fortune. By my calculation, after all bequests were deducted, including the generous contribution to the Mozart Gesamtausgabe, each of the Zerbonis would receive more than 13,000 Gulden, worth between $75,000 and $150,000 today.

Reverting to the will, the next part determines:

> To my young friend, Departmental Councilor Max von Scharschmid, I bequeath two shares of DDSG, i.e., the Danube Steamship Company, and request him to undertake the execution of this my last will.

As a number of further bequests were of identical shares, it was of interest to establish their value. Each of the shares had a nominal value of 500 Gulden, roughly equal to $3,000 to $5,000 today, and the inventory of Köchel's estate shows that at the time of his death he owned thirty-six such shares, which formed some 20 percent of his total fortune. I wrote to the registrar of the Steamship Company in Vienna to try to find out when Köchel had acquired these shares, but the reply indicates that all their old records were destroyed during World War II.

The other bequests, always one or two shares in the aforementioned company, are to the two sisters of Emanuel Mikschick "mein unvergesslicher Freund" (my unforgettable friend): Frau Emilie von Henkel, wife of k.k. major in Teschen, and Frau Sofie Kämpf, widow of an estate director in Teschen; to Frau Theresia von Harasofsky, née Scharschmid; to Wilhelmine Gallasch, Köchel's niece, a milliner in Vienna; to his godson Ludwig Lorenz, a writer on ornithology, geography, and mathematics, son of ministerial secretary Dr. Joseph Roman Lorenz, himself an author of scientific books on geology, a subject of great interest to Köchel; to engineer Paul Sprenger; to his friend Dr. Med. Franz Lorenz in Wienerneustadt (whose pamphlet triggered Köchel's work on the Mozart *Register*); to the brothers Franz Aigner, a merchant in Hainfeld, and Ludwig Aigner, a watchmaker in Kumberg (both sons of the late k.k. Förster [forester] Franz Aigner); to Ludwig Mayer, an artist of historical and religious paintings; and to Ernestine Walcher, daughter of Köchel's friend Court Councilor von Walcher (mentioned in the story of Köchel's romance). Similar bequests to five other beneficiaries were later canceled.

Köchel remembered of his valet as follows: "To my valet who was last in my service, I bequeath my clothes and my linen and half a year's wages." The inventory of Köchel's estate values the clothes and linen at 101 Gulden, but there is no indication of the wages he paid, nor is the name of the last valet known.

Next comes the disposition of Köchel's scientific collections and manuscripts:

> My collections of plants and minerals together with the 5 chests that belong to it and the books on natural history I designate for the Gymnasium [grammar school] in Krems in thankful memory to the teaching establishment where I first obtained my education. I request that these collections be maintained in good order, not mingled with other collections and that they bear my name.

As mentioned elsewhere in this book, most of the minerals with their chests are indeed kept in this way, whereas the herbarium was lost during the wars, as were the books mentioned in the will. The collection of the minerals, incidentally, was valued in the inventory at 760 Gulden, the plants at 250 Gulden.

> To the Society of the Friends of Music of the Austrian Empire I bequeath all my musical belongings among which I attach some value to the collected works of Mozart, assembled for the purpose of my Register of works by this master. These are to their greatest part located in a special chest which may remain with the collection. In accordance with my wish, this last mentioned collection should bear my name and should not be mingled with other collections.

I understand from Dr. Otto Biba, today's director of archives of this society, that the special chest or cupboard no longer exists. He also told me that although most of the items bequeathed to the society are still there, for reasons of "practicality," they are no longer treated as a separate "Köchel collection" as designated in the will. In one of his articles, Dr. Biba said about this collection, "To this day it constitutes an indispensable source for the Mozart research." I would have thought that under these circumstances a "practical" way could have been found to accommodate Köchel's testamentary wish! The inventory value of the musical belongings, by the way, is 470 Gulden, which seems a very modest figure even at that time.

There is an additional bequest of 500 Gulden to the society, "for the acquisition of good works of music literature." Small bequests are made to the fund for schoolteachers' widows in Salzburg and to the elementary school in Köchel's birthplace, Stein, which he attended before entering the Gymnasium in neighboring Krems. (In the will this is described as "Trivialschule." It appears that the original meaning of this term, no longer in use, was any school below the level of a university; but in southern Germany and Austria, from the seventeenth century, it was adapted to indicate schools below the level of Gymnasium.)

Next follows provision for the maintenance of the joint grave of Friedrich and Ludwig Köchel. This is in the form of an interest bearing Papierrente (annuity) of 200 Gulden at 5 percent, specifying the grave in St. Marx and altering this in the aforementioned codicil to the new location in the Zentralfriedhof. This paragraph caused some complication at first but was eventually resolved by making half-yearly payments of the interest direct to the gravedigger who undertook the proper maintenance of the joint grave.

Next comes the following most meaningful paragraph:

> Any settlement with my friend Franz Ritter von Scharschmid, K.K. county court president in Vienna, is absolutely impossible. I request him and his wife to specify an object of their choice from my estate and to kindly accept same in memory of their grateful friend and witness over many years of rare domestic bliss.

In the Verlassenschaftsakt I found the Erklärung (statement) signed by Herr and Frau von Scharschmid, dated 26 June 1877, whereby Herr Franz accepted a copperplate engraving (Kupferstich) of Raphael's "Transfiguration" and Frau Marie a copy of Hanslick's book *Concertsal*. (The expression *durchaus ausgeglichen* in the German text of the testament really means the opposite of "absolutely impossible," but as this is an obvious mistake in the wording I must assume that this is the meaning intended.)

Köchel finally decreed that the legatees receive their legacies free of all deductions.

There are three codicils to the will (apart from the correction relating to the cemetery mentioned before). The first of these, from 7 April 1871, appears to exclude the Mozart autographs from the previously mentioned provisions regarding the musical belongings:

> To my testament of 1st July 1868 I find myself obliged to add the following partly new, partly corrective instructions: a/ my valuable autographs of W. A. Mozart in a brown portfolio I bequeath to the K.K. Court Library in Vienna and wish that this example were followed by others.

From the receipt (Empfangbestätigung) signed for the Library by Hofrath (court councilor) Dr. Ernst Birk, we know that this brown portfolio contained the following original Mozart manuscripts:

K. 193 Dixit et Magnificat
K. 194 Missa brevis in D
K. 260 (Offertorium) Venite populi, venite
K. 122 Minuet (for orchestra) in E flat
K. 337 Missa solemnis in C
K. 618 (Motet) Ave verum corpus (this work was to be performed in 1906 at the ceremony unveiling a memorial plaque on the assumed Köchel birth house)

The official combined value of these autographs is stated as 550 Gulden in the inventory, and this sum also includes the manuscript of a Schubert song, "Vater schenk mir diese Stunde," composed in Vienna in March 1820.

A list of further bequests in this codicil follows: 500 Gulden to Ferdinand Pohl, then archive director of the Musikverein; similar amounts to the Carolino-Augusteum museum, the Mozarteum, and the Institute for Geography, all in Salzburg; the Association for Geography, the Zoological and Botanical Society, the Geographical Society, the Meteorological Society, and the "Musikfreunde" (Friends of Music) Society, all in Vienna; also annuities based on capital sums of 500 Gulden each to K.K. telegraphist Johann Hafner in Salzburg, the economist Franz von Scharschmid (a nephew of Köchel's friend), and Fräulein Fanny von Scharschmid in Linz. There is also an annuity based on 4,000 Gulden capital to Max von Zerboni, one of the principal beneficiaries of the will as a prelegacy. This particular legacy was intended to secure a regular income to Max, who was a minor when the codicil was written, but he had come of age by the time the will was executed, and this bequest was therefore not carried out.

The second codicil, dated 12 April 1874, is mentioned and partly quoted in the chapter dealing with Köchel's contribution to the first edition of the collected works of Mozart. It is this codicil that created the financial basis for the task, as will be seen later. The continuation of the passage quoted there, by which Köchel assured his ongoing contribution to this important venture in case he died before its completion (as was the case), is as follows:

> I wish, however, that my pledged word not be broken by my death and therefore decree as follows:
>
> 1. If the publication of the complete works of Mozart, complementing the opera edition mentioned, becomes a reality, my heirs should at the conclusion of the year pay 2000 Rthlr in silver in my name to Beitkopf & Härtel in Leipzig.
>
> 2. In the same way, throughout the pursuing four years, at the end of each year in which the publication proceeds regularly, similar payments of 2000 Rthlr should be made to the same bookshop-publisher, so that in the course of five years calculated from the beginning of its publication, by which time I imagine this to be completed, the 10,000 Reichsthaler in silver should be paid out without any deductions whatsoever.
>
> 3. Should there be an interruption for whatever reason in the publication, my heirs are not obliged to make payment of the annual quota,

only when publication resumes and continues regularly should the quota be discharged in such manner as to make the final quota payment only at the conclusion of the complete edition.

4. Concerning a reciprocal performance in copies of the complete edition, for the time being nothing is determined; it is my wish, however, that my heirs be advised of this (nb meanwhile I have stipulated for myself in reciprocity two copies). In any event, one such copy I specify for the Mozarteum in Salzburg, another for the Society of the Friends of Music in Vienna.

If I live to see the commencement and continuation of the publication the records of quota payments made by myself will be attached to this statement. The copy of my Register of Mozart's works which is supplemented by handwritten sheets should, for the purpose of the publication, be handed to Breitkopf & Härtel and, on the whole, they should be aided in every way by having access to my Mozart manuscripts.

From the executor of the will we know that the first two installments of this scheme were paid by Köchel himself on 4 September 1876 and 3 March 1877, respectively; 1,500 Gulden equaled 1,000 Reichsthaler each time. It is also stated that, as the actual publication took much longer than anticipated by Köchel, the agreement between the executor and Breitkopf & Härtel stretched out the payments until March 1886.

Two more bequests are the subject of the third codicil, dated 30 June 1875, instructing the monthly payment of 20 Gulden each to Köchel's niece Wilhelmine Gallasch for the duration of her life and to candidate teacher Carl Duffek "who was recommended to me by Dr. Lorenz of Wienerneustadt." The latter was to be paid these monthly sums until the end of 1877, but he was also to receive a bond of 200 Gulden.

This, then, completes the testament. The first task facing its executors after Köchel's death was to prepare an inventory of his possessions and to put a value to them. Köchel died on 3 June 1877; the inventory was ready on 23 June. The final total comes to 85,702.88 Gulden, a very considerable sum, and most of this was in the form of "Obligationen" (bonds), the value of which is given in total at 78,120 Gulden. As all of these are shown with their nominal issue price, they may have been investment bonds bearing a fixed rate of interest, usually 5 percent, not subject to market fluctuations, but this assumption may be negated by one of the receipts in the Verlassenschaftsakt, in which Dr. Joseph Roman Lorenz, Ritter von Liburnan, acknowledges two shares of DDSG and gives their value, with coupons, as 868 Gulden. It is not clear whether this value applies *per share* or for the two shares together. (The nominal value, it will be remembered, was 500 Gulden per share.)

There was also "ready money" listed as "Baarschaft" in the amount of 3,510.62, silver objects and "Pretiosen" (precious items) at 247.96, clothes and linen at 101, furniture and other household goods at 468, and the scientific collections, valued jointly at 3,255.30 Gulden.

13

The Memorial Plaque on the Wrong House

Stein on the Danube, where Köchel was born, is a very small town. Situated some 80 kilometers (50 miles) northwest of Vienna in the wine- and fruit-growing area known as "The Wachau," it is a favorite excursion spot for the Viennese. The main street, running parallel to the river, is Landstrasse, and it was in No. 62, a pretty corner house next to the parish church, where until most recently it was thought that Ludwig Köchel was born. Local historian Dr. Gerd Maroli now states that this building probably housed the primary school Köchel attended.

If you turn left from here and walk along the Landstrasse, past the Pfarrhaus (rectory) where Köchel's birth is recorded in the official register, you come upon Ludwig von Köchel Platz, a small square so named in his memory in 1950, but having no direct connection with Köchel.

Had you turned right from No. 62, a few steps would have taken you to Schürer Platz, a square named in 1866 after Paul Schürer, mayor of Stein from 1858 to 1886. One of the buildings along the street, today No. 76 Landstrasse, is the Grosser Passauerhof, which was known to have housed the office for tax collection, occupied by Köchel's father. According to Maroli, this was also where the Köchels had an apartment before 1803 and where in most likelihood Ludwig Köchel was born.

But it was the house on the corner of Schürer Platz and Landstrasse, No. 8 on the square, known today as Mazzetti Haus, where on 4 October 1906 a memorial plaque was unveiled in the mistaken belief that this was the house in which Köchel was born. The reason for the error is that the Köchel family was known to have lived here for many years, up to the time when Köchel's father died in 1820, and not until 1951 did anyone take the trouble to find out whether this was really the family home at the time of Köchel's birth.

Franz Biberschick reported in *Krems-Stein und Mautern* that year that the true place of birth was the house known today as No. 62 Landstrasse, whereas the house on Schürerplatz was in 1800 not yet the property of the Diocese of Passau, the employer of Köchel's father. On the church registry book entry showing Köchel's birth, the number "124" is clearly in evidence, and until recently it was thought that this referred to No. 62 Landstrasse. It now appears that in 1805 there had been a renumbering process and that the true location of No. 124 at the time of Köchel's birth was the Grosser Passauerhof, then listed as No. 124.

Even now, in the full knowledge of the facts, nothing is being done to correct what is clearly wrong, and music lovers from the four corners of the earth are regularly (mis)guided to the Mazzetti Haus to take their pictures of the supposed birth house. While I was there in 1991, I came across a group from France, and only when I explained what at the time I thought to be the true facts to their leader and guide, Pierre Petit, composer and music critic for the newspaper *Le Figaro*, did they move to have a look at No. 62 Landstrasse as well. (Today I would have to guide them to the Grosser Passauerhof.)

The memorial plaque is nevertheless meaningful, even in its wrong position, as a sign of recognition for the man who, according to one of the speakers at the unveiling ceremony, was better known abroad than in his own country.

The year 1906 is significant in that it was the 150th anniversary of Mozart's birth, and the suggestion for the plaque was closely connected with the celebrations held to honor the composer's memory. It would have been more logical for this event to have been held four years earlier, in 1902, to remember the twenty-fifth anniversary of Köchel's death, or six years earlier, in 1900, to honor the centenary of his birth, but the fact is that his name never occurred to anyone except in connection with Mozart.

The people of Stein and Krems had almost forgotten him in spite of his benevolent bequests to the local schools. Perhaps the fact that no one with the name Köchel had lived in Stein/Krems since 1820 contributed to this lapse of memory, evidenced to this day by the fact that Köchel's name did not appear on the list of local celebrities honored in the town museum of Krems with a special "corner" at the time of my first visit in May 1991, an omission that, according to Herr Dr. Ernst Englisch, local director of culture and archives, was about to be remedied.

The idea of a memorial was first proposed by musicologist Karl Viktor Reusch of Cannstatt, the man who had written a short time before the first biographical article on Köchel (later to become part of the foreword of the second edition of the *Köchelverzeichnis*). He approached the owner of 8 Schürerplatz, Herr Mazzetti, and the authorities at Krems, the twin town of Stein.

After lengthy correspondence between the participants of the scheme, the exact position of the plaque was decided. Discussions followed as to the material to be used: marble, granite, or bronze. In the end they agreed on green syenite because black marble was thought to be more suitable for use in a cemetery. The letters were to be engraved in gold, and the authorities in Stein took it upon themselves to be responsible for the periodic renewal of the gilding. We have no record of the total cost of the plaque, but we know that an initial sum of 100 Kronen (then about $7.50) was donated by a Victor Köchl of New York, who claimed to be related to Ludwig.

In trying to solve the question of how this mysterious Victor Köchl came to be mentioned in connection with the memorial plaque project, I am reminded of Köchel's dedication of the *Register* to his friend and fellow researcher Otto Jahn. He writes about the researcher's joy in finding an answer to a question others were unable to resolve. Indeed, a biographer's duty is to look for solutions of mysteries that had puzzled predecessors, and there is no greater joy in such work than to unearth something that had remained concealed to all previous researchers.

When I read again and again about the "fact" that there are no Köchel descendants, as Köchel never married and his brothers and sisters died young and childless, and then came across the story of the memorial plaque detailing Victor Köchl's involvement in the project, I decided to find out more about this connection. With perseverance (and some luck), I was able to trace a descendant of Victor: his daughter-in-law Charlotte Marshall who had been married to Victor's younger son, Paul (he had had two sons), and who, in her upper eighties at the time of my inquiries, lived in Wilton, Connecticut. There are also two granddaughters, Jill and Penelope Köchl (they are all spelling the name without the *e*), both of whom live in New York.

It appears that Victor, who had a hardware/drugs business in New York and who was born in Ulm, Germany, in 1850, was convinced that his family, which had originated in the Austrian Tyrol, was connected to Ludwig von Köchel. In 1905 he instructed a firm of genealogists to carry out a full study of his family background, and, indeed, they were able to trace his ancestors back to the fifteenth century.

On my request, Mrs. Marshall again looked at all details and concluded that there was no link between the Köchls of Tyrol/Ulm/New York and Ludwig Köchel's family! This fact also appears to have been known to Victor *before* he made his contribution to the cost of the plaque, leaving open the question: Why did he come to Salzburg to the Mozart festivities in 1906, and why did he continue to maintain, as confirmed by the great-granddaughters in New York, that he "must be" related to Ludwig von Köchel? This biographer must conclude that the Victor Köchls are not related to Ludwig's family, and, to go back to the Jahn dedication, it is indeed most deflating to find that having "hoisted the flags on a new discovery," it becomes just one more frustration of a journey taken in vain.

The 100 Kronen donated by Victor were the starting point toward meeting the costs. The rest of the money needed came from people who wished to honor Mozart's memory; these included the director of archives of the Salzburg Mozarteum, k.k. Imperial Councilor Dr. Johan Evangelist Engl, and the publishing firm of Breitkopf & Härtel, Leipzig, famed for the first edition of the *Köchelverzeichnis* in 1862 and for the first ever complete edition of Mozart's known compositions, instigated and financed in part by Köchel through his generous posthumous donation.

The inscription on the plaque reads as follows:

Geburtshaus	Birth house
von	of
Dr. Ludwig Ritter v. Köchel	Dr. Ludwig Ritter v. Köchel
k.k. Rat	k.k. Councilor
dem verdienstvollen Schöpfer	the deserving creator of the
des Mozart-Katalogs	Mozart Catalog
geboren 14. Januar 1800	Born 14th January 1800
gestorben 3. Juni 1877	deceased 3rd June 1877
zu Wien	in Vienna

This was the program of the unveiling ceremony to start at 3 P.M. on 4 October 1906:

1. Symphony, performed by the regimental band No. 84 of Baron von Bolfras
2. Mozart Chorus sung by the students of the State Gymnasium (grammar school) of Krems, conducted by their teacher, Herr I. Christlbauer
3. Speech by school councilor and writer Dr. J. Wichner, a professor at the Gymnasium
4. Mozart Chorus sung by the students of the Gymnasium
5. Closing speech on behalf of the local authority. This was given by the mayor of Stein, Herr F. Müllauer
6. National anthem

The "Mozart Chorus" of item 2 was in fact the "Ave verum corpus," a motet composed for four voices with accompaniment of two violins, viola, double bass, and organ. According to the *Köchelverzeichnis*, it was "probably composed for the Feast of Corpus Christi service held for teacher and choir conductor Anton Stoll in Baden." As mentioned, this is one of the works of which the original autograph was in Köchel's possession at the time of his death and which he bequeathed to the Imperial Court Library, making it an ideally suited choice for performance at these festivities.

A report in the local newspaper *Niederösterreichische Presse*, No. 41, on 6 October 1906 gives a full account of the festivities. This lists among those participating District Commander E. Hufnagel, Dean Dr. Anton Kerschbaumer, five members of families who had life-long friendships with Köchel—that is, Hofrat (Court Councilor) Rudolf Ritter von Walcher-Uysdal; his sister, Baroness Erny Czoernig; Baroness Paula Baltazzi-Scharschmid; and Bruno von Rainer zu Harbach with his wife, Seraphine. Frau Therese von Harrasowsky, née Scharschmid, was unable to attend due to ill health and sent a telegram to the organizers. (Of those mentioned, Ritter von Walcher-Uysdal was a descendant of Ferdinand Walcher, mentioned in chapter 6 on Köchel's romance; he was later in the services of Archdukes Karl and Albrecht and ennobled. I assume that Baron Ritter von Rainer zu Harbach was related to the Archduchess Marie Caroline Rainer, who will get mentioned in chapter 22 on Köchel's work in mineralogy.

Baroness Baltazzi-Scharschmid was the great-granddaughter of Köchel's friend Franz Freiherr von Scharschmid.)

Two important personalities who were missing from the ceremonies were Karl Viktor Reusch, who had first proposed the memorial plaque, and Victor Köchl from New York, the first contributor to its costs. Both these gentlemen had hoped to combine their visit to the Mozart Festival held in Salzburg from 17 to 20 August that year with their attendance at the unveiling of the plaque. This event (namely, the unveiling), however, had to be postponed to enable teachers and students of the local schools that Köchel had attended, and which had been closed during the summer holidays, to participate.

The well-attended unveiling ceremony had the benefit of a fine, sunny day. The plaque was surrounded by a number of floral wreaths, the tributes from many respectful admirers.

The main speech, presented by Dr. Wichner, included the following details: "Ludwig Köchel who was born on 14th January 1800 in this house . . . learned after his father had lost his position (of tax collector for the diocese) to cope with the serious side of life and this surely had a beneficial effect on his scholastic achievements." This is of course wrong: we know that Köchel's father retained the job after the secularization of church properties by becoming responsible for the collection of state taxes. It is unlikely that his income suffered from this change of employer.

He continued:

> Köchel is shown to have been a kind-hearted patriot who gave of his best when educating the imperial princes entrusted to his care and thus the festivity of today, held on the name day of our emperor, may rightfully be called patriotic. . . .
>
> Köchel was the leading Mozart expert of his day. His principal achievement is the compilation of the Mozart Catalogue and the instigation to publish the collected works of Mozart. Toward these aims he donated the many manuscripts he had caused to be copied . . . and it is only fitting that many admirers of Mozart felt that in this anniversary year memory should also extend to the man who accomplished such a prominent service through his distribution of the works by this "hero of sound." In this context I mention first of all Herr Karl Viktor Reusch of Cannstatt who wrote the first biography of Köchel and thus drew attention to the almost forgotten scholar; Victor Köchel of New York, a relative [!] of the celebrant, Dr. Johann Engl, director of archives of the Mozarteum in Salzburg, the Leipzig publishers Breitkopf & Härtel,

and the well-known donor and author of the festive inscription . . . who forbids the mention of his name. [Probably a reference to the dean, Dr. Anton Kerschbaumer.]

This reverential undertaking has been well received in exalted circles as shown by this telegram sent from Innsbruck by the Archduke Eugen, who knew Köchel personally, the son of Archduke Karl Ferdinand, one of the four archdukes whose education was entrusted to the care of Ludwig Köchel:

> On occasion of the festivity of unveiling the memorial plaque for Ludwig von Köchel, most deserving for his knowledge of the immortal works of Mozart and personally known to me, I extend my warmest greetings to the Memorial Committee and to all admirers of Mozart present.

The speech then gave details of Köchel's achievements in fields other than music and refers to him as "a lonely but happy man . . . who found harmony in the shape and color and whose study contained joyful inner tranquility."

Thus, this silent man, this modest scholar, has been escorted through his life by friendship, art, and science and when he realized that the end was near, he bethought of his first place of higher education and bequeathed to the Gymnasium of Krems part of his scientific library and his collections of plants and minerals to act as a stimulant for the youth of this school in its study of natural history. It is very likely that no other Austrian grammar school can pride itself of such wonderful and valuable teaching aids. Therefore, dear students, you have every reason to participate at these festivities in honor of your kind-hearted friend and thus discharge your duty of gratefulness. It is a fitting thought that you should pay homage to this man whose greatest happiness was in the music of Mozart by performing some of his musical compositions.

And you, schoolchildren of Stein, when you see the name of Köchel on the memorial plaque, you must not forget that the man who achieved fame through his tireless creative work, once sat on the same school benches as you, played in the same squares of this town or—in spite of the occasional danger—on the banks of the River Danube.

I hand over in the name of its donors this memorial plaque into the protective care of the community of Stein, and I remove the veil so that the name of Köchel may radiate in golden blaze eternally, to the glory of the deceased and the honor of the town Stein.

After this speech and the unveiling, wreaths were laid in front of the plaque by Court Councilor Ritter von Walcher, descendant of Köchel's personal friend, and Baroness Baltazzi-Scharschmid, great-granddaughter of Köchel's best friend Scharschmid.

The school choir then rendered "O Schutzgeist alles Schönen" (Oh Guardian Spirit of All That Is Beautiful). Then came the speech by the mayor of Stein, F. Müllauer. He thanked those present for their attendance, and extended the town's gratitude to those who caused the memorial plaque to be erected and to Mazzetti, the present owner of the house. He then said, "Whenever we shall pass this house we shall remember the man who is almost more famous and better honored abroad than in his homeland." Herr Müllauer then mentioned the several members of the Scharschmid family and their friends who had come up from Vienna to add a feeling of family participation to the festivities. The national anthem was sung by those present to conclude the festive occasion.

We are left to wonder whether anything will ever be done to move the plaque to its rightful place on the walls of the Grosser Passauer-hof—or whether a new plaque should be made for that house, perhaps to honor the one hundred fiftieth anniversary of the first appearance of the *Köchelverzeichnis* in 2012?

14

Köchel and Mozart

It would be impossible to write about Köchel's life without also providing a brief sketch of Mozart's life, whereas the latter's work must of necessity receive more detailed attention in connection with the *Köchelverzeichnis*. This is almost by way of an apology as most readers assumably sought this book on Köchel because of their interest in Mozart; it is therefore very likely that they already know enough about the composer without reading what I have to say about him.

My reason for including a few words about Mozart's life and character is to demonstrate how very different these were from those of Köchel. Those readers who until now were totally ignorant about Köchel may have thought of him as a contemporary of Mozart, that the two men were perhaps friends, sharing their interest in music, that their origins were similar, and that their lives ran a parallel course.

Nothing could be further from the truth.

Mozart died more than eight years before Köchel was born. It was not until Köchel was fifty that he started on his work of organizing Mozart's compositions, by which time most of the composer's contemporaries had also died.

Köchel's father was a tax collector and may therefore best be described as a civil servant, whereas Mozart's father Leopold, who had come to Salzburg from Augsburg in southern Germany and who took some years to adjust himself to the different world and language of the Austrian town, became conductor of the archbishop's orchestra and was a composer in his own right. He also wrote the "definitive" violin school of the period. He was thus able to help create the world of music in which his son was to live. Wolfgang's sister Maria Anna

("Nannerl"), four and a half years older, was an accomplished pianist at a very tender age. Mozart thus grew up in an environment in which it was natural for him to devote practically all his time to music, at the expense of a childhood like that enjoyed by others his age.

Born in 1756 in Salzburg, by the time he was six Mozart had written his first compositions. As he lived only to age thirty-six and as his total musical output comes to at least 626 known compositions (the number listed by Köchel), in the thirty productive years an annual average of more than twenty works had to be written. Taken over phases of ten years his output is almost completely balanced in numbers.

When Mozart wrote music, nothing could disturb him. In fact, he liked to be surrounded by happy voices and female company; he liked to sip from a tumbler of punch or a glass of champagne. The reason for this detachment from noises that would have distracted most other creative artists is that his music was almost completely "ready" in his head; all that remained to be done was the laborious task of putting it on paper. This also explains why he was able to sit down to the piano and "improvise" a complete work, a gift not granted to many (the other best-known improviser being Franz Liszt), but in Mozart's case it was really a performance of music virtually "written down" in every detail to the last semiquaver. In addition, it explains why so many of his manuscripts have very few corrections.

Those who knew Mozart were surprised by his behavior away from his music. He appeared coarse; he did not choose his words carefully; his relationship with his employers, friends, and women was naive. Having been deprived of natural childhood and reached remarkable maturity in the field of music before he was twelve years old, he remained a child in other respects for the rest of his life. He never developed a sense for domestic order, his household expenses were sky high compared to his earnings, he borrowed money where he could, yet he never denied a loan to a friend even when he did not know how to repay what he already owed.

By contrast, Köchel had a well-organized childhood of a most conventional character; he was studious and ambitious, as shown by his school reports. But he was no genius: he had to work for his results, whereas success in all aspects of music came not only easily but naturally to young Mozart.

Mozart had the support of a loving father for much of his creative life (he died in 1787, four and a half years before his son). Leopold's influence and authority was tremendous. As a child, Wolfgang said "Nach dem lieben Gott kommt gleich der Papa" (after God my father follows immediately), and these sentiments did not change during Mozart's life.

Köchel lost both his parents while still a student and long before the creative part of his life commenced. He had to find inspiration and direction elsewhere.

If Mozart achieved recognition by the imperial house and by monarchs of foreign lands because of his talent at a very early age, an "infant prodigy" if ever there was one, Köchel had to work his way up slowly until he received acceptance by his imperial employers, leading to friendship with at least one of his former pupils, Archduke Albrecht, in later life.

Let me revert to the term *infant prodigy*. Examples abound in modern times of musicians who started their careers as performing artists in early childhood, and some (e.g., Yehudi Menuhin) in later life fulfilled the great promise of their early musicianship. But Mozart was unique in being *creative* at such an early age, in his ability to write *good music* in his childhood, music of sometimes astounding maturity, and in his progression from these early beginnings in an unbroken line to reach the greatest heights of musical composition.

Bruno Walter (1876–1962), the great conductor, was known for his admiration of Mozart's music. Once a journalist pressed him to name the "greatest composer" of all time. Walter, after thinking long and hard, replied, "I suppose if I must make a choice, I would have to pick Beethoven." "But maestro, it was always assumed you hold Mozart in higher esteem than anyone else," said the surprised interviewer. "This goes without saying," replied Walter calmly. "I thought you were asking me to name the greatest *after* Mozart!" This anecdote from the 1930s, nearly 150 years after Mozart's death, serves to prove the unique position held then, as today, by Mozart in the world of musical composition.

Was Mozart "burnt out" by the time he died? We can have no reason for suspecting this because in his last year he wrote some of his greatest masterpieces, works such as the *Magic Flute*, "La Clemenza di Tito," the Clarinet Concerto in A, the "Ave verum," and last, but not least, the Requiem. Although there are many unfinished fragments, nothing is known of any unfinished musical plans he might have had when he died. The main reason for this is that the music in his head at any one time had to be committed to paper in a tremendous hurry, perhaps to make room for new thoughts and phrases that were crowding in. On his deathbed it was still the Requiem that occupied his attention; he knew he would be unable to finish this composition and wanted to make sure that nothing was lost from his concept of this work completed by others after he died.

Was there any envy in Köchel toward the "easy" success of Mozart? Nothing in his writings indicates this. When he tried his own hand at composition, he did not follow in Mozart's path; he attempted neither to imitate him nor emulate him. His total respect was for the genius of the composer whose work became the obsession of his life. He knew that he himself possessed no such genius, not in the field of music and not in any other direction. But he somehow sensed a duty to systematize the composer's musical output, a task for which he was well equipped.

Here is another strange point. Mozart is generally known as a "symmetrical" composer: everything he did in music was written in this way; there are no loose ends, no unfinished phrases, and each composition shows a well constructed balance. Yet, having completed a new work, he seemed to have no interest in fitting it into some sort of sequence; system and symmetry are totally missing. And this is exactly where Köchel came in. With his logical mind and fired by the great respect he had for the composer, he was ideally placed to create the *Register,* to find a thematic order of the compositions *never challenged* by anyone, and to show a chronological order on the basis of his research.

The chronology has been updated a number of times, and this process continues today. Köchel knew this would happen; he himself continued his work and furnished valuable notes to be incorporated by Count Paul Waldersee in 1906, long after Köchel's death, in the second edition of Köchel's work. Today, modern technology is used to analyze the sequence of compositions: the latest is based on the watermarks found on the music paper used by Mozart. But surely, this process is not foolproof either. It assumes that the composer finished one stack of paper before using the next. With an untidy man who probably kept music paper in every corner of his home, he may have used old paper for a new composition when he was unable to find a new batch; he kept moving, no less than fourteen times for instance between March 1781 and September 1790! Here are the addresses as taken from Walter Hummel's book *W. A. Mozart's Söhne* (published by Bärenreiter, of Kassel and Basel in 1956):

1781	16 March	Deutsches Ordenshaus, Wien [Vienna] 865 [now Wien I. Singerstrasse 7]
	9 May	"Zum Auge Gottes" Am Peter No. 577 [now Wien I. Petersplatz 11]
	September	Am Graben No. 1175 [now Wien I. Graben 28]
1782	4 August	"Zum roten Säbel" [now Wipplingerstrasse 25]
	December	Hohe Brücke No. 437 [now Wipplingerstrasse 17]
1783		Kohlmarkt [details not known]
	April	Judenplatz, Stadt 244 [now Wien I. Judenplatz 3]
1784	September	Alter Trattnerhof, Am Graben 591 [now Wien I. Graben 29]
	December	Camesinasches Haus, Schulerstr. No. 846 [now Wien I., Schulerstrasse 8]
1787	April	Landstrasse Hauptstrasse No. 224 [now Hühnergasse 17]
	December	Tuchlauben 281 [demolished since]
1788	17th June	Alservorstadt, Währingerg. 135 [now Wien IX, Währingerstrasse 26]
1789	early	"Zur Mutter Gottes," Judenpl. 245 [now Wien I. Judenplatz 4]
1790	September	Klein-Kaisersteinisches Haus, Rauhensteing. 970 [now Wien I. Rauhensteingasse 8] [This is where Mozart died.]

It would be difficult even for a tidy person to be systematic under such circumstances!

Alan Tyson's contribution to the everlasting question of the chronological order of Mozart's compositions, discussed later, is most valuable where his information is *positive*, as it establishes, on the basis of the paper used, the *earliest* possible time of a composition but obviously not the latest. Also, his work is restricted to those compositions where original manuscripts could serve as a basis for research. Köchel's task went far beyond this, but he was lacking some of the scientific aids available to today's researchers.

Many of Mozart's original manuscripts were lost, and when Köchel established the chronological place of such a work, he had to use a copy of uncertain date. The haste with which Mozart finished his compositions was followed by a similar hurry to "get rid" of the manuscript. Often this was a necessity, because the work was commissioned and the money was needed. But even where this was not the case, Mozart tried to get the completed work out of the way, and he kept no records at all to show where these manuscripts could again be found. Somehow he seemed to lose interest in what had been finished; the next task urged him to dispense with the previous one.

Köchel's greatest achievement is perhaps the detective work in tracing the early compositions—those not recorded by Mozart himself in his little "register" started in 1784, which is now in the manuscript department of the British Library. (It got there via the estate of novelist Stefan Zweig, together with some Mozart manuscripts and other items.) We have no sure indication as to what triggered Mozart into starting this register, but it is perhaps significant that his wife Konstanze started to keep domestic accounts at about the same time!

Having thus referred to Mozart's wife, this is a good place to show the contrast between the two men's attitudes toward sex and domestic life. Mozart married Konstanze in 1782 after courting her elder sister Aloysia for several years. Even before this romance, there were other attachments that could have led to a serious involvement or to marriage.

Köchel, as we know, remained a bachelor all his life, and we only know about the one romantic interlude described by Sophie Kleyle, which may well contain a fair amount of imagination on her part.

Mozart had the pleasure of seeing his wife bear seven children. Although only two of these survived, there must have been some family joy, an experience that Köchel had only "by proxy" in the household of his friend Scharschmid.

Mozart's professional life shows an unbroken progression from his early days as infant prodigy to his creation of immortal masterpieces. Nothing could disturb the concentration of this musical career that lasted to his deathbed.

Köchel first prepared himself for a legal career, but having obtained his degree, he never practiced law. Years of tutorship followed in which there was no direction toward future activities. Having attained a post at the highest possible level in this field, it must in fact have been an anticlimax to find, at the age of forty-two, that he was not "prepared" for the next phase of his life—prepared in the scientific sense of the word. But this final period, lasting thirty-five years, brought out his true abilities, allowing him to accomplish all the things for which he is now justly remembered—and many more that have wrongly been forgotten.

When it came to the final chapter, death and funeral, the contrast between the fates of Mozart and Köchel was tremendous. Mozart, a young man who should have been in the prime of his life, fell ill and died within a matter of weeks. The illness itself is mysterious enough to give rise to the ill-advised rumors of poisoning. We now know that sufficient medical grounds existed to cause his death from an ailment with its origin in earlier illnesses.

Köchel reached an advanced age, and whereas no accurate reports are available as to the ultimate cause of his death, we know that a journey to Italy three years before he died was the start of his physical demise, and another trip taken some months before his death triggered the final collapse. Even so, it took a considerable time before he actually died, and when this happened, it was a gentle death, entirely in character with the way he had lived.

There are many versions as to the cause of Mozart's unheralded funeral, and it is not for this work to try to find the true reason for what happened or the true circumstances of the act itself. The fact is that his final resting place is an unmarked grave, and all efforts of posterity to create a "Mozart grave" in the central cemetery of Vienna cannot alter this situation.

By contrast again, Köchel was ceremoniously interred in his own grave after a funeral service attended by members of the imperial family, the nobility of Vienna, and members of many branches of art and science.

An untidy end for the genius—an orderly one for the man of systems!

15

Köchel as Others Saw Him

Nearly one hundred forty years have passed since Köchel's most important work first appeared in print. Since then every Mozart researcher—and there have been a great many of these—started his work on the foundations laid by Köchel and paid homage to him in so doing. The tributes are often mixed with criticism. Some musicologists have found it difficult to place themselves and their work into the environment in which Köchel worked; they conveniently forget the utter confusion surrounding Mozart's artistic output at the starting point of Köchel's activity. Yet Köchel would be the first to admit modestly his own shortcomings, to point out again and again that what he did was a mere beginning for others to continue.

The greatest tribute to Köchel's work is contained in the fact that all references to Mozart works still bear the "K" numbers as an absolute means of identification. In his *Mozart in Retrospect* (Oxford University Press, 1955), Alec Hyatt King, the eminent musicologist and Mozart expert (who died in 1994), says:

Few men of the nineteenth century or any other century have become universally known through a single letter of their name. Outside the field of science—where for instance the "M" numbers of certain nebulae have perpetuated the name of Charles Messier, the French astronomer—it is doubtful if this honor has come to anyone save Ludwig Ritter von Köchel, the "K" of whose surname is seen in print wherever Mozart's music is played. Such literal distinction is of course facilitated by the passion of the twentieth century for compressing organizations and persons into strings of unpunctuated letters, GATT, GBS, SHAPE and so on ad nauseam. After some sixty years of general acceptance as "KV," Köchel's great Mozart catalogue has now become known simply as "K."

This view adds a different dimension to Köchel's destiny. The abbreviation to the single letter K has led to total ignorance regarding the man behind it, yet it is true that this rare distinction was afforded to very few men. Alec Hyatt King has more to say about him:

> He showed intellectual and personal qualities which . . . were to mark him as one of the great men of his age. . . . All the more credit, therefore, must go to Köchel for his pertinacity. . . .
>
> His great achievement lay in the chronological order which he established on a basis of musical style and paleography for the works composed before 1784 [that] . . . bore no dates. . . . In order to round off the whole, Köchel classified Mozart's entire output into the twenty-three categories which were later adopted unchanged for the publication of the Complete Edition. . . .
>
> A lesser man might have rested content with these laurels but Köchel's final service was still to come. He realized that the publication of his catalogue marked only the first stage in making Mozart's genius fully and widely known. The second stage necessarily entailed the establishment of a definitive text of each composition, to be published in a standard edition.
>
> . . . Current interest in Mozart was still limited. Clearly, a definitive edition could not be undertaken as an ordinary publishing venture. Enthusiasm and financial support were essential. Köchel supplied some of the latter himself and devoted all his energies to arousing the former.
>
> His eminence in the world of learning and his privileged position in court circles enabled him to evoke some interest among musicians and the aristocracy. (The thirteen patrons ultimately included 8 German crowned heads.) He himself gave Breitkopf 15,000 Gulden (app. £1,500 at the time) to finance the project, but had his name withheld until later.

After quoting from the prospectus offering the complete edition on a subscription basis, Alec Hyatt King continues:

> But notwithstanding the low price, few subscribers came forward and the somewhat anxious tone of the prospectus proved to be justified, for the first list, published in 1877, contained only eighty-four names. Clearly, the edition could hardly have been undertaken but for Köchel's generosity. . . . Köchel died revered by all who knew him for

his deep and varied learning, for his dignity and nobility of character and for the generosity of his mind and fortune.

In dealing with Mozart's lost and fragmentary compositions, King states, "When Ludwig von Köchel affixed the number 626 to the 'Requiem,' he could not have foreseen the emphatic finality which that number would come to impose upon the general conception of Mozart's output . . . probably few people realised that the total of works which he actually composed falls not far short of 700."

The tributes started much earlier and included those by persons who knew Köchel. A very interesting one comes from Karl Mozart, the composer's son. In 1856, as mentioned before, a Mozart Festival was held in Salzburg between 6 and 10 September to mark the centenary of Mozart's birth, and Karl Mozart received an invitation as guest of honor. Köchel intended to use this opportunity to obtain a memento in the hand of the man whose father he honored and admired so greatly. To his most pleasant surprise, on 16 September 1856, Karl Mozart wrote the following:

> The honor awarded me by such an excellent man as you, dear Herr von Köchel, is justified only by the merits of my father; therefore in order for my participation in a personal measure of your request, may I instead take this opportunity to express my most sincere thanks for everything you have contributed to the glorification of my father's name and for your efforts to propagate his praiseworthy remembrance unto future generations. Your most respectfully devoted Carl Mozart.

It is noteworthy that these sentiments were expressed *six years* before the first appearance of the *Köchelverzeichnis* and therefore reflect the esteem in which Köchel's work toward the popularization of Mozart was held long before he accomplished the task for which he is known today!

Karl Thomas Mozart, by the way, had lived for many years in unrecognized obscurity in Milan, Italy, and had been "found" by the organizers of the festival. He was to die two years later on 31 October 1858, the last of the Mozarts, his composer brother Franz Xaver Wolfgang having died on 29 July 1844 and neither having had children to carry on the name.

Joseph Bergmann, one of the biographers of Archduke Karl, Köchel's erstwhile employer, a man who knew Köchel well (and who was to partake in the official valuation of his scientific collections after Köchel's death), says of him in his *Medaillen auf berühmte und ausgezeichnete Männer des österreichischen Kaiserstaates vom XVI. bis zum XIX. Jahrhundert* (Medals Honoring Famous and Excellent Men of the Austrian Empire from the Sixteenth to Nineteenth Century): "Köchel was well versed in the classical and modern languages and their literature, a thorough expert of music, an excellent botanist, a man of versatile education and a keen admirer of all arts and sciences."

A long and much-treasured tribute comes from Köchel's contemporary Otto Jahn (1813–1869), the man whose *Mozart*, with its detailed appreciation of each composition mentioned therein, was of such tremendous help to Köchel that he dedicated the *Register* to him in glowing terms. This is what Jahn wrote in the foreword to the second edition of *Mozart* in 1867:

> The most significant advance for me and for readers of this revision has been brought about by Ludwig von Köchel's "Chronological-Thematical Register of Wolfgang Amadeus Mozart's Compositions" (Leipzig 1862). The need for such a register had become so inevitable to me that I was determined to undertake such a work when, at the appropriate time, I learned that Köchel had been busy on this task for some considerable time. Contact, first in writing, then in person, soon convinced me that this work was in much better hands [with him] and it was to my satisfaction that in some matters of detail, at any rate, I was able to lend a helping hand.
>
> Through unparalleled devotion that shrank not from sacrifice or effort, a work has been created which through its reliability of research and clarity of execution may be considered exemplary. Naturally, individual additions and corrections are unavoidable in this field; Köchel himself has already published some (Allgemeine Musik Zeitung 1864, page 493 on); a few trifles you will also find here. Incidentally, I was able to dispense with all footnotes and comments as regards chronology and bibliography of individual Mozart compositions which I was obliged to include before in the absence of the Register. Now in most instances reference to the numbers in Köchel's Register suffices and these are used unsparingly here; only when it was required for my specific purpose did I go into further detail. The corrections made of some of the mistakes noted in printed versions of the scores by reference to the original [manuscript] could also be obviated as they have found their proper place in Köchel.
>
> Köchel's friendship which I consider the most beautiful benefit of joint endeavor, accompanied me and supported me with the most

faithful participation on all paths I had to tread in my new revision. What he proved to me, I cannot name—he knows it and how cordially I thank him for it. With him, Sonnleithner, Karajan, Pohl and Julius André, were tireless in pursuing my queries and requests. To all of them go my very special thanks if my book, and to this I attach great weight, can be reliable in its details.

When Hermann Deiters prepared the third edition of Jahn's book, published in 1889 (i.e., long after Jahn and Köchel had died), he mentioned in his foreword, "The Köchel register was at my disposition in the form of the original proof copy which contained numerous handwritten additions." This "Handexemplar" is now again in the possession of the original publishers, Breitkopf & Härtel, who kindly sent me copies of some pages.

Dr. Anton Kerschbaumer, a writer who lived in the area of Austria in which Köchel was born and who commented on his "masterful cello playing," has this to say: "Toward his friends Köchel was full of sincere sympathy. To those who did not know him closely he seemed proud, unfriendly, remote. In social circles he excelled through his wit, and his rapturous admiration of Mozart alleviated the rigors of his scholarship. . . . His healthy round face was always clean shaven, the curls of his hair surrounded his high brow. The impression he gave was not so much that of a scientist, rather that of a well-bred man of culture with a sense for what is noble."

The Austrian composer Wilhelm Kienzl (1857–1941), who at one stage of his career was very close to Wagner at Bayreuth and whose work as a composer had been greatly encouraged by Franz Liszt, knew Köchel and was most impressed as a young man by the achievement of the *Köchel Register.* The following are extracts from his diaries as told by Hans Sittner in his book *Kienzl-Rosegger,* published in 1953:

> Around this time the capable German composer Ferdinand Thieriot (1838–1919) was active in Graz in his capacity of artistic director of the Steiermark Musical Society. I still remember most vividly his sympathetic merriment in hearing about my suggestion to perform, strictly in their chronological order all of Mozart's 626 works, as listed in the well-known Köchel Register, in the course of one year in Graz, in three concert halls of varying size, in the church and in the theater.

And later in the *Diary:*

> On occasion of the "Vienna Days" I called on the two well-known music researchers Ludwig Ritter von Köchel and August Wilhelm Am-

bros. The old councilor Köchel who has knowledge of many dead matters and who has achieved high merit through his publication of the "Chronological Thematical Register of All of W A Mozart's Compositions" and a biography of the "Austrian Palestrina" Johann Joseph Fux, showed himself in the course of our conversation to be most conservative in his [musical] taste, whose empathy did not extend beyond the first stylistic period of Beethoven.

One of Köchel's best-known contemporaries among musicologists was Leopold von Sonnleithner (1797–1873). Soon after the appearance of the *Köchelverzeichnis,* this expert wrote an article about the work for the publication *Recensionen,* which was printed on 28 September 1862 and from which I wish to quote the following relevant passages:

> If I speak again about a book which has been repeatedly reviewed in this and in other papers, it is not only to strengthen with my voice the general chorus of those singing its praises, but to illustrate on the one hand the difficulty of this achievement from an aspect not so far sufficiently appreciated, on the other hand to meet the wish expressed by the author in his own Foreword (P. XVIII) that everyone, who is able to do so, should contribute to filling the gaps evident in the work.
>
> Not a few artists "of the métier" consider the friends of the arts (the dilettanti) only with a sort of condescension, considering their achievements only as poor, barely tolerable attempts. In many instances this view is actually well founded, because many dilettantes are concerned merely with their own entertainment, diversion, whereas the seriousness of art bars them from entering into its inner sanctum. . . .
>
> In bygone centuries musical literature was almost exclusively in the hands of so-called dilettanti, that is: men, who in possession of musical and literary knowledge, were at the same time, through their office or wealth in an independent position without the necessity of looking elsewhere for their livelihood. . . .
>
> In this field there are enterprises which can only be carried out with great sacrifices of money and time and which can, therefore, only be undertaken by an enthusiastic friend of the arts who, equipped with the knowledge and talent of an expert, leaving aside all gain, employs his means and his spirit from his pure love of art to reach a preset target and who finds in this the true reward for his devotion.
>
> One such task was the work in front of us and Dr. Köchel is the man who embraced within himself all necessary attributes. Anyone who has ever had occasion to deal with similar works even on a much smaller scale, will know to appreciate the colossal difficulties encountered. There is no special skill in utilizing the well-known and easily

accessible resources, to review and to muster what has been gleaned from these. But to seek out the concealed sources and to make them accessible, to win over the usually jealous proprietors and guardians of unknown treasures, to recognize and utilize with swift and sure eyes what has been sought, often after being granted but a cursory glance, to supplement in the most feasible way the unavoidable gaps by reasoned deduction and to put in order and present lucidly the whole with comprehensive circumspection—this is a task to which only true dedication could render its force and perseverance.

Dr. Köchel in his Foreword tells us specifically only that he had obtained benevolent furtherance of his task both from his countrymen and from the owners and principals of libraries and art collections abroad. In his modesty he silently omits to mention that because of his endeavor, for several years he undertook long and expensive journeys; that he went to Vienna (etc. as above) and many more places, that he stayed sometimes for weeks and months, sparing neither effort nor expense to be able to scrutinize the desired manuscripts, if possible to obtain copies of same and to receive information and clarification about them. If in the process he succeeded in bypassing numerous obstacles and to overcome, in particular, the reservations of some of the owners of Mozart autographs or of rare copies thereof, this can only be ascribed to the impression made by his confidence inspiring personality and by his ability to instill in their minds the conviction that no manner of self-interest or vanity, only pure love of art and deep reverence for the great composer were the mainspring of his undertaking. This then was the key that opened all archives and libraries, all private collections and transformed into collaborators all admirers of Mozart to whom he turned.

Sonnleithner then, after explaining the activity of Alois Fuchs toward creating a comprehensive register of Mozart's works and detailing the assistance he himself gave toward this enterprise, resulting in a "ganz ansehnliche, alles bis dahin Dagewesene überragende Arbeit" (quite considerable work, surpassing everything so far in existence), continues to say, "But although this preliminary work was utilized by Dr. Köchel, it fades into insignificance when compared with his magnificent achievement, which as a necessary complement to Otto Jahn's classic Mozart biography will from now on endure as an example for similar undertakings and will adorn every music library." Sonnleithner, by the way, assisted Jahn in his work on Mozart.

After this lengthy introduction come the specific comments relating to entries in the *Köchelverzeichnis,* but as it is not the task of this book to go into such detail, suffice it to say that they serve mainly the purpose of supplementing the information given by Köchel and not to contradict anything contained in the *Verzeichnis*. In fact, Sonnleithner concludes by saying, "In the work that is in front of me and which I scrutinized repeatedly with all due attention without finding any significant shortcomings therein."

Concerning the comments made by Sonnleithner in relation to specific entries, these, together with other facts discovered by Köchel after publication of the first edition, were included in Köchel's article published on 20 July 1864 in the *Allgemeine Musikalische Zeitung* to which I refer in a different place in greater detail.

Dr. Constantin von Wurzbach, the author and editor of the *Biographisches Lexicon* (Biographical Encyclopaedia) of Austria's famous men, also wrote a *Mozart-Buch*, published in 1869. In its foreword he links Otto Jahn's *Mozart* and the *Köchelverzeichnis* and refers to them as "two works so unique in their format as to enrapture to the utmost everyone who has occasion to occupy himself with distinguished persons and with their activities."

In a different place in the book, Wurzbach, in quoting a comment by Köchel on Mozart's Quintet for Piano and Wind Instruments, K. 452—"from beginning to end a true triumph of purest harmonious sound"—calls Köchel "undoubtedly a competent judge."

Wurzbach's comments on Köchel's "Mozart Canzonen" are that they are "full of vitality, of enthusiasm, rhythmically accomplished, it could be taken for a work by Leopold Schefer." (Schefer was a well-known German poet who lived 1784–1862.)

Wurzbach also quotes the following comments by Dr. Franz Lorenz, whose pamphlet, as mentioned, inspired Köchel to start work on the *Verzeichnis:*

As a worthy pendant to Jahn's biography, Köchel's great Mozart Catalogue appeared whose accomplishment in every respect leaves nothing to be desired. It was made possible only through its author's self-sacrificing devotion coupled with his independent situation which permitted him to seek out the still existing 440 manuscripts of the master which were scattered over Europe in all directions of the compass, at their place of existence and to stay as long as necessary for their close scrutiny. Anyone willing to form even an approximate opinion of the extent and laboriousness of this work, comparable only to its meritoriousness, should take it to hand and should, as an example, thumb through the hundreds of thousands of bars of music Köchel had to

count in the original manuscripts thus to enable the owner of the catalogue to obtain his own control over each edition of a Mozart composition as regards its integrity [i.e., entirety] or its fragmentation. Jahn's
and Köchel's works are of a kind which, subject to some specific corrections and additions, will not be surpassed in times to come.

Prophetic words these proved to be!

Franz Giegling, one of the three revisers of the sixth edition of the
Köchelverzeichnis (which in its reprinted eighth edition is the one in
current use as no further update has been prepared since its appearance in 1964), writes in the *Neue Zürcher Zeitung* to commemorate
the centenary of Köchel's death in 1977:

> His humanism . . . was based on a profound systematic and methodical
> study of jurisprudence and natural sciences. To this was added the per-
> sonal impetus of an enthusiastic urge for research which went hand in
> hand with an incredible workload to produce beautiful results in many
> fields. . . . Köchel's work and merit in creating a chronological order in
> Mozart's total output cannot be over-emphasized. Even today . . . his
> solitary path of scientific achievement must amaze.

Ludwig Schrott wrote in Munich in 1950, "This high-minded gen-
tleman with his bright eyes and high brow . . . the sympathetic actor
face . . . with whom one needed closer acquaintance to know that he
was not proud and unfriendly, but a man who in spite of his superi-
ority possessed real piety and humor."

Erich Valentin enthuses in 1962, "He occupied himself out of sheer
joy with matters concerning Johann Joseph Fux, Mozart, Beethoven
and the Imperial Court Orchestra of Vienna . . . a lover of music who
set himself as his life's task to be active in the arts and sciences . . .
well-known but still unknown . . . whose name became a concept of
which one always thinks in context with Mozart."

Dr. Otto Biba, director of archives of the Gesellschaft der Musikfreunde in Vienna, wrote in 1977, "The energy and diligence behind
all his work is inestimable. And we have no knowledge of any helpers
of Köchel's, even of a copyist who might have assisted him in the
copying and scoring of the works of J. J. Fux in 21 volumes. In relation
to this action and workload all gratitude must seem modest."

Biba also gives details of the collection of musical manuscripts
and copies bequeathed to his society: the "complete works of Wolfgang Amadeus Mozart both as regards scores and individual parts

and of the works of numerous other composers, in approximately 700 note books. . . . In judging this collection two aspects must be appreciated: the activity of the collector as determined by the high quality and scientific points of view and the minutely accurate copying of the works of Mozart."

The society acknowledged Köchel's contributions to its activities and finances in earlier statements. In a memorial volume published in 1937, for instance, it is emphasized that "he was one of the first promoters of the Society's collections to contribute a considerable sum for the acquisition of worthwhile musical properties for its archives and library."

The selection of these tributes has been kept relatively short to avoid repeating the same sentiments over and over. Köchel's life, or what is known about it, was one of hard work coupled with the intense joy of achievement. The fields in which he excelled were all self-chosen, and he brought the enthusiasm of the self-taught amateur of noble thought to them. All this will be described in Part II.

16

Nineteenth-Century Man

To understand Köchel's life and work, we need to consider the period in which he lived. Many of the things we take for granted today simply did not exist for him, and without making allowances for this situation, it is almost impossible to appreciate what he has achieved. The nineteenth century saw tremendous changes in all fields of human existence, and a man born just a fortnight into the century lived through most of these.

Austria was a monarchy under emperor Franz II at the beginning of the century and had not changed constitutionally by the end when Franz Joseph I was the emperor; but this seemingly uneventful position ignores the period of tremendous upheaval between 1847 and 1849 when the whole of Europe went through the turmoil of revolutions, causing in Austria the abdication in 1848 of Ferdinand I. His nephew took the throne and became the longest-ruling monarch—and almost the last one—of the Austro-Hungarian Monarchy.

The days of Köchel's childhood were under the influence of Napoleonic wars; Vienna was occupied in 1809, as was Stein, Köchel's birthplace. Although Archduke Karl, his future employer, scored a morale-lifting victory against Napoleon at Aspern, the French were able to bring up reinforcements in time for the battle of Wagram, some six weeks later, whereas Archduke Johann's troops were held up by a skirmish in Raab (Györ in western Hungary) and failed to arrive in time. The Austrian army was defeated, and after another defeat at Znaim, Karl agreed to a cease-fire with the French and withdrew from the command of the Austrian army.

Economically, the country was bankrupt. In 1811, by special charter, the value of the Gulden was reduced to one-fifth. Not until the end of the Napoleonic wars did the currency become stable again. With the introduction of the Krone, the gold standard was adopted.

As mentioned earlier, Köchel's liberal views led him to relinquish the post of school inspector in 1850. Although nothing is on record to demonstrate an actual political involvement before or after, the very fact of his *withdrawal* into the world of science indicates a disenchantment with the establishment.

The revolutionary thoughts traversing Europe around the middle of the century were given a systematic backbone in the *Communist Manifesto* published by Karl Marx (1818–1883) and Friedrich Engels (1820–1895) in 1848. The process of popular uprising, somewhat in reverse since the heady days of the French revolution of 1789, was given fresh impetus. Liberal-minded members of the establishment knew that the only chance of maintaining the existing power base was a gradual improvement for the *lower classes*. The industrial revolution had changed the pattern of domiciles. With the need for more and more industrial workers, the urban population increased dramatically everywhere, and Vienna was no exception. The Austrian capital had a population of 235,098 in 1796; by 1851, this number had risen to 431,147, and the figure for 1890 is 827,567, indicating that in Köchel's lifetime the urban population had just about tripled in size. Similar figures apply to other Austrian towns.

Life in the cities always moved at a faster pace. The development of book printing, newspapers and periodicals, the first public libraries, even reading for the blind—all emanate from this period. (Louis Braille, 1809–1852, was blind from the age of three. At sixteen he invented his system of reading for the blind, still in use today. He was, by the way, a church organist and played the cello as well.)

Inventions dominated the scientific world of the century. Think of electricity, *discovered* in 1831 by Michael Faraday (1791–1867); the first locomotive in 1804 (Trevithick), which hauled ten tons of iron and seventy men in five wagons at five miles per hour for nine and a half miles in the mines of Pen-y-daren near Merthyr Tydfil; followed by Stephenson's 1829 *Rocket* on the Stockton-to-Darlington line and by the rapid development of a railway network everywhere in Europe, including Germany (1835) and Austria, where the first tracks were laid in 1836.

In 1801 the first practical steamboat, the *Charlotte Dundas,* appeared on the Forth and Clyde Canal; by 1829 there was also a steamboat on the Danube, and it was possible by 1834 to travel by steamboat from Vienna to the estuary of the river at the Black Sea.

After the hobby horse, the predecessor of the bicycle invented in France in 1811, there was an early example of a real bicycle in 1844. Carriages became more comfortable; the brougham was built for Lord Brougham in 1838, and the hansom cab invented by Joseph A. Hansom (1803–1882).

At the beginning of the century, the average speed of a mail coach, the *only* means of long-distance travel, was eight miles per hour. This had not changed since Roman times—that is, for some two thousand years! Within the century the speed would increase almost *tenfold* by switching to rail travel, leaving a further, almost similar, increase for the twentieth century with its travel by jet airliners.

Candles were the only form of lighting at the start of the century; good oil lamps existed from 1836, paraffin ones from 1853. Gas was first used for lighting in 1803; by 1810 gas street lighting commenced, but in domestic use it first appeared toward the end of the century. Gas cookers were first seen at the Great Exhibition in London of 1851.

The first sewing machine was patented by the American Isaac Singer in 1851, although Austrians may know that the Viennese tailor Josef Madersperger had invented the principle of machine sewing in 1815, but he lacked the necessary funds to develop his invention and died in obscure poverty in 1850—one year before Singer introduced his successfully developed model. In a similar vein, Austria could claim the invention of the typewriter via Peter Mitterhofer in 1866, when some of his working models were sold to the emperor, but the commercial possibilities were overlooked, and it was again left to the Americans to introduce the article years later.

Looms for weaving first appeared in 1835, and Vienna had no less than 450 silk weaving mills by 1845. Ladies' handbags were introduced early in the century; until then there were pockets concealed under the dress and outside the petticoat.

The first cable was laid under the English Channel in 1851, to be followed by the first transatlantic one to America in 1858. Suddenly communications, which had also not progressed since Roman times, changed dramatically, with almost instant transmission of important (and not so important) events, something we take for granted in today's world of television and satellites.

Charles Darwin's (1809–1882) journey on HMS *Beagle* was in 1831, and 1 July 1858 was the date of his first public statement of the modern theory of evolution. Friedrich Nietzsche (1844–1900) published his *Untimely Observations* between 1873 and 1876, and Edgar Allan Poe (1809–1849) published his *Philosophy of Composition* in 1846. Charles Dickens (1812–1870), whose works were translated into German as well, was one of numerous contemporaries in the world of literature.

Louis Pasteur (1822–1895) developed the heating process of milk; also applied in the production of wine and beer, it is designed to keep out harmful vegetation. His paper was first published in 1857. Samuel Lister (1815–1906) and Robert Koch (1843–1910), whose activity and discoveries were destined to revolutionize medicine, commenced work in 1867 and 1876, respectively. The Austrian Academy of Science came into being in 1847, the Vienna Technical High School in 1866 and the High School for Agriculture in 1872.

Although the motor car was not invented until after Köchel's death, its forerunner, the first mechanical vehicle powered by a gasoline engine, appeared on the roads of Austria in 1865, developed by Siegfried Marcus and capable of speeds of only four miles per hour (half that of a horse-drawn carriage!). Marcus produced a more viable model in 1875, but it was left to the Germans Daimler and Benz to come out with a commercially marketable motor car another ten years later.

London's sewerage system was installed in 1864; the Suez Canal opened in 1869. Even Alexander Graham Bell's (1847–1922) telephone was invented a year before Köchel died, in 1876.

The world of music, after the giants of the eighteenth century—Bach, Händel, Mozart, and Haydn (who lived until 1809)—moved into the most productive and versatile period it had ever known. Ludwig van Beethoven (1770–1827), Louis Berlioz (1803–1869), Georges Bizet (1831–1875), Aleksandr Borodin (1833–1887), Johannes Brahms (1833–1897), Anton Bruckner (1824–1896), Fréderic Chopin (1810–1849), Gaetano Donizetti (1797–1848), Anton Dvořák (1841–1904), César Franck (1822–1890), Fëdor Glinka (1803–1857), Edvard Grieg (1843–1907), Franz Liszt (1811–1886), Felix Mendelssohn (1809–1847), Modest Musorgsky (1839–1881), Jacques Offenbach (1819–1880), Niccolò Paganini (1782–1840), Nikolai Rimsky-Korsakov (1844–1908), Gioacchino Rossini (1792–1868), Franz Schubert (1797–1828), Robert Schumann (1819–1856), Bedřich

Smetana (1824–1884), Johann Strauss, son (1825–1899), Sir Arthur Sullivan (1842–1900), Piotr Tchaikovsky (1840–1893), Giuseppe Verdi (1813–1901), Richard Wagner (1813–1883), Carl Maria Weber (1786–1826)—the list is endless.

For a man who looked on music as the motivating ingredient of his life, these must have been exciting times. Yet it is a well-known fact that Köchel shunned most music written after Mozart's death, the only notable exception being Beethoven, whom he treated with equal respect.

17

Remaining Mysteries Surrounding Köchel's Life

Köchel's whole life was something of a mystery, as so little was known about him by so few people, and nobody thought of him as a worthy subject for a clear and comprehensively detailed study of his life and achievements for more than 120 years after his death. During his lifetime, some suggested that the most suitable writer for this task would be Otto Jahn, whose *W. A. Mozart* (1856–1859) was the most detailed description to date of the life and work of the composer and who, since 1851, had known Köchel well. Both men had given numerous examples of their mutual respect. Without Jahn's book it would have been almost impossible for Köchel to have compiled his *Register*, leaning as he did again and again on the facts therein.

Jahn died in 1869 (i.e., eight years before Köchel), and in this way this possibility was lost. Other learned friends or contemporaries, such as von Waldersee, Sonnleithner, Nottebohm, or Hanslick, never showed sufficient interest.

In spite of this neglect, Köchel's scientific heritage is well documented, and we assume that in this respect there are no significant gaps. The dispositions of his last will, moreover, were to ensure that his various collections got into the right hands.

This, regretfully, does not apply to anything connected with his private life.

The few facts that were to be found had to be dug up almost from nowhere. There are no surviving descendants of the Köchel family—at any rate none I could trace (in spite of all possible efforts). Because neither Ludwig Köchel nor his brother, Fritz, married, there could in any case only be more distant relations whose descendants may be alive today. I made contact with all Köchels living today in Vienna and in Salzburg without finding anyone who could verify a relationship. After strenuous efforts, I succeeded in locating surviving relations of Victor Köchl in the United States, only to ascertain that they have nothing to do with Ludwig Köchel. A niece, Wilhelmine Gallasch, is mentioned in Köchel's testament, but the exact degree of relationship could not be established (the term *Nichte,* niece, being more broadly used in German) or whether she had married and whether there were any surviving descendants.

There must have been a legacy of personal papers and notes, but no disposition appears in the will in this respect. Max von Scharschmid was instructed to execute the testament; theoretically, therefore, such papers should have come into the hands of the Scharschmid family, the more so as the three principal beneficiaries, the Zerboni boys, were, as mentioned, the grandchildren of Köchel's friend Franz Freiherr Scharschmid von Adlertreu. But again, I had to establish with regret that there are no surviving descendants in this family, either, and consequently any personal papers that may have been in their possession have been lost.

The testament gives information about some friends and godchildren not connected with Köchel's professional life, but when these bequests of 500 or 1,000 Gulden are related to his total estate, we can see how insignificant these contacts must have been.

In the absence of all personal documents and records, the first "mystery" is the uncertainty surrounding Köchel's love life. The only romance of which we know is the Sophie Kleyle story, and, in fact, all we have is the diary of a young girl, inexperienced in matters of love, who enthuses about an impressive and somewhat mysterious man. Whether her feelings were reciprocated by Köchel and whether the possibility of marriage figured in his thoughts at all we do not know; his own diary of these events is lost. Whether his restraint in the affair was for financial or professional reasons or whether perhaps latent homosexual tendencies were to blame cannot be proved one way or another.

Köchel did have a number of friends from his early youth who remained bachelors throughout their lives. In pursuance of his botanical studies, he went on many excursions, and one of his regular companions on these was August Neilreich, who later became a famous botanist. He also never married and was to express his "love" for Köchel in an almost rapturous way. Still, not too much should be read into this matter, either, because the mode of expression was very different at the time.

The fact that Köchel never married could have had other reasons. When he first became acquainted with Sophie, he was a penniless student at the University of Vienna who earned his pocket money, lodgings, and sustenance by his employment as tutor and educator to the children of noble families. In those days it was still customary to marry only after securing one's basis of existence.

In the years to follow, right up to his forty-third year, Köchel was engaged in the archducal household, which meant that he had virtually no time to himself—no private holidays or even occasional free weekends in which he could have pursued his own aims. As he gave absolute priority to his career, seeing in this—correctly—the security of his future, all thoughts of private life had to stay in the background.

When in 1842 he was decorated with the Leopoldsorden, which afforded the statutory right for an application to be granted the hereditary Ritter title, Köchel made full use of this. Here we have another "mystery": if he had no plans to marry and start a family, why take the trouble to make the petition that eventually led to his becoming a Ritter (knight, or chévalier) of the Austrian Empire? It is therefore possible that at the time he still had plans to find a suitable girl, or perhaps there was already a candidate selected for this purpose—without anything becoming of the matter.

The succeeding eight years, when he lived in Vienna and Teschen as Privatgelehrter (private scholar) and during which he undertook a number of long foreign journeys, must have given him ample opportunity to find a companion. He preferred his privacy, and the joy of "family life" (Familienglück) to which he often referred and which also figures in his testament is that of the family of his friend Scharschmid in whose household he had lived for a number of years. What attracted him to this family? Was it just a continuation of the friendship started in their youth when both men studied law at the University of Vienna, or could it be that he was secretly "in love" with Scharschmid's wife, Marie? Or later with daughter Johanna, whose three sons were to become the main beneficiaries of his testament? It remains a mystery!

To mention again the wording of the last will, he cannot "square accounts" with Scharschmid and decides to leave him nothing, except a small token, yet it is a Scharschmid (i.e., Max von Scharschmid) who is given the responsibility to execute the provisions of the will, and other members of the family receive bequests, whereas about one half of the total estate goes to the three Zerboni boys, the sons of Johanna. Why?

Another "major mystery" emerges from the testament. The total estate amounted to some 85,000 Gulden, a considerable sum, estimated to equal perhaps $750,000 in today's terms. (The calculation of comparable values is not easy; the true worth may have been considerably more.) Köchel had started out as a student of no means, his father left him nothing at all, and in the absence of personal papers, we cannot establish whether he had made some other inheritance. His elder brother, Fritz, who had worked as a qualified engineer and died in 1836, also remained a bachelor. His total estate, left to Ludwig, came to less than 1,000 Gulden, and this includes the 200 left him by their father in 1820.

In search of an answer as to where Köchel's fortune had come from, I calculated that one possible solution is that Köchel himself was able to save the whole amount. Considering that for fifteen years he had lived almost as a member of the archduke's family, during which time it was just about impossible for him to spend any of his own money for private purposes, he might have saved nearly his total earnings during this long period.

The archives of Archduke Karl contain no details of Köchel's salary; they refer merely to "norms" applying to all tutors. (Dr. Otto Biba, archive director of the Gesellschaft der Musikfreunde, suggests in one of his articles that the archduke "must have paid him well.") Let us assume an average salary of only 1,000 Gulden per year. If this was consistently deposited at the then-customary 5 percent annual rate of interest, after fifteen years, with compound interest, a sum of over 22,000 Gulden would have accumulated. If it is further assumed that the pension granted him by the archduke after completion of his service was sufficient for his ongoing cost of living (and this is most likely, because for the bulk of the time he lived in the house of his friend Scharschmid and for the last few years in the archducal palace, thus having no household expenses of his own) and that he did not have to withdraw anything from his earlier savings, these could have remained on deposit for another thirty-five years, during which time the amount would have grown to nearly 120,000 Gulden!

This demonstrates that even with a smaller average salary than the 1,000 Gulden suggested here, or allowing for some of the interest to have been spent, this calculation may represent a mathematical solution of the puzzle.

I have repeatedly attempted to convert the 85,000 Gulden to today's terms but have found it difficult to do so. What is known is that at the time of Köchel's death, a conversion into pounds sterling would be roughly ten to one, producing a value of £8,500 (about $12,750) in 1877. Using the price of gold, a multiplier of 60 only would apply to this sum. Taking average earnings as a basis, the multiplier could be 300. Prices of food, housing, and so forth all produce different figures, and I am lost as to which formula to adopt. Taking my starting point of a "good" salary of 1,000 Gulden, Köchel's fortune could have paid eighty-five such salaries. If a person in a similar position would today earn perhaps $30,000 to $45,000, a figure of up to about $3.6 million results. I rest my case.

One of the smaller "mysteries" is where Köchel lived in Vienna between 1843 and 1848. Possibly he lived with the Scharschmids, as in later years in Teschen and in Salzburg, the more likely because with several long journeys undertaken during this period, he did not really require a home of his own.

Another unsolved question is whether and to what extent he was remunerated for his scientific writings—this could have supplemented his pension. Similarly, it is not known when he first came into contact with the publishers Breitkopf & Härtel.

I revert once more to the Scharschmid matter. When Köchel followed his friend to Vienna in 1863, he did not rejoin his household but accepted a "grace and favor" apartment in the archducal palace in Hofgartengasse (today Hanuschgasse). After many years, and for the first time, he did not live under the roof of his friend. Might there have been a dispute between the friends, or at least a "misunderstanding"? Could this be the explanation of the sentence in Köchel's will whereby Scharschmid was only to select a token from the estate, whereas other members of his family were to be main beneficiaries, executors, and legatees? The testament was made in 1868, a few years after Köchel had left his friend's house, although it is reliably reported that he continued "to share his table and leisure time."

Someone, somewhere, may exist who has some of the source material in his or her possession that contains the answers to these questions. It is best if I turn to this person (or persons) with the same request made by Köchel at the end of his foreword to the *Register:*

> As no one can be better convinced than the author how much of what is submitted here had to remain fragmentary because no further sources opened up, and that the publication of this piece of writing will give occasion to entice some of the unknown from its hiding place, thus the urgent request is made to all proprietors of autographs [and other personal details] . . . to contribute through friendly advice to the author or publisher in the interest of all music lovers, to a task to which this individual, on his first attempt, cannot have been equal.

II

His Work

18

The Writer

The old coat of arms of Niederösterreich shows, as is well-known, "five larks ascending in a blue field." Can there be a more apt symbol for a cheerful, singing and song-loving people, even though the designers of the coat of arms gave no thought to such an interpretation? Yes, these harmless Austrian larks warbled their happy song in spite of attacks by Turkish, Swedish and French invaders; they may have ducked in the furrows during the blaze of warfare; but as soon as they felt themselves safe again, they fluttered upwards and blared their suppressed airs with renewed fervor. Austria's opponents, both those of foreign language and of German tongue, would gladly have berated or stifled our very pride, our warm-hearted sensibility and our distinct aptitude for music-making, after overwhelming our poor land with all manner of abuse; but the subject matter and the famous names of those celebrities who, either by birth or through permanent domicile, belonged to Austria, succeeded in pervading all countries on this earth with their irresistible fame—leaving nothing but envy and speechlessness to their adversaries.

Thus started the lecture Köchel gave to members of the Geographical Society about the rather dry subject of Court Music at the Imperial Court during the fifteenth, sixteenth, and seventeenth centuries and up to the mid-eighteenth century. The lecture was published in the society's report in 1866, and Köchel arranged, at his own cost, a reprint in the form of a separate brochure.

Köchel was not a "writer," not in the accepted, conventional sense of the word. He did not make a living out of his written work, and, with one exception, his writings relate very closely to his scientific work and were therefore an extension of this activity rather than a separate matter. The exception is his poetic output, which is the subject of the next chapter. Some bibliographical notes also mention a Schwank (a farcical story), but after a great deal of fruitless search, this turned out to be one of the poems entitled "Eine Walfahrt zum Laudachsee am 18. Schewwal 861 der Hedschra"; this again is mentioned in greater detail in the poetry chapter.

The passage quoted earlier demonstrates clearly that, whatever his subject, Köchel found scope to diverge into the various fields of his pleasurable activities, his love of nature and music. It also shows that instead of treating his subject in a cool, matter-of-fact way, he lets his imagination loose and becomes poetic when others may be content with simple language, stating their facts and figures. And the quotation furnishes proof once again of his ardent patriotism, his love of Austria and his closer home, Niederösterreich.

At the end of this book, I give a list of all books and articles by Köchel, as published. I must add the usual proviso: although my list is longer than any previously published, there may be other writings I was unable to locate. Many of the books and articles on the list are analyzed in detail in other chapters; passages are quoted, and their interrelation is explained. The nature of these works is such that it can readily be seen that they were not written for "profit"; in fact, I very much doubt whether Köchel ever received payment for any of them, including even the Mozart register! Several were published by himself in "private editions," probably in a few hundred copies; others were included in specialized periodicals or in the annuals of societies.

Here is an extract from his Nachruf (obituary) for Joseph Freiherr von Spaun:

> From these pages emerges, if often between the lines, the true picture of this honorable man, his fortunate abilities, the earnestness with which he undertook his training, the deftness, zeal and perseverance in official matters, his happy, sincere spirit, his susceptibility for everything beautiful, particularly in music, but foremost his total disposition for everything humane, his gentle, conciliatory feeling for the failings of others, his self-sacrificing love for his family.

The way in which Spaun's character is described here in one sentence, albeit a long one, is typical of Köchel's writing style. Much of what he says about Spaun could be said about himself, but the essential point is that having read this description, we can almost see the man before us—his very being comes to life.

Köchel mentions Spaun's ability as a violin player and of conducting a small orchestra, performing in front of archduke Rudolf (Beethoven's sponsor) and accompanying the archduke's solo playing of a Mozart concerto. Then comes this sentence: "He noticed . . . behind him a small boy with spectacles who played the violin with great skill. This was Franz Schubert who even as a child was a maestro."

Köchel then mentions that Spaun provided the young aspiring composer with a supply of music notepaper, implying that this act of friendship and recognition may well have led to the first compositions of Schubert (whose first composition was made at the age of thirteen.)

In his article about Theodor Kotschy, the scientist who named several newly discovered plants after Köchel, he says:

> It was providential that the distressed traveler in faraway lands was to receive a helping hand from another voyager who, when he learned of his straitened circumstances, was able to arouse sympathy for the luckless absentee at home in the highest and most exalted circles, the result of which paved the way for his homecoming. It is almost superfluous for us to provide here the name of this high-minded person, baron Karl von Hügel: his name would have been guessed in any case.

I could obviously go on to quote from Köchel's writings, but I think the reader will get the gist from these few examples. His ability to characterize a person known to him in one or two sentences, to tell about the person's ability and work in conjunction with his personal attributes, the way in which he never says anything detrimental about any of these people, in spite of the fact that he himself was often criticized by some of his contemporaries, reflects on his own character.

I came across some letters that Köchel had written between 1859 and 1861 to Dr. Leopold Sonnleithner. In the most humble and friendly way he seeks information, transcripts, and so forth, partly in connection with his work on the Mozart register and partly to further the work of Otto Jahn, who at this time was studying Joseph Haydn's compositions. (It will be remembered that Köchel had much help from Jahn's notes on Mozart: could it be that they were together contemplating a Haydn register?) Yet soon after the appearance of the Mozart register, it was Sonnleithner who wrote, while acknowledging Köchel's merit in creating the *Register,* some fairly severe critical notes about some of Köchel's "mistakes" in an article published on 28 September 1862 in *Recensionen,* which led to Köchel's own corrections published in 1864. Had it been the other way round, we can be sure that Köchel would have given the necessary information to Sonnleithner beforehand, thus avoiding the "mistakes" in the first place!

Now let us consider the other aspect of Köchel's written work: his letters. He was a prolific letter writer. Correspondence was far more important in his time than today: there was no telephone (let alone Internet!), and travel was far more cumbersome and time-consuming; an exchange of letters often had to serve instead of a meeting.

Köchel himself made no arrangements to preserve the letters he received; thus, with a few exceptions in which copies of such letters were made and kept by the persons writing them, hardly any letters addressed to him have survived. One reason for this is that apart from the last fifteen years of his life, he never had a permanent address, and to keep stacks of letters received, and move them from one temporary abode to the next, would have been an added burden. And, although the size of the "grace and favor" apartment in the archducal palace is not known, the fact that he had only one servant at that time indicates that it must have been small.

Fortunately, many of the letters written by Köchel do still exist in the various archives, and I was able to see a number of them and obtain copies. There are several to the prior of the Stift of Kremsmünster, to the International Mozart Foundation in Salzburg, and to the Imperial Office dealing with his application to be ennobled. Elsewhere in this book I also refer to the five letters Köchel wrote to fellow Mozart researcher Dr. Josef Hauer, and details are given of the letters he wrote to his erstwhile employer, Archduke Karl.

Here I give the entire text of three letters because of the importance of their content. The first of these, addressed to the prior of the musically prominent Stift of Kremsmünster, demonstrates the high esteem in which Köchel was held there for his knowledge of music.

Most Reverend Herr Prior!

I believed to best satisfy your wish of having your Requiem which you sent to me, independently assessed by an unprejudiced acknowledged expert, by handing this to my friend Josef Laimegger (director of the Assistance Board of the Department of Criminalogy, k.k. District Court of Vienna). His testimonial should convince you that he discharged his task with as much love as expertise. While fully appreciating the value of your work, he repeatedly emphasized to me verbally that an abridgment of the passages indicated, before publication, would be most advisable. Assistant Court Conductor Rotter also remarked that a performance in front of cognoscenti would be most conducive to a suitable estimation. In this connection I was reminded of your able contrapuntist and organist Joh. Ev. Habert in neighboring Gmunden. Should your reverence, on the explicit request of Laimegger, wish to communicate some other compositions of yours, the route of direct dispatch would seem to be most advisable (L. resides in Wien, Alserstrasse 61).

While offering with pleasure to be of further service to you, please accept my most sincere respect.

Your Reverend's most obedient L. R. v. Köchel
Wien, 18th March 1873.

Some of the names mentioned here need further explanation. Joseph Laimegger (1814–1895), apart from the prestigious position to which Köchel refers, was a noted musicologist, a self-taught scholar of Mozart's compositions. He also taught music theory, and his pupils included the composers Karl Millöcker (1842–1899) and Karl Zeller (1842–1898). In his career job he was later (1879) appointed imperial councilor, and he retained his directorial appointment until his retirement at the age of seventy.

Ludwig Rotter (1810–1895) was chorus director, composer, music teacher, and organist. His appointment as assistant conductor of the Court Orchestra dates from 1870. His sacred compositions were more frequently performed between 1867 and 1896 than those of any other composer, assuring him of fame during his lifetime.

Johann Evangelist Habert (1833–1896) received his appointment as organist at the parish church of Gmunden in Oberösterreich in 1860. The list of his compositions is long and varied. Later he was decorated with the papal order of Gregorius.

As to the prior to whom the letter is addressed, he was Pater Maximilian Kerschbaum (1805–1874), son of a Niederösterreich peasant—that is, a close Landsmann (fellow countryman) of Köchel. After completing the Kremser Gymnasium, Köchel's school, which Kerschbaum attended as a correspondence student, he took holy orders and rose to the position of prior of Kremsmünster in 1869. His compositions consisted of masses, vespers, and other sacred works. (Köchel's connection to Kremsmünster is explained elsewhere in this book.)

The next letter, to Karl Freiherr (Baron) von Sterneck, president of the Mozarteum, shows Köchel's standing in this most prestigious organization, which invited him to comment on their plan to purchase the house in Getreidegasse, Salzburg, where Mozart was born. It will be seen that Köchel, prudent as ever, counseled against the acquisition at that time to prevent overextension of the institute's finances. As we know, the house was nevertheless purchased not much later and opened to the public as a museum on 15 June 1880, four years after this correspondence. (In the first two and a half years, until December 1882, a total of 4,688 persons visited the house, paying an entrance fee of 50 kreutzer, equal to 1 mark; the number of visitors increased steadily over the years; by 1900, the annual figure had risen to 3,516, and by 1905, a total of 72,335 had paid the admittance fee. In 1926, there were more than 17,000 visitors, and on a recent visit to Salzburg, I verified that the place is as popular today as ever.)

Most nobly born Baron!

For the words which go far beyond my true merit and which your Excellency had the kindness to address to me in the name of the Mozart Foundation, I am obliged to express my special thanks. Let the enterprise of the Mozart edition now proceed undisturbed toward its complete realization.

Your Excellency suggests in your esteemed letter a second subject, namely the purchase of Mozart's birth house and about this may I be permitted some comments.

The purchase of real estate at a time when there are insufficient funds available invokes some serious doubts in me, however beautiful the thought behind it. Firstly, it must be questionable whether the rents of the house would suffice to maintain it in good condition, to discharge the tax liability and to meet the costs of administration, particularly if parts of the premises are to be devoted to the archives and the music school of the Mozarteum. It is even more questionable to me whether there would remain a balance of income for statutory pensions and scholarships.

Whatever views one holds on this, at the present time when everybody holds back with donations of all kinds as a result of the general monetary crisis, the emergence of a new demand on the money bags in favor of a second Mozart enterprise could cause precarious competition to the Mozart edition already in progress and could thus work to the detriment of both.

Never in my recollection have we been in the midst of a more disastrous monetary crisis and even the swimmer who can usually keep his head above water is in great danger of sinking. Hopefully, better times will come.

With this hope please permit me to assure you of my humblest respect.

Your Excellency's most obedient servant
L. R. v. Köchel
Wien, 22nd May 1876.

The other letter to the Mozarteum (which predates the one printed above) is even more important. It underlines the discreet way in which Köchel negotiated with the publishers Breitkopf & Härtel (who had previously published his Mozart register) to bring about the first collective edition of "all" Mozart compositions. The Mozarteum was obviously approached by the publishers seeking an opinion and requesting part of the subsidy required to make the edition a reality. The institute in turn asked Köchel for his opinion on the project—without realizing that he was its prime motivator!

Köchel's reply to the Mozarteum contains the fact that he had given a "guarantee" of a substantial sum toward this enterprise, but without disclosing the fact that he was not only the guarantor but also the provider of the sum.

To the most highly esteemed Mozart Foundation in Salzburg.
Highly esteemed Committee!

I have two letters in front of me to which I reply hereby. The first, dated 1st February this year, expresses the wish to receive a sheet of my Mozart Register manuscript and my portrait. You will find both enclosed herewith. The second letter, dated 27th February this year, signed by committee member Herr Hans Schläger, seeks to learn my views about a critically revised collected edition of the works of Mozart. I believe my best way of meeting this wish is by notification of what I have so far undertaken in this matter.

That a great genius could not be more worthily honored than through a correct edition of all his works has long been my firm view and does not seem to require a more detailed exposition. Since for Händel, Bach, Beethoven and shortly also for Mendelssohn similar editions have either been completed or are in the process of completion, it seemed to me a debt of honor—if not to say a reproach, particularly as regards Austria—to have delayed for such a long time to envisage a similar and worthy publication of Mozart's collected works thus creating a lasting memorial to this most peerless personage amongst composers.

These thoughts of mine received further stimulus when the Leipzig music publishing house Breitkopf & Härtel presented to the world of music the beautiful scores of the last eight great operas of Mozart in critical review. As I know neither in Germany nor in France and England of a similar enterprising and experienced publishing firm, I turned to them with the question of whether they might be inclined to attach to this edition of operas the scores of the complete works of Mozart, similarly as in the case of Beethoven, whereas I would be in a position to secure in this event a considerable sum as a subsidy for the undertaking. Breitkopf & Härtel assured me that they had parallel thoughts and that they had received instigations from various directions. For the purpose of constructing a plan it would first of all be essential to prepare a cost estimate and for this and so as to judge the scope of the enterprise it would be necessary to sight those scores which were not published before, representing nearly one third of the 623 [!] numbers making up the Mozart Register. As my collection of Mozart manuscripts, consisting of some 600 items, belongs to the most comprehensive ones, I dispatched everything to them and they in turn proceeded without delay to prepare a reasonably accurate cost calculation.

According to this estimate it will be required to engrave approximately 13160 plates (=3500 sheets), the production costs of which they assess as 40 to 50,000 Reichsthaler. Considering the resulting high price of a complete individual copy (about 350 Reichsthaler) only a modest number of purchasers can be expected, therefore the publishers could only proceed with their task on the assumption of obtaining an actual subsidy of about 25,000 Reichsthaler.

To obtain this subsidy by founding a Society, in a similar way as was done with Händel and Bach, also received some airing, but this scheme was discarded, as with such societies past experience shows that publication can drag out for many years, several of the participants die or drop out without new ones taking their places and in this way the most beautiful enterprises can fade away.

We therefore concluded to proceed on the route of a subsidy and later a subscription scheme and to knock first of all on the doors of high and highest patrons. Meanwhile steps were also taken towards the critical revision and it seems this was the way Herr Joachim came to know of the plan of the undertaking.

I can only reiterate and emphasize that I can think of no more beautiful and worthy a task for the International Mozart Foundation than to support most powerfully an enterprise directed toward the publication of Mozart's works, so splendidly commenced by the firm Breitkopf & Härtel and promising the best results in its further development. It would also afford me the not inconsiderable satisfaction to be able to say that by my explanation of the circumstances I have contributed within my own scope to the advancement of this honorable enterprise.

With the assurance of my most particular respect
Your most humble Dr Ludwig R von Köchel
I. Hofgartengasse 3
Wien, 3rd March 1875.

Apart from the obvious mistake of the number 623 when there are 626 numbers in his register, it must be assumed that the 600 manuscripts mentioned include those copied out by Köchel or copies picked up by him in the course of his research. The participation of the composer and violinist Joachim (Brahms's close friend) is suitably explained in the appropriate place in this book (i.e., chapter 33). In the same place Köchel's own participation in the costs is detailed.

From the way these letters are written, Köchel always seemed sure of his ground and precise in his comment. There is, in fact, little difference between his style of letter writing and that used in his work intended for publication. A ring of authority is evident in everything he writes, coupled with the humble, yet self-assured way in which he expresses his strongly held opinions. His gift as a writer is evident, and his great intellect was in no way diminished, even a year or two before he died.

19

The Poet

One of the little-known facts about Köchel, seldom mentioned to-day, is his poetry. From his early youth, he often expressed his thoughts in verse. The story about his "romance" refers to the poems written to impress Sophie Kleyle, handed to her with the request not to show them to her mother. These, and presumably many others, are lost. What we have is a small volume of some 150 pages, obviously a mere selection of the poems written throughout his life, privately published by Köchel in 1872, enabling him to send personally dedicated copies to his friends.

One of these dedications, for instance, reads as follows: "Der Hochgeborenen Frau Philippine Gräfin von Thun-Hohenstein, geb. Gfin v. Thun-Hohenstein, meiner Gnädigen Gönnerin huldigend dargebracht" (To the high-born countess . . . my gracious benefactress, offered in homage), then "zu wohlwollender Erinnerung" (for kind remembrance), followed by a simplified version of Köchel's heraldic shield and his signature "Ludwig Köchel," quite simply, without his title, then in print again "Als Manuscript gedruckt 1872" (printed as manuscript). This particular copy found its way into the library of the International Mozarteum Foundation in Salzburg. (Interestingly, it was Count Leo Thun who, in his position of minister of education, appointed Köchel in 1850 to the post of provisional k.k. school councilor in Salzburg and supervisor of all grammar schools in Oberösterreich.)

A complete list of the poems included in the volume appears at the end of this chapter.

Köchel's poetic ability was held in high regard by those of his contemporaries who knew about it. They compared his style to that of

Johann Wolfgang von Goethe (1749–1832), Adalbert Stifter (1805–1868), and Ernst Freiherr von Feuchtersleben (1806–1849). Stifter was not so much poet as novelist, yet Robert King says about him in his *Deutsche Literaturgeschichte* (History of German Literature), "a transitory great success was enjoyed by the Austrian poet Adalbert Stifter . . . whose 'Studien' (studies) . . . describe nature and the world of feelings with loving intensity and equal masterliness." Hermann Bahr wrote in 1918, "for us Austrians Stifter is particularly valuable because he expressed the meaning and mission of our origins as clearly as Fischer von Erlach and Hildebrandt, as Mozart and Schubert, as, among the poets, Grillparzer and Stelzhamer." And in the "Moderne Klassiker" (modern classics) series, published in 1854, we read "the description of the countryside, still life, nature, and of the impulses of those human feelings which belong mainly to the natural life of the intellect, is majestically beautiful in Stifter . . . as a poet he is essentially an artist."

Feuchtersleben, who *was* a poet, is best known for his "Diätetik der Seele" (Dietetics of the Soul). Grillparzer and Hebbel were his biographers. I included these critical comments to explain the merit of comparing Köchel's poetry to the style of "real" exponents.

Dr. Heinrich Rauscher, in an article published in *Waldviertel* in 1956, talks of the "sincerity, maturity, harmony, calm and noble restraint" evident in Köchel's poetry.

Köchel dealt with subjects close to his heart; there is, for example, an ode to the famous mineralogist Friedrich Mohs who had influenced him greatly. This poem, dating from 1829, was probably composed to commemorate the conclusion of a series of lectures by the professor, which also signified the starting point of Köchel's own collection of minerals.

Another poem recalls Dr. Johann Bihler, who was Köchel's immediate superior during part of his time as educator of the children of Archduke Karl. Other titles mention "Meinem lieben Wilhelm Mikschik" (To My Dear W. M.) and "Dr. Andr. Baumgartner," a professor of natural sciences and mathematics.

Köchel's patriotism is expressed in "An Österreichs Krieger" (To the Warriors of Austria) and in the following "Radetzky" (translated by George Szirtes):

Sein Name schallt durch alle Welt,	All the world rings with his name,
Der Kaiser kronengleich ihn hält,	The Kaiser owns his equal claim,
Den Seinen weckt er Thatendrang,	His kinsmen's hearts it greatly cheers,
Die Feinde macht er kampfesbang,	But weighs the foe down with his fears,

Dem Unglück tönt er mild in's Ohr,
Des Kriegers Herz schwillt hoch empor,
Wenn man des "Vaters" Namen nennt,
Den Jedes Kind im Lande kennt;
Der Kaiser kronengleich ihn hält,
So schallt Sein Name durch die Welt:
Radetzky!

Consoling when the soul's oppressed
It swells the warrior's martial breast,
And children up and down the land
Hear "father" called, and understand.
The Kaiser owns his equal claim
So all the world rings with his name:
Radetzky!

To this sequence also belongs the "Prolog zu einem Fest-Concerte in Salzburg" (Prologue to a Festive Concert in Salzburg). His life-long friend Scharschmid is thus described in two lines:

Heiser klingt der Name,
  doch kenn' ich besser nicht einen
Nicht als Bruder und Sohn,
  Gatten und Vater und Freund.

Although your name speaks huskily,
  I know none better,
Neither as brother, as son,
  as husband, as father, nor as friend.

But one of the most beautiful poems is the "Festgabe" (Festive Offering), which bears a subtitle indicating that it was written for the silver wedding anniversary of Franz and Marie von Scharschmid (my translation):

Im Maien ward der schöne Bund
  geschlossen,
Im Wonnemond die Wonnezeit
  genossen,
Wo geist- und herzvereint Ihr
  jubelnd-trunken
Zur Welt Euch wurdet,
  Brust an Brust gesunken.

In May, by wondrous nuptial bond
  united
The merry month with merry times
  delighted,
Entwined by heart and spirit were
  you thrilled,
Each other's world by your
  embrace now filled.

Fünfmal der Jahre fünf sind heut
  verflossen,
Und noch, wie damals,
  sehe ich verkläret
Von Aug' zu Aug'
  des Mitgefühles Funken.
Ist spurlos denn an
  Euch vorbeigeglitten
Des Lebens Ernst,
  dess kaum sich Einer wehret?
Ward Euch wohl stets,
  was Euer Herz begehret?
Hat nie die graue Sorge Euch
  inmitten
Der Freude Rosenschimmer
  leis beschritten?

Five times five years elapsed,
  but still excited
I see, as then,
  transfigured in your gaze
Compassion's
  spark, in all this time not stilled.
Is there no sign,
  no trace of earnest sorrow?
Have you escaped
  this inescapable phase?
To get from life what you
  had wished for always?
Did never serious worry come to
  borrow
From rosy joy expected on
  the morrow?

Ward jede Knospe Euch zur vollen
  Blüthe
Und manche nicht zuvor durch
  Frost verkümmert?
Ward fremden Glückes Bau niemals
  zertrümmert
Und liess als Schutt Euch Kummer im
  Gemüthe,
Bis wieder neu ein Schutzdach war
  gezimmert?
Kam Euch die Habe in den Schooss
  gefallen
Von selbst und ohne dass die Hand
  sich mühte?

Bedenk ich's recht, so habet Ihr
  von allen
Den Freudedämpfern Euer Theil
  bekommen
Und wart nicht von der Regel
  ausgenommen.
Doch wie macht ab Ihr die Geschosse
  prallen,
Die gegen Euch das Leben hält
  gezücket?

Ihr sagt: "Wir wandern vorwärts—
  unbeklommen,
Und das, was kommen kann—
  und was uns glücket,
Wird uns zum Sporn erneuten,
  kräft'gen Strebens.
Wir klimmen fort zum
  Ziele unverrücket
Durch Sonnenschein und Stürme
  dieses Lebens,
Und ringen so und rangen
  nicht vergebens.
Denn droht des Einen Kraft auch zu
  ermatten,
Belebt sogleich sie neu den Blick
  des Gatten;
Vereint wird, was zu tragen,
  leicht getragen.
Ergebung war's und ernstes
  Gottvertrauen,
Womit wir uns in Noth gewappnet
  hatten;

Would every bud of yours burst into
  flower
And none succumb in time to icy
  frost?
And why was envy in your
  thoughts not uppermost
When other people had their
  lucky hour?
You never rued the fortune that
  seemed lost.
Did in your laps fall everything
  you needed?
Success move effortlessly in your
  power?

I do consider that you were
  impeded
By all those mishaps that may
  blight one's day;
You, too, were subject to the rule
  of play.
Yet, blissfully, you seemed to
  have succeeded
To fend off all the shots that life could
  fire.

"Forward we go, and fearless,"
  so you say,
"And if we strive to
  reach positions higher,
Determined by each other's
  aspiration
To reach our targets,
  never shall we tire,
Through rain and sunshine,
  through all tribulation
So shall we fight and win
  without frustration.
And if it seemed that one of us
  would falter,
Encouraging the partner's will
  must alter
To jointly overcome severest
  plight.
In deep submission, humble
  humility,
We kneel and pray to God before the
  altar

So durften wir in keinem Kampfe
  zagen."
Ich weiss genug: Ihr braucht nicht
  mehr zu sagen;
Hier kann ich ja den Baum in
  Früchten schauen.
Wohl mögt Ihr fest auf aller Achtung
  bauen,
Wenn selbst des Kaiserthrones Huld
  belohnet,
Geschmückt die Brust mit des
  Verdienstes Zeichen
Um das, was in der Brust ihr
  edles wohnet

Ihr habt erreicht, was Wenige
  erreichen:
Euch hat geschont die Zeit, die
  selten schonet,
Um Euch steh'n wack're Kinder,
  Euch zu gleichen,
Grossältern freu'n sich noch der
  Enkelsprossen!
So schreitet froh denn,
  Silber-Eh' genossen,
Der gold'nen Zeit entgegen
  festgeschlossen!

And cannot fail to conquer every
  fight."
I know enough: you led me to
  the light,
As I behold the fruit sprung from
  your tree.
You brought the Emperor's
  throne tranquility
And earned reward for splendid
  service rendered.
Befittingly, the noble
  decoration
Is on your breast, your heart for
  all to see.

Successful, where most others may have
  tendered
In failure and despair their
  resignation,
You never faltered,
  from your course meandered.
Your children's children make
  you feel elated.
Your silver time for which today you're
  feted
Leads to your golden times
  consolidated.

I assume that the "Stimme eines verstorbenen Kindes" (voice of a departed child) is about one of Scharschmid's children.

Most of the titles are followed by the year in which they were written, but the sequence is not chronological (somewhat surprising with this man of systems!) and the dates not wholly reliable. The following poem, "Mein Fritz" (My Fritz), remembers Ludwig's older brother fifteen years after his death. The year printed after the title is 1841, but Fritz Köchel died on 3 November 1836; the poem must therefore have been written in 1851. (At first I thought that perhaps Fritz Köchel's death was wrongly recorded by the sources, but after locating his "inheritance file" in the Vienna Rathaus, I realized that the date is correct and that therefore the date in the book of poems must be wrong.)

Fünfzehn Winter stürmten an
  deinem Grabe vorüber
Fünfzehn Winter allein wandl' ich
  auf Erden herum,

Fifteen long winters
  have blown over your grave,
Fifteen long winters I
  have walked the earth alone.

Nicht doch allein! dein theures
Bild lebt tief mir im Herzen,
Während die Hälfte vor mir mit
    dir im Grabe schon weilt.
	Ah! but not alone—your
	dear image lives deep in my heart
	Already half my heart
	    is buried in your grave.

This poem is prophetic in as much as Ludwig was to share his brother's grave twenty-six years later, albeit as a result of the disposition of his last will. As mentioned, by then the grave was no longer in St. Marxer cemetery where Fritz's earthly remains were first interred but in the central cemetery of Vienna to which they had been moved.

Some of the poems deal with Köchel's mountaineering passion: "Die erste Alpenbesteigung" (The First Alpine Ascent), "Montblanc," "Ampezzo"; others demonstrate in general his great love for nature, for instance the following "Die Monate" (The Months):

Januar

Ueber die Rinde von Eis und des
    Schnee's weissglitzernde Decke
Gleitet beschienet der Fuss, klingelnd
    der Schlitten hinweg.

January

Over the crust of ice and the
    dazzling mantle of snow
Glides the steel-shod slipper
    of the jingling sleigh.

Februar

Stürmt frostbringend der Nord
    heran über starrende Oeden,
Dreht sich im wogenden Saal tanzend
    das heitere Blut.

February

The North wind howling through
    the frozen Steppe
But in the ballroom dancing
    and the heart athrob.

März

Schüchtern zagt hier ein Blüthen-
    knöspchen und dorten noch eines
Oeffnet beklommenen Muth's
    fragend den reizenden Kelch.

March

The blossom hesitates in bud
    and then
The calyx breaks uneasily
    but brave.

April

Regen jetzt und Sonne zugleich:
    was willst du denn, Mädchen
Das mit Thränen im Aug' lächelt
    und trauert zugleich?

April

Showers and fleeting sun, what moves,
    you, maiden?
Tears in your eyes are smiling and
    mourning all at once.

Mai

Blumen quellen hervor;
    der Lüfte liebliches Kosen
Hat die Triebe geweckt bis
    in die Wurzel hinab.

May

Flowers deck the land;
    the gentle caress of the breeze
Awakes and stirs the sap deep
    into the roots.

Juni

Ist ein glühender Brand die
    Sonne in Bergen versunken,

June

The sun declines a blazing orb
    behind the peaks,

Neiget die Rose ihr Haupt,
tönet der Nachtigall Ruf.

The rose reclines its head;
the nightingale hymns the dark.

Juli

Wetterwolken durchzucket der Blitz,
es rollet der Donner,
Auf das lechzende Feld strömet
der Regen herab.

July

Storm clouds pierced by lightning,
the rumble of thunder
And the rain slakes
the thirsty fields.

August

Erntevoll ist die Scheune;
die Stoppelfelder durchschneidet
Furchen ziehend der Plug,
knüpfend an's kommende Jahr.

August

The harvest in the bounteous barn.
The stubble fields are cut
By the plough in furrows
for the year to come.

September

Halb im Laube versteckt hängt
schwellend die Traube am Weinstock,
Nicket der Apfel am Baum,
locket die saftige Birn.

September

Grapes swell on the vine
curtained in foliage,
Ripe apples nod on the trees
and the tempting juicy pear.

October

Schwirrend zieht nach Süden die
Schwalbe, es sinket von Bäumen
Raschelnd das trockene Laub hin
auf das flüchtige Reh.

October

The swallow chatters and
flies for the South,
The autumn leaves fall on
the fleeting deer.

November

Nebel ziehen herauf,
der Reif glänzt bärtig an Zweigen,
Flocken fallen, man eilt
rascheren Schrittes nach Haus.

November

Season of mists and the morning dew
beardlike glistens on the trees,
Snowflakes fall and warmth and home
beckon in the dusk.

December

Blattlos streckt der Baum
zum Himmel die zackigen Aeste:
Mit der längsten Nacht endet
das sinkende Jahr.

December

The trees point to heaven
their barren hands of twigs,
The longest night the nadir
of the year.

Köchel's employer, Archduke Karl, was not forgotten. Under the title "Die Kinder am Geburtsfeste des Vaters" (The Children at a Birthday Celebration of their Father's), with the subtitle "Aus einem Festspiele am Geburtstagsfeste des Erzherzogs Karl 1828" (From a Festival Performance at the Birthday Celebration of Archduke Karl), follows a dialogue between Archduke Albrecht and the chorus of the other children. From the subtitle it may be assumed that this is an extract from a longer work specially written by Köchel for the occasion and rehearsed with the children. Archduke Albrecht, who was eleven at the time, followed his father in a military career, as forecast in the poem.

A few translations from Latin and Greek (from Vergil's *Aeneid,* Martial's epigrams, Ovid's *Heroides,* Horace's "The Sermondes," and Homer's hymns) also find their place in the volume.

Before turning to his poems connected with music, I wish to mention the final work in the book, which is also the longest. In the inventory listed merely as "Ein Schwank," best translated as "A Prank," its full title is "Die Pilgrimfahrt zum Laudachsee am 18. Schewwal 861 der Hedschra" (A Pilgrimage to Lake Laudach on the Eighteenth Shawwal of the Year 861 of the Hegira). This title caused me some problems. On the basis of remarks in several articles about Köchel, I first supposed this to be a humoristic anecdote (in prose), but I was unable to locate it in print or manuscript. The references always mentioned "Landach" instead of Laudach, and wherever I looked, I could not find a lake by that name. Eventually I stumbled upon Lake Laudach, a tiny mountain lake in the Austrian Alps of the Salzkammergut, near Gmunden and the well-known Traunsee. (In Gothic script, which Köchel frequently used, the letters *n* and *u* are very similar, and it is obvious that once the mistake was made, one writer copied from the other, without any thought of verifying the existence of a lake by that name.)

The critical comment I found about this "anecdote" mentioned "humor and waggishness in this witty story." Let me explain the title. Naturally, we have a date here. The "Hegira" was the flight of the prophet Mohammed from Mecca to Medina which constitutes the starting point of the Muslim calendar. This corresponds to 16 July 622 A.D. in our calendar. The Muslim calendar, which is lunar, consists of twelve months, each of twenty-nine or thirty days. The year is thus only 354 days long, or, when the last month, Dhu al-Hijjah, has 30 instead of the usual 29 days, it has 355 days. For this reason, the months of the calendar are moving through the seasons in a complete cycle of thirty-two and a half years and this makes it difficult to calculate the date represented by the title. Eventually, I found a formula for the exact calculation and on this basis can say with reasonable certainty that the year 861 commenced on 3 February 1456 and that the Eighteenth Shawwal was 14 November of that year.

Considering that in 1456 the Turks had not yet entered Austria (and bearing in mind that the story and the date in the title indicate that it took place under Turkish occupation), it is likely that Köchel did not make an exact calculation of the date, wanting merely to write a humorous "prank" about persons of no historical background. True, there had been a Persian poet named Hafiz (the name of the central character of the farce), but he had died in the year 791 of the Hegira. On the other hand, the name Hafiz can apparently be applied to all scholars who undertook a detailed study of the Koran.

With all his other highly regarded abilities, humor was not one of the special attributes of Köchel, a fact recognized by Sophie Kleyle early on and by others who came in contact with him later. The poem itself is too long to print here. My reason for dealing with its story and background at such length is only because of the mistaken belief expressed in some articles that this is a humorous short story.

Köchel would have been a very different person if he had not left us some poems with a musical connection. "Der Meister auf der Geige," 1837 (The Master on the Violin), "Tonkunst," 1835 (Musical Art), and "Beethoven," 1827, which follows, all emanate from a period when his main interest was still the study of natural sciences.

Wenn dein Lied ertönt,	When your song is heard,
Gewaltig die menschliche Brust ergreift,	Majestically gripping each human breast,
Dein Genius, erhabenen Schwunges fort,	When your genius with noble fervor
Mit sich fort die begeisterte Seele reisst:	Carries with it enthusiastically the soul;
Dann hast du ein Denkmal dir errichtet,	Then you have erected your memorial,
Dir selbst errichtet,	Erected it for yourself,
Deiner würdig, unabhängig vom Wandel,	Worthy of you, untouched by change,
Unvergänglich, so lang' ein	Immortal so long as
Fühlendes Herz in eines Sterblichen Busen schlägt.	A compassionate heart beats in a mortal's bosom.

But for us, most important is Köchel's contribution to the centenary festivities of the birth of Mozart. The "Mozart Canzone" for the celebrations in 1856 was written during the period when Köchel worked hectically on the register of Mozart's compositions. This ode to the composer appeared at the time as a privately printed publication, and it has been reproduced since several times in part or in full. It also features, of course, in the book of poetry from which the other examples are taken. An English translation by Martin Cooper also appeared in print, but this is not, in my opinion, an adequate translation, and mistakes appear in the printed version I came across. I give here my free translation in which I have tried to reflect as closely as possible the original structure and sentiment of Köchel's work. The reader will find here what is best in Köchel's poetic output, closely linked with the respect and honor always expressed toward the composer.

Als Welten einst in unermess'nem
    Bogen
Wie Ball um Ball des Schöpfers
    Hand entrollten,
Begann um Sonne—
    Sonne bald zu kreisen.
Ob auch sie ziellos erst
    entweichen wollten,
Anziehend doch und
    wieder angezogen,
Umwandeln sie in abgesteckten
    Weisen
Jahrtausende in Gleisen.
Und ähnlich auf der
    Erde heit'ren Räumen
Strebt auch der Mensch,
    die grosse Welt im Kleinen,
Mit seinem Ebenbild sich zu vereinen:
Bewusst, und unbewusst in
    wachen Träumen,
Anziehend angezogen, seinem Triebe
Nachgebend, leitet fesselnd ihn die Liebe.
	Far in the past primeval worlds
	    emerged,
	Inchoate spheres from the
	    Creator's hands,
	Swept in the void
	    encompassing the sun,
	And into space in
	    ever-widening bands.
	Our sun, as one of many
	    new stars, surged,
	Constrained by God,
	    to take the course begun,
	Its predetermined run.
	Eons have passed and on
	    the face of Earth
	Mankind attempts to curb
	    his mighty sphere.
	Endeavoring to impress his image here,
	To tame the wildness of our
	    planet's birth.
	Man, driven by his instinct from above,
	Toils ceaselessly to forge a life of love.

Und wie's die Mutter drängt, mit
    süssen Namen
Den Liebling an der Brust
    auch zu benennen,
Der Freund dem Freund sein
    Inn'res will erschliessen,
So lehrt die Liebe selbst die
    Sprache kennen.
Doch will das Herz aus seinem
    engen Rahmen
Im Ueberdrang der Liebe überfliessen,
Aufjubelnd sich ergiessen,
So strömt es aus in vollen
    Seelentönen:
Das erste Lied, die Liebe hat's
    erfunden,
Und seinen Klang die Liebe
    nachempfunden.
Die Liebe ward Erfind'rin jedes Schönen,
	Just as a mother feels a
	    natural urge
	To pet and nurse the baby
	    at her breasts,
	As friend to friend will act
	    with good intent,
	So love in its own tongue will
	    make requests
	And rising out of solitude
	    emerge
	In overwhelming flow, intolerant,
	But joyful, jubilant,
	Thus is the world surrounded by sweet
	    sounds,
	Echoing love and, flowing from the
	    heart,
	Creating song, to sound in
	    every part,
	Wherever opportunity abounds,

Ein trittst du in die
   Hallen ohne Worte.

Wie das Metall in glühendem Ergusse
Durch alle off'nen
   Bahnen sich gewaltsam
Fortwälzt, in jeder Form sich zu gestalten:
So muss ein reicher
   Geist auch unaufhaltsam
Anscheinend leicht
   in anmutvollem Flusse
Zu mannigfacher
   Schöne sich entfalten.
Mit stürmenden Gewalten
Ergiesst sich seiner
   Symphonien Rauschen;
Und wie entkörpert klagen Instrumente,
Als ob zur Seele sich die Seele sehnte,

Durch sein Quartett,
   Gefühle auszutauschen.
So war's,
   wie Vater Haydn ihn erkannte,
Der Meister ihn den.
   ersten Meister nannte

Des Lebens Höhepunkt hat
   er erklommen,
Der Liebe Sonnenglut hat
   ihn entflammet:
Aus Mozart und Constanzens
   Liebessehnen
Ist Belmont und Constanzens
   Lied entstammet
Von heit'rem Lebensgrunde
   abgenommen
Scherzt Figaros
   mutwill'ges Liebeswähnen.
Zum Tönemeere dehnen
Sich stürzend
   Melodien-Klanggewimmel,
Besäumt, umdämmt
   von Harmonienschranken,
Des edlen Geistes
   edelste Gedanken,
Durch Schrecken führend
   zu des Glückes Himmel,
Der reinen Liebe schüchternde Gesänge,
Der "Zauberflöte" zaubervolle Klänge.

The captive world acknowledges
   this hour!

As molten metal pours upon its course
Through channels, molds,
   and glowing ferrous streams,
To cool in varied and protean forms:
So potently his
   restless genius gleams
From form to form,
   to rise from calm to force,
And move from charm to
   violent vocal storms,
Creating his new norms.
In symphonies, the laugh and
   cry of strings,
The bodyless lament of instruments
Exchange from soul to soul
   their sentiments.
The music of quartets
   originally brings
To Papa Haydn's ears
   young Mozart's name;
That master's praise soon added to
   his fame.

He reached the very pinnacle
   of life,
And turned to love as to the blazing
   of the sun.
From Wolfgang and Constanze's
   loves and joys
Belmonte and Constanze's
   songs were spun.
He set Beaumarchais's comedy
   of strife,
A social farce,
   portrayed by Figaro's voice
With jesting, cunning ploys.
Cascades of sparkling
   melodies conspire
Constrained and framed
   in harmony to bind
The noblest thoughts expressed by
   noble mind,
First hesitant,
   then tested through the fire,
The "Magic Flute" in cadences refined
Reaches the height of Mysteries defined.

Die grosse Kraft will nur
  an grossen Stoffen
Sich messen, kann nicht
  am Gemeinen kleben.
Der starken Leidenschaften
  hohle Brandung,
Der würdelosen
  Liebe sträflich Treiben,
Vom Strahl des ewigen Gerichts getroffen,
Des frechen Mörders
  frevelhafte Handlung
In grauenvoller Ahndung:
Du hast's mit
  markerschütternder Vollendung
Uns vorgeführt, doch weisst
  du zu versöhnen
Durch weises Mass,
  der Züglerin des Schönen.
Du wirst bestehn,
  Wahrzeichen Seiner Sendung,
"Don Juan's" Musik,
  ein Canon allen Zeiten,
Kostbarstes du,
  von Mozarts Kostbarkeiten.

Wie sollte nicht nach
  allen Läuterungen
Der Liebe höchster Schwung,
  der Zug nach oben,
Das weiche, fromme,
  volle Herz entzünden,
Mit heil'gem Sang
  des Höchsten Kraft zu loben!
Auch hier ist
  dir Erhabenstes gelungen;
Es scheinen andachtvoll
  aus fernen Gründen
Sich Engel zu verbünden,
Wenn rieselnd klar in
  himmlischen Akkorden
Dein "Ave verum corpus"
  fort sich windet;
Und wieder jubelnd,
  sieggewiss verkündet
Trompetenschall,
  was uns gewähret worden,
"Pignus futurae gloriae"
  —auch deines Ruhmes

Unbridled power was in
  Mozart's mind
Which needs material
  commensurate.
The chatter of the day,
  the commonplace
Must yield to passion
  and deserved fate.
There is a legend, ready to unwind
Of love and lust,
  of lecherous embrace,
Of treachery and menace.
From this same tale
  his deepest masterpiece
Of crime and punishment
  in time unfolds,
But balanced,
  so the listener beholds
A peaceful ending
  to adversities.
"Don Giovanni,"
  though carried down to Hell
Stays with us as a
  solemn warning bell!

When all his passions,
  all his pains of heart
Were satisfied,
  the time came to endorse
His firm belief in the
  Almighty's reign,
—As if ordained by
  supernatural force,—
His Sacred, Holy Song,
  will play its part.
Devoutly comes from
  mythical terrain
Angelical refrain.
In "Ave verum corpus"
  angels sing
Majestically reverberating
  chords.
Like clarion sounds,
  the Lord's eternal words,
Translated here in
  Mozart's rendering,
"Pignus futurae gloriae"
  these words that wing

Zukünft'ges Pfand,
  du Stolz des Sängertumes.

Wenn sinkend sich die
  Sonne neigt zur Rüste,
So sammelt sie in voller
  Kraft die Strahlen
Und streut ein goldnes
  Netz auf alle Lande
Zum Abschiedsgruss
  und Perlen ohne Zahlen.
Noch einmal flammt
  es auf dem Prachtgerüste
Des Genius und—löset seine Bande.
Vom letzten Lebensrande
Ertönen Weltgerichtsposaunenrufe,

Das "Requiem"
  im strengen Schritt der Fuge
Bewegt sich ernst,
  in geistergleichem Fluge
Entschwebt dein,
  Sang zur höchsten Thronenstufe
Dein Requiem—
  du sangst es dir—und Frieden
Und Ruhe sei
  dem Schlummernden beschieden.

Wer sagt, du sterbst,
  Unsterblicher? Du schwandest
Nur aus der
  Sterblichen getrübten Augen,
Um von den Höh'n
  ein heller Stern zu leuchten.
Begeist'rung muss
  aus deinen Werken saugen,
Und nachempfinden,
  was du einst empfandest,
Die Nachwelt beugen
  sich dem Unerreichten.
Wie Wolkenquellen feuchten
Die Flur befruchtend,
  dass sie blühe, grüne,
So dringe deiner Melodien Maienregen
Hinein ins Herz,
  dass es auf seinen Wegen
Dem Meister nachzustreben

Eternally their way for men
  to sing!

At close of day
  the dying sun descends
In glory and a golden
  web unfurls,
Transmutes the peaceful,
  placid countryside,
Before the dusk with strings of
  countless pearls.
Once more, inspired,
  his genius ascends
To build an edifice of glorious sounds,
Where sanctity abounds.
For Judgment Day last trumpet's call is
  heard.

His Requiem,
  in measured fugal tone,
In ghostly flight ascends the
  timeless throne,
Life's utmost bounds
  transcended by His Word.
The Requiem—
  you wrote for your own death—
God grant you peace and
  soothe your final breath!

To us, mere mortals,
  with our clouded eyes
Immortal though you are,
  we could not see
That like a star,
  eternally you shine
And each performance
  gives posterity
Another chance to learn
  and recognize
Your genius, unreachable,
  divine,
An everlasting sign.
Like land enriched
  and fructified by rain,
So will your melodies resound and soar,
From your day forth,
  and forth for evermore
To give us joy again,

sich erkühne.	and yet again.
Ihm aber Preis,	To God Almighty
dem Höchsten auf dem Throne,	we give grateful praise,
Der uns erhebt in diesem Erdensohne!	Whose gift to you has thus enriched our days!

List of Poems Published in Köchel's Selection

"An die Freunde"
"Der Mensch und die Welt"
"Der junge Strom und der alte Fels"
"Die Henne, der Hamster und die Lerche"
"Das Gebeth"
"Distichen"
"Die Monate"
"Glaube, Hoffnung, Liebe"
"An eine Erzieherin"
"Der Bohnenbau"
"Die Wolken"
"Die Genesende"
"Die Kinder am Geburtsfeste des Vaters"
"Abends"
"Die erste Alpenbesteigung"
"Montblanc"
"Ampezzo"
"Am Meeresstrande"
"Stammbuchblätter"
"Mein Fritz"
"Scharschmid"
"Stimme eines verstorbenen Kindes"
"Meinem lieben Wilhelm Mikschik"
"An eine Verklärte"
"An Therese zum 18. Geburtstage"
"An Dr. Johann Bihler"
"Prolog zu einem Festconcerte"
"An Oesterreichs Krieger"
"Radetzky"
"Dr. I. B. Kapsinger"
"An Dr. Andr. Baumgartner"
"An Friedrich Mohs"
"Festgabe"

"Sonettenkranz"
"Wenn nur—"
"Mit einem ausgestopften Kätzchen"
"Am Erinnerungstage eines Hochzeits-Festes"
"Zu Ende des Schuljahres"
"Der Meister auf der Geige"
"Tonkunst"
"Beethoven"
"Mozart. Canzone"
"Uebertragungen."
"Aus Vergil. Aeneid."
"Aus Martial. Epigramm."
"Aus P. Ovid. Nas. Heroid."
"Aus Horat. Satir."
"Aus Homer. Hymnen."
"Ein Schwank"

20

The Composer

I should start with a personal confession that also explains how this book came into being. I already mentioned that when I first set out to write it, I knew no more about Köchel than the average concertgoer: he was the man who "organized" Mozart's compositions. I did not know when and where he lived or what else he did.

It all began for me as a flippant remark made in conversation when the enormous productivity of Mozart was discussed and when someone present raised the possibility that he may not have written all of the works attributed to him.

"Could it be that Köchel," I said, "instead of just collecting the works, may in fact have written some of them?" I carried the joke a little further by claiming that I had come across a descendant of Köchel who showed me some remarkable "proof" to this effect. A journalist who was present said to me that if I could prove this, it would make a sensational story. When I confessed that the whole thing was a joke, he suggested that there was a story in this somewhere and that it was worthwhile to investigate. Who was this Köchel, anyway?

Let me now reassure the reader: Köchel did *not* write any of Mozart's compositions! Nevertheless, it came as no major surprise to me that he was a composer in his own right, albeit never published and, apart from some private performances in his circle of friends, never performed—that is, not until 1996, as explained later. It is indeed fortunate that a few of his compositions survived at all, in manuscript form, in the well-guarded sanctuary of the archives of the Vienna Gesellschaft für Musikfreunde. They were among a batch of original manuscripts collected by Köchel and bequeathed in his will to the archives of the Gesellschaft.

As far as can be established, these compositions were publicly mentioned on two occasions only: in 1912 by Eusebius Mandyczewsky in the centenary edition of the society's report and by Dr. Otto Biba, the present archives director of the society in a detailed article published in 1977 in *Oesterreichische Musikzeitschrift* to commemorate the centenary of Köchel's death.

I have already mentioned the skepticism with which some professional musicologists treated Köchel's musical proficiency and have provided their comments that he was not a sufficiently well-trained musician for the task. This, in spite of the fact that he was an accomplished cellist and that his written music is most accurate; in fact, many of Mozart's compositions only exist today as a result of his painstaking copying of some fragments or of inaccurate copies of original manuscripts, long since lost. Interestingly, the whole manuscript of the *Köchelverzeichnis* (which is also in the archives of the society and which I recently had the privileged pleasure of thumbing through) is written on music note paper.

And so to the compositions. To help in their assessment, I have solicited the help of two internationally known concert performers, the violinist Ruth Waterman and the pianist Leslie Howard, and, in particular, the choral conductor Richard White, who in 1996 gave a world premiere with the Phoenix Singers of Shrewsbury of one of the works set for four male voices with piano accompaniment. This is a setting of a poem by Philipp Mayer; I prepared an English translation of the words, but, in the event, the part song was performed in German. The event was also mentioned by the BBC. I was of course present and this now belongs to my most pleasant recollections in connection with my work on Köchel. May I repeat here my profuse thanks to all three of my helpers!

A performance of some Köchel compositions was also held in Krems, organized by the local Ludwig v. Köchel Gesellschaft on 17 May 1996. It is not known which of his works were performed. The compositions were written between 1815 and 1828; Köchel was between fifteen and twenty-eight when he wrote them. Whether he ever composed anything thereafter is not known; his frequent moves and long journeys could easily account for the loss of subsequent works. It is in fact almost miraculous that these early works are in existence. It is also not known whether he ever attempted to get any of these published, but the answer is very likely to be negative because in other fields, like poetry or mineralogy, he often took the trouble to arrange for private publication. By the time he had funds available for such a venture, he probably felt that his musical works were not worthy to be published, and, with his having spent many years on the study of Mozart and Fux, this is not altogether surprising.

His own musical taste was very conservative. In spite of the fact that he lived at a time of tremendous development in the world of music, with composers like Brahms, Schumann, Mendelssohn, Chopin, Liszt, and Wagner spreading their wings, he never considered anyone later than Beethoven and Schubert.

This view is also apparent in his own compositions. They are not Mozartean, which would perhaps be logical, but bear some similarity with the styles of Schubert and Beethoven.

Mandyczewski describes them as "Hausmusik"—that is, music to be performed at home rather than in the concert hall—and Biba repeats this assessment in his article. They are mostly songs, set for one or several voices, and there are a few piano pieces—nothing for the cello, Köchel's instrument. The poetry settings are based on works by Schiller, Goethe, and, particularly, the previously mentioned Philipp Mayer, his friend and future coeducator in the household of archduke Karl. There is no setting of any of Köchel's own poems, although he later published a volume of these. We are left to wonder at this omission.

The first and most noticeable thing in looking at these pages of manuscript is that whereas Köchel's ordinary writing tilts to the right, his music writing (apart from the earliest pages) leans heavily to the left. This is most unusual. One would almost think that he was either ambidextrous, using his left hand for music writing only, or that he had a split personality of which one part was his literary trend, the other the musical. A simpler explanation may be that he disliked his rather untidy style of music script in the early works and labored to gradually improve this by the tilt to the left. This was fully developed by 1825 and retained in later examples, such as the manuscript pages of the *Köchelverzeichnis*.

The most elaborate manuscript is "Sehnsucht," the aforementioned four-part song with piano accompaniment, based on a Mayer poem. This constitutes seventeen pages of the total of forty in the archive. The parts are two tenor and two bass voices. The work dates from 1822, indicating that the friendship with Mayer predates their tutorial period and probably comes from being fellow students at the Vienna University. This is a pleasing melody; the harmonies are also easy on the ear, and the counterpoint is mostly in canon form. There are eight stanzas, the last being identical to the first. The care with which Köchel prepared the manuscript, copying out the four parts separately, indicates that this was intended for performance, even if only among friends.

There is also a setting of another Mayer poem, "Romanze," for single voice and piano accompaniment (which accounts for a further eleven pages) where the attached poem shows the date of 1819, but there is no date on the music. Because it is not likely that Köchel and Mayer were acquainted at that time, the music was obviously composed a few years later, a fact also confirmed by the style of music script. There are also settings of two love poems by Philipp Mayer, composed in May 1822: "Gewährung" and "Begegnung." But it is another "Begegnung" (Encounter), a setting of a poem by Goethe, composed in July 1823, that I find the most beautiful and original of the works.

The earliest compositions, some dances—"Ländlers," in the Austrian idiom—date from 1815 and 1816. Three of these brief compositions are on one manuscript page; the first and second fairly primitive, the third a little more sophisticated. Each consists of sixteen bars only; there is no development of the ideas.

Three more of these appear on another manuscript page, undated, but from the style of composition and the nontilting music writing, they are probably from the same period. There is a title to this second page: "Schlittenfahrt, Deutscher und Ländler" (Sleigh Ride, German, and Ländler), indicating the types of these dances, all in three-quarters beat. It should be noted that the Ländler, from which the waltz developed, not only is an Austrian dance but originates in Niederösterreich, Köchel's homeland.

All of Köchel's compositions, with the exception of the settings of the Mayer poems, must be considered sketches, never completed. The music writing on the two early pages is very straight, but in "Begegnung" from 1823, it begins to tilt somewhat to the left, and this trend had become the style of Köchel's manuscript writing by 1825.

There are two short "Minuettos" for piano, composed in October 1823. One of these has a canonlike counterpoint, pleasing to the ear. The sixteen bars of this composition are followed by a trio of much simpler construction, but again with promising counterpoint.

The instructions for performance on the various compositions, the dynamic notations, and so forth, vary in language: they are sometimes in Italian, sometimes in German, and even sometimes in French. On the early works Köchel gives his own name as Luigi K.; later he uses his initials only. Four songs, composed between 1823 and 1825, are a good example. "Ich hab' mein' Sach'," based on a poem by Goethe, has Italian notations; the "Punschlied" (Schiller), German (mit Feuer, lebhaft); "Mihi est propositum," French; and "Chor kreuzfahrender Matrosen" (based on Graf Platen's poem), again Italian notations.

There is a three-page composition based on Goethe's poem "An Mignon." It dates from 1828. Attached is, in Köchel's hand, a partial copy of "Lied der Mignon" by Reichardt, a German composer of songs, a forerunner of Schubert, who also wrote music for Gotter's "Geisterinsel," a free adaptation of Shakespeare's "Tempest" to which I refer in chapter 30. Reichardt, whose name is spelled here as *Reichart*, was a near-contemporary of Köchel's (1752–1814). Although the subject matter of the song is similar to Köchel's, there is no similarity in the treatment, which makes me wonder why Köchel should have copied this work and kept the copy among his own compositions.

From the same year, 1828, which was the last one in which Köchel seems to have composed music, comes "Der Sänger," also based on a poem by Goethe.

Apart from these pieces are some twelve pages of various fragments—sketches of ideas.

My conclusion is that Köchel was not destined to become a "great composer." It is more than likely that he was aware of his limitations in this field and decided to give up and turn his attention to other things. Undoubtedly, he had sufficient musical education to be able to read and write music, to create pleasing sounds, both in harmonies and counterpoint. It may be that at the time these works of his were created he did not possess sufficient musical training for the task that lay ahead of him. Whether he did any more musical studies between 1828 and 1850, when he started work on the Mozart manuscripts, is not known, but his preoccupation with other scientific matters makes this unlikely.

What is probable, therefore, is that when he set out in 1850 to look for manuscripts, to place these into chronological order, to assess which ones are not by Mozart, and so on, he had a sound musical basis, sufficient for the initial task. Given his general abilities and this fundamental grounding, it must be accepted that during the eleven years he spent on his research, he acquired the additional knowledge needed for the work. By the time the manuscript was complete and handed over to the publishers, no one in the world had greater expertise on Mozart's compositions. It may well be that he would have turned his back on this job, had he had more specific knowledge, which is what the other musicologists of the day had done. Köchel was to rise to the challenge, and the results of his accomplishments prove that he was worthy of it.

21

The Botanist

The wide scope of subjects of interest to Köchel needs no better proof than the almost surprising fact that this "doctor of law" who spent more than half his working life researching the compositions of great musicians also found time to devote to natural phenomena. His activities in the fields of mineralogy and botany made important contributions to research and teaching. Even today, when you ask people in Austria what they know about Köchel's background, many answer, "He was some sort of a botanist, wasn't he?"

He first became a full member of the prestigious Austrian Society for Zoology and Botany on 1 May 1857, and we know from Dr. Elisabeth Hübl's account that he made regular financial contributions far beyond his normal membership fees. Between 1864 and 1871, he was vice president for a full year on four separate occasions. In the course of these periods he often deputized for Prince Colloredo-Mannsfeld, president of the society, and in the in-between periods he was a member of the Select Committee of the Society. In 1870 he became a "life member" by paying 100 Gulden, about $15 at the time. (The name *Colloredo* is of course well known to all admirers of Mozart: Count Hieronymus Colloredo von Waldsee und Mels, archbishop of Salzburg, who carried the title "Primate of Germany," was Mozart's first employer as well as Mozart's father's for many years.)

In 1871 Köchel wrote an obituary for the society's publication on Dr. August Neilreich, the eminent botanist, author of close to fifty books, articles, and other contributions on the subject. Neilreich had maintained a lengthy friendship with Köchel, whom he considered his mentor. In fact, as will be seen from the excerpt presented later, it was Köchel who first awakened Neilreich's interest in the subject.

A long section of the obituary is Neilreich's own account of his life, and as this contains some important references to Köchel, I quote from this autobiography written in 1869 (in my own English translation):

> In describing my botanical activities perhaps I lingered longer than jus-
> tifiable, but this description is also the story of my life since 1856. At
> the same time I must, before leaving this subject, pay homage to the
> man who in recent times has been a faithful friend to me and has stood
> by my side with loving devotion. As already mentioned in my preface
> to "The Flora of Vienna," I received my initial tuition in botany from
> Hofrath [Privy Councilor] Karl Enderes and Imperial Councilor Dr.
> Ludwig Ritter von Köchel and that it was these two gentlemen who
> were the real cause of me becoming a botanist. For family reasons En-
> deres became more and more estranged from botany and therefore for
> many years now he had no influence on me in this field. He died at
> Kremsmünster on 3 October 1860, a man of benign character with a
> heart of gold and a deeply felt sense for truth and justice.
>
> Köchel, too, had left Vienna in 1848, first moving to Teschen and
> then to Salzburg. But he returned to Vienna in 1863. Since then our
> friendship became ever closer. His considerable scientific education,
> his sharp intellect and his paramount knowledge in so many different
> fields of human learning were to instigate and enlighten me. He was
> the fountain offering me refuge to which I could always return. This
> not only refers to matters of science; he accommodated me with lov-
> ing willingness in all affairs of life. A bright point in the dark night of
> my life.

Neilreich's autobiography mentions examples of joint study excursions, sometimes with the participation of their mutual friend
von Scharschmid. He says, for instance, "During the summer of 1859
I lived in Hitzing, in the autumn I called on my relations in
Kitzbühel, Gastein, and Salzburg where I met Köchel and together
we visited the Königssee near Berchtesgaden and the Hochmoor at
its source."

In a different section he writes, "The philosophical faculty of the
University of Vienna awarded my doctor's diploma on 3 August
(my name day) and the Emperor of Austria honored me with the order of the Iron Crown. Naturally, I would never have received this
without the effective intervention by our president, Prince Josef Colloredo, and the devoted activity by my noble friend Köchel and by
the court president von Scharschmid."

In the obituary (which precedes the autobiographical notes) Köchel describes the "close bond of friendship" between the two men. He then proceeds as follows:

> In the description of my friend's life my name appears often, far too often for my liking . . . but in my duty as biographer . . . I am obliged to include his references to his relationship with his friends and this has forced me to mention the friend [namely, Köchel] who unswervingly stood by him unto his last breath and who found, after his death, this touching piece of writing, a farewell full of love and loyalty.

Here is the translation of the posthumous letter from Dr. August Neilreich to Köchel, included in the obituary notice, which will help us to appreciate the relationship between the two men:

To my noble friend Dr. Ludwig Ritter von Köchel.

I cannot part this life without expressing my sincerest thanks to you for the countless proofs of your tender devotion and unlimited love which you proved through a long sequence of years at every opportunity. Not only have you provided in the final helpless period of my life so much stimulation for my occupation and diversion, but your comprehensive knowledge and your sharp intellect have often served to educate and enlighten me, to sweeten the sad days of my old age. Regretfully, I can only thank you with words. It would have given me great satisfaction had I been able to bequeath you my herbarium and my library, the fruits of forty years of diligence, but I know only too well that under the present circumstances such a legacy would only place a great burden upon you. I therefore beseech you to make your own selection of a souvenir from my estate because I own nothing that would equate with so much love. May God grant it that you may for a long time and with happiness continue the eve of your life preserving your robust constitution and acute freshness of your wit until in times to come—or so we believe and hope—we may see each other again in another life.

Your intimately loving Dr. August Neilreich.

Whether Neilreich's flowery style is just a typical example of the period, or whether the fact that he, like Köchel, remained a bachelor suggests that the two men may have had a more passionate connection than mere friendship, cannot now be determined. The general sentiments he expresses about Köchel are similar to those voiced by others who knew him, and the comments he makes on Köchel's scientific and intellectual acumen are shared by other notable contemporaries. The remark about Köchel's "present circumstances," which make it impossible for Neilreich to legate to him his collections of books and plants, is a reference to the fact that Köchel lived in a small apartment in the archducal palace where there would have been no space for these treasures.

This testimony, by the way, is not the first Neilreich wrote about Köchel. When in 1846 he published his *Flora von Wien,* he said this of Köchel (and of Enderes) in his foreword: "You have introduced me into the realm of the most lovable of all sciences, you have generously opened for me the richest treasure of your knowledge and have created for me the wide field of nature with all its happiness and enjoyment which now I wish wholeheartedly unto those who, similarly to myself seek recreation and enlightenment in botany." And in his *Geschichte der Botanik in Niederösterreich* (History of Botanics in Niederösterreich) published in 1855, he praised Köchel's merits in his research of the flora of the Baden area. (Readers will remember the summers spent in the Weilburg near Baden during Köchel's tutorial work with Archduke Karl's children.)

Köchel wrote an article about another noted botanist-zoologist, the Austrian Theodor Kotschy, a widely traveled scientist who had then just returned from an eight-year study trip to the Middle and Far East. The article (from which I quote in chapter 18) appeared on 9 February 1844 in the supplement section of the *Allgemeine Zeitung* in Augsburg, Germany.

One of the newly found plants brought back from this trip was named after Köchel: *Reseda affinis Koechel.* It is obvious that Köchel participated in the discovery and classification of these newly found plants, but in line with his usual modesty, it was his fellow scientists who named them after him. Other botanists who named plants after Köchel were Stephan Ladislaus Endlicher, *Koechlea mitis;* E. Fenzl, *Bupleurum Koechelii;* and W. D. Joseph Koch, *Verbascum lyratifolium.*

The article about Kotschy is a descriptive account of the journey to many lands and a detailed appreciation of its results, which included the collection of some four thousand species of plants with more than two hundred thousand examples of these from the regions visited.

During the years spent in Salzburg (1850–1862), Köchel became a member of the Society of Salzburg Geography (Gesellschaft der Salzburger Landeskunde), established in 1860. The *Bulletin* of the society often mentions him in a way that makes it obvious that he took his membership most seriously and that he contributed to the activities of the group, which in 1867—by which time he lived in Vienna—made him honorary life member. This was after he delivered a lecture to the members to honor the 100th anniversary of the birth of Freiherr (Baron) K. E. von Moll, a great naturalist of the eighteenth century. Köchel's lecture was about the baron's literary activities; Anton Ritter von Schallhammer spoke about the historical circumstances and about Moll's life.

Köchel was also responsible for a contribution to a book by A. Sauter published in 1866 and entitled *The Flora of the Salzburg Principality*. His chapter dealt with the geological and meteorological influence on the plants of the region.

No other specific work of Köchel's survives on botany, but this account on his activities in the field would be utterly incomplete without mention of his own herbarium. The collection of plants, painstakingly assembled by Köchel over several decades, unfortunately succumbed to the ravages of time. There is no list, no "Köchel Register," to tell us what it originally contained.

We know from a report by the erstwhile guardian of the department of natural sciences at the Gymnasium of Krems, Professor Konrad Twdry, that there were "180 bundles (or folios) in three tall cabinets each containing 60 shelves." Until very recently, a small collection in the Gymnasium was thought to represent the remnants of this herbarium; some doubts existed and with the help of Dr. F. Speta, head of the biology department of the Oberösterreich Landesmuseum, it was established that these bundles could not have come from Köchel's collection.

One of the documents I found in the file containing matters of Köchel's estate (i.e., the "Inheritance File" kept at the Rathaus archives in Vienna) is a Bestätigung (receipt) for the items bequeathed by Köchel in his will to the Gymnasium in Krems. This bears the signature of Twdry and is dated 28 July 1877.

The cabinets described in Köchel's last will were perhaps used for firewood during World War II. From the description of Köchel's many travels we must assume that some of the collection was of exotic and unusual plants found by him on his journeys to many lands. We can also calculate from the records available that the collection must have contained more than thirteen thousand specimens.

22

The Mineralogist

One of my great experiences in tracing Köchel's life was to see his huge collection of minerals bequeathed in his will to the Gymnasium (grammar school) in Krems where he received his education. The collection, now kept in the school's natural history department, is housed in three huge polished wood cabinets; there are seventeen drawers in each of these, divided into eight rows for the display of eight or nine specimens per row, making a total of 3,288 pieces. Some of these were lost over the years, but the bulk of the collection is intact and can be used as an aid for day-to-day teaching at the school.

There is a complete inventory of the minerals, in Köchel's own handwriting. This is arranged on the basis of the hardness classification established by the famous mineralogist Friedrich Mohs (1773–1839), whose lectures awakened Köchel's interest in the subject. In 1829 he honored his teacher by writing a poem, "An Friedrich Mohs," in which he enthuses about Mohs's teaching that had opened his eyes to the wonders of nature and had made clear to him the systematic connection between all that had seemed chaotic before. (Heinrich Niebler, in an article published in 1980, explains that the hardness classification invented by Mohs "is the basis of all tables of definition of minerals because of its simplicity.")

He also honored Mohs in his introduction to the register of the minerals collection, as follows: "Stimulated by the incomparable lectures given by the deep thinking founder of the natural history method of mineralogy, Prof. Friedrich Mohs, I started to collect in 1830 and have continued to do so until this day." (This was written in 1875.) In a way, this is the only autobiographical note by Köchel! Whereas he kept copious notes on the lives of others and wrote a number of biographical works, he never bothered to record anything connected with his own affairs.

Mohs's classification, based on a scale of hardness of the minerals, gained recognition in the world of science through its simplicity and logic. (*Chambers Concise Dictionary* defines the Mohs scale as follows: "a scale of numbers from 1 to 10 [1 representing talc, 10 representing diamond] in terms of which the relative hardness of minerals is measured. [F. Mohs, 1773–1839, German mineralogist]"). Mohs was a disciple of A. G. Werner, the famed "father figure" of German mineralogy and geology. He followed his teacher in 1818 in the position he had held at the Bergakademie (mountain academy) in Freiberg, Germany. In 1826 he transferred to Vienna and as professor of mineralogy gave a series of lectures at the Court Minerals Cabinet between 1827 and 1829. Köchel attended these, and the poem must have been written upon their conclusion.

The membership Köchel had with the Salzburg Society of Geography, already mentioned in connection with his activities as a botanist, shows his deep interest in and dedication to natural sciences. Among the many bequests he made there is an annuity of 500 Gulden (then £50) in silver to this society, which gratefully acknowledges this "unexpected addition to our wealth" in its *Bulletin* on 25 October 1877.

To revert to Köchel's collection of minerals, it appears that the initial pieces were purchased from a private collector. Later Köchel received several substantial additions from various sources, including the collection owned by the Archduchess Marie Caroline Rainer. He further supplemented the collection during his many trips throughout Europe and North Africa. There are specimens from places as far apart as Siberia and Egypt, Hungary and Brazil.

A scientific assessment of the collection was made for the Kremser school by its Professor Dr. Georg Weinländer a few years after Köchel's death. He starts by explaining Köchel's motive for bequeathing the minerals to the school—namely, to improve the poor resources available there for teaching. He then demonstrates Köchel's expertise in mineralogy by referring to Köchel's work *Die Mineralien des Herzogtums Salzburg, mit einer Übersicht der geologischen Verhältnisse und der Bergbaue dieses Kronlandes* (The Minerals of the Duchy of Salzburg, with a Survey of the Geological Conditions

and the Mines of This Crownland), published in Vienna in 1859 by
Gerold, and evidencing its author's deep knowledge of the subject.
This work is still in use as a textbook. It first describes, on pages ix to
lxvii, the geological conditions of the area; next come details about
mining activities (on pages lxviii–lxxix); and the actual study commences on page 1 and continues to page 145. This is followed by a
compilation of minerals based on their local occurrence, followed by
a complete register of the 320 minerals mentioned in the study, in alphabetical order and cross-referenced with the page number where
details of the mineral are given.

There is a map, presumably drawn by Köchel himself, to introduce the work; this is followed by a foreword in which the activity
of Karl Erenbert Freiherr von Moll (the subject, as mentioned, of a
separate detailed study by Köchel who dealt with Moll's literary activities) and of his mentor, Friedrich Mohs, is mentioned.

Köchel then makes reference to an earlier work of similar content, Kaspar Melchior Schroll's "Grundriss einer Salzburgischen
Mineralogie" (Basis of Salzburg's Mineralogy), published in 1797;
he makes a favorable comparison between this and an even earlier
(1786) work "Grundlinien einer Salzburgischen Mineralogie"
(Outline of Salzburg's Mineralogy) by Werner. He states that since
the appearance of Schroll's "Grundriss," research has led to many
new discoveries and therefore a new work is timely in its appearance.

In particular, he mentions the two mineral collections of the
Salzburg Bergrath (Director of Mines) Mathias Mielichhofer
(1772–1847) located in the Joanneum in Graz and in the Benedictine
Stift St. Peter in Salzburg, respectively, the free use of which was permitted for Köchel's study.

As regards the geological survey itself, this is meaningful and interesting for experts only; there are tables and groupings to aid their
general scrutiny. A compilation follows of various mining activities,
metal by metal, followed by salt, chalk, and peat and terminating
with a description of the gold-panning work on the riverbank of the
Salzach (Salzburg's river).

The main study covers a detailed, systematic survey of all minerals to be found in the Salzburg "Kronland," together with their
chemical analysis, specific weight, and other attributes, as needed
by the expert. The nonexpert can only wonder at the well-versed
and knowledgeable depth Köchel had on the subject.

Referring to Köchel's own collection of minerals, Weinländer informs us that

> the collection can be considered substantial both as regards the number of specimens and their selection, also by the variety of their places of finding. The pieces consistently measure 5 centimeters in length and width (with the exception of crystals and a few other specimens that usually occur in smaller dimensions only, platinum for instance). As regards types, 440 different ones are represented and this must be set against a total of 650 known minerals which number, however, includes some uncollectable types, such as water and ice and others which are extremely rare in their occurrence and sometimes not definitely confirmed in their existence.

Special tribute is then paid to the beauty of the specimens included. I can vouch for this fact because what I saw was all very special indeed.

The appreciation of the collection proceeds by explaining its practicability as a teaching aid by the inclusion of excellent examples of crystal formations demonstrating the deviations from regularity and uniformity, which is indeed the way most minerals appear in natural surroundings. There are specimens with stripes, opacity, roughness, and other irregularities from perfect crystal surfaces.

Next is a detailed analysis of the more important pieces of the collection, drawing attention to those that deserve very special mention. The way in which the minerals were assembled took account of all aspects to be considered with such a task. Whereas originally not intended for school use, due to its consideration of all necessary points and because of the rich variety and careful selection, the collection is now imminently suitable for this purpose. And the availability of such material makes for tuition far beyond what may be expected to be in the curriculum of a provincial grammar school.

Weinländer's list runs over some thirty pages, but even this is incomplete as it is restricted to making a single mention of each type found, whereas there are numerous examples, and to pointing out those that merit particular attention due to their beauty or other special attributes.

The handwritten register by Köchel was used as a basis for the listing as the systematic approach applied by him could not be bettered. The original register itself was lost soon after Dr. Weinländer's appreciation was written, but it reemerged in the 1970s and is now also at the school. At the time of my two visits it was on display in a glass case that formed a permanent exhibition of Köchel's activities, particularly as regards his attachment to the school. Its title page calls it simply "Mineralien Sammlung Köchel" (Köchel Minerals Collection). As mentioned, it lists every piece, which enables us to see not only what is still there but also what is now missing from the original assemblage.

It is interesting to note here that part of the collection was almost lost at one stage. Some time after completing his work on the *Köchelverzeichnis* in 1862, Köchel suddenly remembered that he had arranged storage of some possessions in the cellar of the house in Stein in which he had spent his childhood. He wrote a letter to the authorities at Stein to ask whether the two large wooden chests in question still existed at "house No. 26." The mayor, Herr Schürer, passed this query on to Herr Mazzetti, the current owner of the house, who located them safely and arranged for their transportation on the new railway line from nearby St. Pölten to Salzburg, where Köchel lived at the time. The huge weight of the chests indicated that they contained part of the minerals collection. (This episode is mentioned in an article written in 1906 by local historian Dr. Anton Kerschbaumer.)

23

Köchel and the Beethoven Letters

The important work Köchel did in connection with the compositions of Mozart and Fux is the subject of detailed attention in this book. His taste in music was most conservative; it is said that he did not "approve" of music written by anyone after Beethoven.

That he was interested in Beethoven's work is evident from the fact that he undertook the printed publication in book form of eighty-three letters written by Ludwig van Beethoven to his Imperial Highness the Archduke Rudolph, one of his patrons, to ensure they were not lost to posterity. He later also arranged to publish four letters by Beethoven to Count Brunswik with whose sister Josephine Deym Beethoven was in love at one time; these appeared with Köchel's comments in the publication *Musik und Bildende Kunst* (Vol. XIII, no. 34) in Vienna in 1867.

The small volume discussed here in fact contains eighty-six letters, as three written to Kammerherr (chamberlain) Freiherr (Baron) von Schweiger are also included. These three are on very much more "intimate" terms than the eighty-three to the archduke in which Beethoven endeavored to be most respectful.

In his foreword, Köchel explains how the letters became available. When Archduke Rudolph's elder brother and heir, Archduke Ludwig Josef, died on 21 December 1864, they formed part of his documentary estate. His nephew, Archduke Leopold, permitted publication of the letters on the behest of Dr. Kaspar Freiherr von Seiller and Dr. Leopold Edler von Sonnleithner, both noted musicologists of the day. (Sonnleithner, to whom I referred before, was a close friend of Schubert and of Austrian dramatist Grillparzer; he also assisted Otto

Jahn in his biographical work on Mozart and, as mentioned, wrote a critical assessment of the *Köchelverzeichnis* upon its publication.)

Köchel prepared explanatory comments, added footnotes where necessary, and arranged the publication of the letters. The title page of the book says:

Drei und achtzig	Eighty-three
neu aufgefundene	newly discovered
Original-Briefe	original letters
Ludwig van Beethoven's	by Ludwig van Beethoven
an den	to the
Erzherzog Rudolph	archduke Rudolph
Cardinal-Erzbischof von Olmütz K.H.	cardinal-archbishop of Olmütz IH
herausgegeben	published
von	by
Dr. Ludwig Ritter von Köchel	Dr. Ludwig Ritter v. Köchel
Wien	Vienna

Beck'sche Universitäts-Buchhandlung (Alfred Hölder)
1865

(*IH* stands for "Imperial Highness.")

Archduke Rudolph (1788–1831), who later became cardinal-archbishop of Olmütz, was a lifelong supporter of Beethoven. He was seventeen when he first met the thirty-five-year-old composer in 1805. In his detailed explanatory introduction on pages 3–16, Köchel talks about the "beautiful relationship" between the composer and his archducal friend, as displayed for the first time in its entirety in these letters from "a titanic, creative genius to a gifted, generous patron." The connection between the two men lasted until Beethoven's death in 1827.

The letters are mostly undated but appear to have been written between 1812 and 1823, although the earliest is now assumed to date from June 1811. The absence of dates is not surprising because without a postal service and telephones, the quickest way of communication was to send letters by hand, usually taken by a servant who was sometimes asked to await an immediate reply. The recipient would know that the letter was written the same day, thus obviating the need to put a date on it, a fact that sometimes adds to our confusion.

Whereas all of Beethoven's letters seem to have been retained by the archduke and are thus available to us, his replies were not kept by Beethoven. It cannot be doubted that they were part of a two-way correspondence as frequent reference is made by the composer to those he received.

The general tone of the letters is one of respectful friendship. The requirements of formal address were always observed; "Ihre Kaiserliche Hoheit," abbreviated in print to I.K.H. (= Your Imperial Highness) stands at the beginning of each, whereas Beethoven signs as I.K.H.'s "unterthänigster" (most humble), "treuergebenster" (most faithfully devoted), or "gehorsamster" (most obedient) "Diener" (servant).

In his editing of the letters, Köchel states the assumed date of each in parentheses based on their context. In some of the letters reference is made to "Thayer": this relates to the "Chronological Register of Beethoven's works" recently published by the American biographer Alexander Wheelock Thayer (1817–1897), from which Köchel says he "gained welcome instruction on numerous points." The opus numbers in the letters are those used by the publishers Breitkopf & Härtel in their thematic register of Beethoven's works.

The letters are of varying content and length. Some very brief ones merely serve to confirm an appointment or to apologize for one not kept. A great deal of very personal content relates to Beethoven's struggle to obtain the guardianship of his nephew Karl, son of brother Karl who had died on 15 November 1815. (Young Karl over the next ten years was to give Beethoven a great deal of trouble.)

Money matters are another recurring subject. Köchel tells us that initially three regular sponsors jointly contributed 4,000 Gulden (florins) per annum to Beethoven's finances: the archduke, Prince Ferdinand Franz Josef Kinsky (1781–1812), and Prince Franz Josef Lobkovitz (1772–1816). The money paid by the two princes later ceased, causing severe financial problems for the composer. Even when payments were resumed by the executors for the two patrons—both of whom had died—on the agreed basis, due to the devaluation of the currency that had taken place through the so-called "Finanzpatent" (finance charter) of 1811 and reduced the purchase power of what Beethoven received to *one-fifth*, the composer experienced considerable financial strain.

Money received by Beethoven was not subject to any return services by him, but he provided musical tuition to the very gifted Erzherzog Rudolph (for which separate payments were made) and to show his gratitude, he dedicated a number of his compositions to his patron, which are listed by Köchel as follows:

a. The 4th Piano Concerto in G, Op. 58   published 1809
b. The 5th Piano Concerto in E flat, Op. 73   1811

c. The "Lebewohl" (farewell) Sonata for Piano in E flat, Op. 81a   1811
d. The Sonata for Violin and Piano in G, Op. 96   1816
e. The Piano Trio in B flat, Op. 97   1816
f. The "Hammerclavier" Sonata for Piano in B flat, Op. 106   1819
g. The Piano Sonata in C minor, Op. 111   1823
h. The "Missa Solemnis" in D, Op. 123   1827
i. The Fugue for two Violins, Viola and Cello in B flat, Op. 133   1825/6

(The fifth piano concerto is known to us as the "Emperor"; the trio as "The Archduke," because of its dedication; the Missa Solemnis was written by Beethoven for the occasion of Erzherzog Rudolph's enthronement as cardinal archbishop of Olmütz; the fugue is the one known as "Grosse Fuge"; and the "Lebewohl" Sonata is the only one of Beethoven's sonatas to which he gave a name.)

Beethoven also dedicated important compositions to Prince Lobkowitz, who played the violin and had his own private orchestra. These include the six string quartets, Op.18, and the one in E flat, Op. 74, and also the song cycle "An die Ferne Geliebte," Op. 98. The C major Mass Op. 86 is dedicated to Prince Kinsky.

The archduke was an able pupil, and at least one of his own compositions, a set of forty variations on a theme set by Beethoven, was dedicated to his teacher and was published by Steiner & Co. in 1819 under the title "Aufgabe von Ludwig van Beethoven gedichtet, vierzig mal verändert und ihrem Verfasser gewidmet von seinem Schüler Rudolph Erzherzogliche Hoheit" (Exercise composed by Ludwig van Beethoven, forty times altered and dedicated to its author by his pupil His Archducal Highness Rudolph). Beethoven was delighted with this composition—it is surprising that it is not performed nowadays!

One of the subjects mentioned in most of the letters is the mutual state of health of the correspondents. Recurring illnesses by both (in the case of the archduke, usually gout) led to frequent cancellations of meetings planned, visits arranged.

Here are my translations of a few of the letters.

No. 1 [To Chamberlain Schweiger, marked 1812 by Köchel, but now believed to be from June 1811] The smallest of the small has just been at the most gracious Lord where everything was locked up, then here where it was all open, but nobody about except the faithful servant. I had a thick stack of music on me to procure as a fitting conclusion a good musical soirée—nothing—Malfatti insists I should go to Töplitz which is not at all to my liking.

I can't help hoping that the gracious lord will not be as well entertained without me—o vanitas—it cannot be any other way.—Before I
go to Töplitz I shall come to see you in Baden or I shall write.

Farewell, all the best to his Lordship, stay fond of
Your friend, Beethoven.

Köchel's footnote: "The very popular (medical) Dr. Malfatti of Vienna was at that time regularly consulted by Beethoven. The journey
to Teplitz (note the different spelling!) took place in 1812."

No. 7. Vienna, 24th July 1813.

From day to day I hope to be able to return to Baden, but meanwhile
the dissonances that keep me here may still drag on till the end of the
following week.—For me to remain in town during the summer is tor-
ture and when I consider that on top of it I am prevented from calling
on Y.I.H. [Your Imperial Highness], I suffer and feel even more repug-
nance. Meanwhile, it is really the matters relating to Lobkovitz and
Kinsky that keep me here; instead of reflecting upon the number of
bars (of music) I must memorize the number of errands I have to make;
without this I could hardly hope to survive.
    Y.I.H. will have heard about Lobkovitz's accidents. One must sym-
pathize, but to be so rich cannot be lucky! Count Fries is reported to
have paid 1900 ducats in gold on his own to Duport, whereby the old
Lobkovitz house had to serve as security. These details are beyond all
belief.
    I hear count Rasumovsky will come to Baden and will bring his
string quartet, this would be quite nice as Y.I.H. would find it good entertainment. In the country I know of no better delight than quartet
music. Y.I.H. should graciously accept my most sincere wishes for your
health and please commiserate with me who has to vegetate here under such adverse conditions. Meanwhile I shall strive to make up twice
in Baden for all you are missing.

In his footnotes to this letter, Köchel gives a long "explanation"
about the financial contributions by the Kinsky and Lobkovitz families, but frankly the conversions between the value of the Gulden
before and after the devaluation do not make complete sense. The
gist of the matter is that since Kinsky had died after a riding accident
in 1812, and Lobkovitz had found himself in some financial difficul-
ties (the "accidents" to which Beethoven refers in the letter),
Beethoven's total income had shrunk from 4,000 Gulden to the

equivalent of about 2,000 Gulden in real value. Still, Köchel says "a single man could live quite decently from this amount." Köchel also says that the quartet employed by count Rasumovsky (to whom a number of important compositions of Beethoven are dedicated) consisted of "the virtuosi Schuppanzigh playing first violin, Sina second violin, Linke on Cello and Weiss on the viola."

The reference to Duport might relate to Louis Antoine Duport (1783–1853), a successful ballet dancer who later leased the Kärtnertor Theater in Vienna (between 1821 and 1828 for two periods), or possibly to Jean Pierre Duport (1741–1818), a French composer who spent considerable time at the court of Frederick II of Prussia and whose Minuet served as a basis for Mozart's pianoforte Variations K. 573.

No. 13 [marked 1814]: I hope to obtain forgiveness for my non-attendance. Your disfavor would punish the innocent; in a few days I shall catch up with everything.

A new performance of my opera "Fidelio" is contemplated (a). This gives me much to do, yet in spite of my healthy appearance I am not well.

For my second "academy" (b) the arrangements are partly made. I must write something new for Milder. (c) I hear meanwhile, and to my comfort, that Your Imperial Highness is well again. If I don't flatter myself too much I hope to contribute to this state soon. Meanwhile I have taken the liberty to advise "Mylord Falstaff" (d) that he will soon have the favour to appear in front of Your Imperial Highness.

Köchel's footnotes to this letter explain that (a) there had been no performances of *Fidelio* since 1806; (b) a "1st academy" (concert) consisting of "Wellington's Victory" was given on 2nd January 1814 and a second, to consist of the "Egmont Overture" and again the above work, was planned for 26 March 1814, both conducted by Beethoven himself; (c) Milder referred to court opera singer Anna Milder who sang the part of Leonore in the first production of *Fidelio*; and (d) "Mylord Falstaff" probably referred to corpulent violinist Ignaz Schuppanzigh who, as mentioned, was playing first violin in Count Rasumovsky's string quartet.

No. 18 [1814] My deepest thanks for your present, I only regret that you could not participate in the music. I have the honor to transmit herewith the score of the Cantata. Your Imperial Highness can retain it for several days after which I shall see to it that as speedily as possible it is copied for you.

Still exhausted from the exertion, vexation, pleasure and joy! everything together and intermingled; I shall have the honor to attend Y.I.H. in a few days.

I am hoping for favorable news in Y.I.H.'s state of health: how gladly would I sacrifice many nights completely if only I were thus able to aid your total recovery!

Köchel explains here that the "present" probably referred to the "academy" of 29 November or 2 December 1814. The cantata "Der glorreiche Augenblick" set to a poem of Dr. Alois Weissenbach for Choir and Orchestra by Beethoven (Op. 136) was first performed in Vienna on 29 November and repeated on 2 December.

No. 37 [1819] I have the honor to send herewith through the copyist Schlemmer the masterly variations of Your Imperial Highness's; tomorrow I shall personally attend Y.I.H. and am most joyful to be able to serve my exalted pupil in the role of companion [or accompanist—the German *Begleiter* could mean either] in his famous career.

This letter refers to the archduke's composition mentioned earlier.

No. 42 [1819] Because of my inability to alter the appointed time of some legal proceedings concerning my nephew, I must regretfully forego the pleasure of attending Y.I.H. tonight; the more shall I hurry tomorrow to call on Y.I.H. at half past four.—Because of the matter itself, I know I shall find you indulgent. May heaven end this [matter] finally, because my emotions suffer sensitively in painful rage.

Köchel's footnote to this letter reminds the reader that the guardianship procedures concerning the nephew who had turned out badly and his ill-spoken mother (i.e., Beethoven's sister-in-law) were in full swing at the time. This year (1819) finally saw nephew Karl enter a reformatory.

The booklet of the Beethoven letters concludes with a list of those Beethoven compositions that are mentioned in the course of the correspondence.

24

Johann Joseph Fux: The Second "Köchel Register"

Johann Joseph (or Josef) Fux is a name not too familiar to the average music lover. His works are now seldom performed, few recordings are available, and these are bought mainly by people particularly interested in baroque music. These facts relate even to his native Austria.

Yet, this man, who was "court composer" and "court conductor" of the imperial court orchestra for over forty years was not only a famous writer and performer of music in his time, whose compositions were well known and praised abroad, but he attained lasting fame among generations of composers through his "Gradus ad Parnassum" (loosely translated as "The Steps Leading Up to the Abode of the Gods"), a treatise of counterpoint in musical composition. (*Counterpoint* is, put simply, the joint and pleasing sounding of different melodies.)

Fux died in 1741. He was a contemporary of J. S. Bach, Händel, Vivaldi (who died in the same year), and the Scarlattis. When Köchel decided, after completion of his work on the register of Mozart's compositions, to undertake a similar task of "organizing" Fux's artistic output, very little was known about this composer, and few of his works were being performed. But Köchel had shown an early interest in Fux, having prepared a register of his church compositions found in the abbey of Göttweig, which was published in 1834 (i.e., sixteen years before he commenced work on Mozart's opus!). He probably became aware of his compatriot's work while visiting the Stift at Göttweig during his schooldays and perhaps even at that time he had plans to devote his attention to this "forgotten master" and to assist in efforts to resuscitate the melodious sounds that had by then been dead for nearly a hundred years.

Göttweig is a magnificent edifice, and the musical treasures housed in its archives are equally unrivaled in their splendor. Pater Gregor, the custodian of the abbey at the time of my visit, allowed me a glimpse into this treasure trove, an experience not to be forgotten: I held some of the original manuscripts by Fux and by many others, also some rare first editions, all of which are now listed in a two-volume splendid work entitled *Der Göttweiger Thematische Katalog 1830* (The Thematic Catalogue of Göttweig 1830) compiled by Professor Friedrich W. Riedel, director of music at the Abbey's music archives.

After a gap of some thirty years, Köchel turned his attentions again to Fux, and he continued to research his life and work. In the course of sorting those compositions, the manuscripts of which lie in another famous Stift, Kremsmünster in Oberösterreich, a separate study was compiled and published in 1867. Kremsmünster has always been associated with musical culture and continues its tradition today under Dr. Pater Alfons Mandorfer, who most helpfully showed me the dedicated copies of Köchel's works to the abbots Pater Altman and Pater Amand Baumgarten. The reader may remember that Köchel's maternal grandmother was the sister of Abbot Fixlmillner of Kremsmünster, a fact that must have been known to Köchel.

Köchel's work, entitled "Johann Josef Fux, Hofcompositor und Hofkapellmeister der Kaiser Leopold I, Josef I und Karl VI, von 1698 bis 1740" (J. J. Fux, Court Composer and Conductor of Emperors Leopold I, Josef I and Karl VI from 1698 till 1740) was published in 1872 by Alfred Hölder's Beck'sche Universitäts-Buchhandlung in Vienna. This book is much more than just a register of Fux's compositions (which are listed as an appendix over separately numbered pages 9–174 at the end of the book). The preceding 584 pages give a detailed account of Fux's life and work from the earliest known facts up to his death.

Several more appendices contain documentary evidence of the Fux family's economic circumstances; Fux's employment and promotions record; his reorganization of the court orchestra; his solmization dispute with J. Mattheson (1681–1764), a German writer on music and organist/composer; dedications of his "Gradus ad Parnassum"; the ranks of the Imperial Court Orchestra from 1680 to 1740; his personal testimonials of the musicians employed at court from 1715 to 1740; a listing of the musical compositions by the emperors Ferdinand III and Leopold I used by Fux; a register of the operas, serenades, "Feste teatrali" (theatrical performances), and oratorios performed at the imperial court in Vienna between 1631 and 1740; and a list of church texts.

This definitive work on the composer is one of Köchel's greatest achievements and was the theme of Sonnleithner's recommendation to grant him honorable membership of the Society of the Friends of Music in Vienna.

The foreword of the book gives us a strong lead into Köchel's character, the man who undertook a number of laborious tasks, never expecting to be rewarded for them and always displaying his modesty. It also explains the state of knowledge, or rather the lack of it, as regards the life and work of Fux at the time Köchel decided to commence his research, and as it shows his dogged, detective-like investigative work, I wish to quote from it as follows:

> Although no treatise on the history of music can bypass the name and activity of the famous author of the "Gradus ad Parnassum," they all conclude by saying that detailed information on the circumstances of his life, his birth and development is missing. . . . The world of music, not counting a few unauthenticated anecdotes, has remained in total ignorance regarding the life and the greatest part of the works of this worthy man, therefore Fux must in this respect number among the "forgotten ones."
>
> That there was no notion of the existence of such an outstanding fellow countryman in his native Styria I was able to ascertain in the course of my own research; but it is more difficult to comprehend that even in Vienna, the scene of his forty or fifty years of brilliant activity, no trace of private records or tradition survives about his life.
>
> As a more distant person, equipped with goodwill and some perseverance, I have undertaken to collate material . . . and to deliver this in some coherence into the hands of a future researcher.
>
> Restricted to the meagerest of information, without the ascertained place or year of his birth, or even the year in which he died, it meant to start the research at random. The opening consideration that Fux must have died in Vienna and probably left a will behind, led to the first portentous results. . . . In the archives of the k & k district court of Vienna I found the hoped for little gem that became the seed of all further research.
>
> From his last will, written in his own hand, it became clear that Fux had been married, but had no children, had become a widower and that, apart from other siblings, he had a brother, Peter; that there ex-

isted a Fux house in Hirtenfeld at St. Marein near Pickelbach and much more. . . . The existence of the Fux family in that area having been ascertained together with a surviving grandson of [the aforementioned] Peter Fux . . . a journey [was made] to St. Marein . . . where the local registers of christenings, marriages and deaths . . . enabled me to compile the family tree of the Fux family; the ninety-four-year-old Johann Fux, a well-to-do farmer in Obergogitsch, well remembered the family birth house No. 50 in nearby Hirtenberg, and [he recalled] a relation who had featured in a painting with other musicians.

Unfortunately, neither he nor others could advise on the circumstances of how the Kapellmeister [conductor] came to Vienna or where he had obtained his [musical] training. No letters could be found; this was later explained by the fact that the whole Styrian kinship . . . lacked the art of writing. . . .

It emerged that Fux, then organist in the Schotten abbey in Vienna, married in 1696 and became widower in 1731. But no chronicle . . . gave any hint as to how long before his marriage Fux had been working at Schotten, nor where he received his education.

Köchel's foreword next lists the names of various archives that have provided information on his further life and of his compositions, the court performances of his operas and oratorios, and so on, concluding with the customary thanks to those individuals who helped him with his research. It should be mentioned here that whereas Köchel spells Fux's second forename *Josef*, the signature on Fux's testament is *Joseph*.

As next to nothing is known about Fux's early life and not even the date of his birth can be firmly established, Köchel, after dealing with Fux's family tree and place of birth, jumps to 1696 when, at the approximate age of thirty-six, he was established as resident organist at the Viennese Stift (abbey) zu den Schotten (to the Scots) at an annual salary of 400 florins, probably with free living quarters and the opportunity to supplement his income with teaching and other musical activities. This same year he married Juliana Clara Schnitzenbaum in the parish church of Schotten, and the marriage registry entry gives the first information on Fux's presence in Vienna, together with his occupation. How and when he got there, under whose tutorship he studied to play the organ or the art of composition, are not known.

Köchel's book continues with a graphic description of the musical world of Vienna under emperor Leopold I (1660–1705). Although remote in terms of population from the six hundred thousand in

Köchel's days, the city of Vienna nevertheless occupied an important position among other German cities. The emperor had a keen interest in music, operas in particular; the performance of such works as "Il Pomo d'oro" by Cavaliere Marc'Antonio Cesti (1623–1669) and "La Monarchia latina trionfante" by Antonio Draghi (1635–1700) with libretto by Niccolo Minato in 1666 and 1667, respectively, was lavish, with extravagant machinery for special effects built by Ludwig Burnacini. These were court performances; the general public was not admitted.

In this period, music in Vienna was the domain of the Italians, as was the case in other centers of music, such as Munich, Dresden, Hamburg, and London. A long section is devoted in the book to the "invention of the opera" by the Italians; this is ascribed to Jacopo Peri (1561–1633) of Florence, who was the first composer to combine a dramatic scenario with musical arias and simultaneous songs of several voices. The first opera, based on a poem by Ottavio Rinuccini and with music by Peri, was first performed in 1594 or 1595 in Rome under the title "Dafne" (the score is now lost). The immediate success spurred Peri to compose the music for "Euridice" to words by Rinuccini, which was first performed in 1600 to even greater acclaim on occasion of the marriage of Henri IV of France and Maria di Medici in Florence.

When Claudio Monteverdi (1567–1643) turned his attention to opera, says Köchel, the continuing triumphant success of this new genre of art was eternally assured and was to be sustained by Alessandro Scarlatti (1660–1725), who wrote more than one hundred operas (apart from two hundred masses, seven oratorios, and more than five hundred cantatas!).

Köchel next deals with Fux's musical career. He was appointed Kaiserlicher Hohekomponist (imperial court composer) in 1698 at a monthly salary of 60 florins; this was increased to 90 florins in 1701 by special imperial decree. In 1702 Fux gave up his post of organist at Schotten and requested a further increase of salary from the emperor, which he duly received. He was now paid 120 florins per month.

Fux's satisfactory contribution to court music continued during the reign of Josef I (1705–1711). In 1705 he was appointed Kapellmeister (conductor) of the St. Stephan Dom in Vienna. He remained in this prestigious post until 1715, but from 1713 was also acting as conductor of court music of the Dowager Empress Wilhelmine Amalia's orchestra. The empress maintained an orchestra of twenty-eight musicians.

By 1715 his annual court salary had reached 3100 florins. This was under Karl VI (1712–1740). The year 1716 saw the first performance of his opera *Angelica vintricite d'Alcina* with words by P. Pariati; although this was not the first opera Fux wrote, it marked an important point in his operatic career (he wrote eighteen operas in all). A glowing account of the performance was given by Lady Mary Wortley-Montague in a letter to Alexander Pope.

The years 1717–1718 were marred by the solmization dispute with Johann Mattheson of Hamburg. This matter is too technical for this book, but suffice it to say that Mattheson, who represented the advancing concept of musical modes as we know them today, was abrupt in his treatment of the previously dominant church modes as represented by Fux, and the resulting dispute brought a lot of bitterness to the Austrian composer. (By the way, Köchel says, before giving a technical explanation of the basis of the dispute over several pages, "it must not be expected for me to give here a detailed treatise of the different views expressed by Fux and Mattheson. For the connoisseur this would be superfluous; for those to whom these matters are alien, tiring." I cannot express this any better!)

The next chapter deals with Fux's church music, focusing on the composition in 1718 of his Missa Canonica (most of his other church compositions are uncertain as regards their date). There are 289 known church compositions of a total of 405 works, which highlights their importance in the composer's musical output. Strict settings characterize Fux's music, and this is even more true regarding church music. In dedicating the Missa Canonica to his employer, Karl VI, he declares, "I flatter myself Your Majesty will recognize in this Mass that old music has not totally disappeared as yet . . . and that its taste and dignity continue to live on." The Mass is based on the style of the sixteenth-century Italian composer Giovanni Pierluigi da Palestrina (ca. 1525–1594), whose church music had served as a model for generations. (Fux was often referred to as the "Austrian Palestrina.")

Fux's church compositions include 57 masses and requiem masses, 57 vespers, 22 litanies, 12 graduals, 14 offertories, 12 motets, and 106 hymns. Köchel shows some examples in this chapter; a more detailed examination follows in the thematic register.

And so to the "Gradus ad Parnassum" written in Latin in 1725, the work that secured everlasting fame for Fux among musicians of the world through its clear and concise definition of composition and of counterpoint in particular. Köchel quotes from the subtitle of the book that it should be "a guideline for systematic musical composition based on a new and reliable method, the like of which had never before been published in such logical sequence." In his introduction to the work, Fux explains that whereas much had been written about the theory of music, very little material was available about the practice of writing music, and what existed lacked clarity. Köchel praises the well-chosen Latin expressions, stating that the work is easy to understand as its language is neither stilted nor artificial in its style.

The format is a series of lessons given by an experienced and well-meaning master named Aloysius (to honor Palestrina—Aloysius = Luigi?) to an eager and gifted pupil given his own name Josephus, who is taken through the whole sphere of musical composition with encouragement, teaching what is necessary, correcting what is wrong. Köchel praises this "admirable method of retaining the reader's attention throughout."

The first part of the "Gradus" concentrates on theory ("Musica speculativa"), the second on practice ("Musica practica") in composing. Everything is covered in great detail, which is obviously the reason for the "Gradus" to have become the definitive textbook for centuries to come, a fact that Köchel underlines with examples of praise by the great masters of later years. Josef and Michael Haydn, J. S. Bach, Händel, Mozart—all studied the work and made use of its teachings.

Fux's oratorios are chronicled in the next chapter of Köchel's book, and then the "opera-poets" or librettists Pietro Metastasio and Claudio Pasquini are brought to our notice who between 1730 and 1742 provided texts for several of Fux's operas. The operas themselves are next discussed in detail, covering, as they did, nearly thirty years of musical activity starting in 1702 with "La Clemenza d'Augusto" and ending with "Enea negli Elisi ovvero Il Tempio dell'eternita" in 1731.

This year brought the death of Fux's wife, Juliana, who had been "for thirty-five years a loyal friend and sympathetic nurse in his long sufferings." The shock of this event induced Fux to write his testament in the following year, in which he named his niece Eva Maria Fux as main beneficiary. Eva had lived for thirty years in the house of her uncle. For his nephew Matthäus Fux, in addition to a substantial legacy, he negotiated a permanent grant to be paid upon his own death by the treasury.

The next chapter details the activities of the "Hofkapelle" (court orchestra) under Fux between 1715 and 1740; these matters are also related in Köchel's separate book on the history of court music. (See the next chapter.) This is followed by a list of Fux's pupils. One of these was Georg Christoph Wagenseil (1715–1777), who in 1739 became court composer and remained in this position until his death. He was for many years music instructor of empress Maria Theresia. When in 1762 the six-year-old Mozart was to perform for the empress at court, he asked, "Is Herr Wagenseil not here? He understands this." When Wagenseil came, Mozart said to him, "I am playing a concert by you, and you must turn the pages for me!" (This episode is also mentioned by Köchel in his poem "Mozart Canzone.") The book also contains a list of portraits of Fux, followed by a list of apartments in Vienna in which he had lived.

When Fux died in 1741, his approximate age was eighty-one; the exact age cannot be stated because of the uncertainty of the date of his birth. From his sixtieth year, he greatly suffered from gout; this chronic condition was to persist for the rest of his life, first affecting his feet only, later also his hands, so that after 1737 he had to rely on another person's hand even for his signature. He died of "hectic fever," a form of consumption.

Köchel theorizes about the influence Fux's music and his teaching in the "Gradus ad Parnassum" must have had on Bach and Händel, both of whom were twenty-five years younger, but he concludes that there is no likelihood of either of these great masters ever having been in direct contact with him.

This far goes the story of the composer's life and work, given in great detail over 272 pages in Köchel's book; he then fills another 300 pages with documentary evidence backing up all he had written, before coming to Appendix X, the "Thematic Register" of compositions by Johann Joseph Fux. This, however, is again preceded by some general explanations. Köchel tells us that in searching for manuscripts or copies of Fux's compositions, he first visited the archives of several Vienna churches with which he knew Fux had been associated, such as St. Augustin, St. Peter, St. Michael, and Von den Schotten—with most disappointing results. The more surprising were "the rich stocks of music found in the Stifts of Göttweig and Kremsmünster," where the respective Chorus Masters Hermann Moser and Maximilian Kerschbaumer were most helpful to Köchel. He also states that the fire at Göttweig in 1718 "destroyed all stocks of music there," which would indicate that the manuscripts found in this abbey all date from a later time. Other archives that housed some Fux autographs were the k.k. Court Library in Vienna, the Archives of the k.k. Court Orchestra, the Wiener Musikverein, the Royal Library in Berlin and the Royal Library in Dresden. Köchel then says that he made great use of a thematic register by Alois Fuchs (no relation to J. J. Fux!), who, as a well-known collector of manuscripts, was well placed to prepare his listing.

As a further clear example of his modesty, Köchel says that he makes no claim to completeness, and that without dates on most of the manuscripts, it proved impossible even to attempt a chronological order. Although "first performances" of a work are often recorded, these do not serve as a guide as to their date of composition, except in a "negative" way by the certainty that they must have been written *before* and not after that date!

With one exception, nothing leads to an earlier date than 1698, by which time the composer was approximately thirty-eight years old! This one work is the Requiem Mass (K. 51), which was apparently written for the funeral service of Archduchess Eleonore, widowed queen of Poland, who died on 16 December 1697. Under these circumstances, Köchel concentrated his efforts on setting up a thematic register only.

We are further told that Fux's operas and oratorios were not performed in Vienna after he died, whereas his church compositions remained popular for decades, the last known use being in 1775. In Göttweig and Schotten, his works continued to be performed even to the time of Köchel's research activity in the 1860s. He concludes these comments by suggesting that "perhaps Fux's music will deservedly undergo a similar resurrection to that of the works by Bach and Händel whose music enjoyed renewed popularity a long time after their respective deaths."

Of the "Gradus ad Parnassum," Fux's treatise of composition, translations were made from the original Latin into many modern languages. Köchel mentions the English translation of "Faux's Practical Rules for Learning Composition, London 1791"; the composer's name is further misspelled as "John Joseph Feux" in another edition of the same translation, and Köchel comments that this is "a totally useless extract compiled with as much ignorance as frivolity." His opinion of the French translation is not much higher: "written in poor French with many deliberate alterations and omissions." He is less critical of the German and Italian versions.

Fux's 405 compositions are grouped in eleven sections in the register, and these are not in any chronological order, even where this would be possible. As mentioned, very few details exist of dates of composition. More puzzling is the absence of any early works—none were ever found, yet it is impossible to believe that Fux composed *nothing* until he was thirty-seven. (Compare this with Mozart, who did not quite live to that age.)

The structure of the register is the following: Each work is given a serial number, followed by its title and by the voices and/or instruments for which it was written. Next comes the name of the movement or part (e.g., "Sanctus" in a mass or "Ouverture" in an opera), followed by one line of music with words where applicable. Underneath comes information regarding the manuscript, if found, or copy, together with their location and then under the title "Anmerkung" (remark) as much as Köchel was able to find out about the work and its origin. For instance, after No. 16 "Missa Fuge perversum mundum," he says, "The cover [of the music] calls Fux assistant conductor, thus the manuscript must originate between 1711 and 1715; by the way between March 1730 and 24th February 1732 three performances are noted."

Some of these notes by Köchel are most detailed—for instance, those on the opera *Angelica*—but usually very little is mentioned, obviously because so little is known about the origin or even the performance of the work.

25

Music at the Imperial Court

For those readers who had known the name of Köchel in one connection only—namely, as the man who "organized" Mozart's compositions—it must come as a surprise that he devoted much time to other matters related to the history of music. If we leave aside the publication of the Beethoven letters, where he fulfilled an obligation of making public what had come to him privately, adding some notes of explanation only, we know of three works that cover in great detail the activity of composers and musicians of an earlier period and also right up to his contemporaries.

One of these works, his biographical study of Johann Joseph Fux, together with a register of Fux's compositions, the only one in existence, was the subject of the previous chapter. Köchel's other two works in this field are "Die Kaiserliche Hof-Musikkapelle in Wien von 1543 bis 1867" (The Imperial Court Orchestra in Vienna from 1543 till 1867) and "Die Pflege der Musik am österreichischen Hofe vom Schlusse des XV. bis zur Mitte des XVIII. Jahrhunderts" (The Cultivation of Music at the Court of Austria from the End of the Fifteenth to the Middle of the Eighteenth Century).

There is a thematic overlap among these works: Fux was a court musician, and his activity falls into the period of the title of both works. These works themselves overlap; the period between the mid-1500s and the mid-1700s being covered in both. The treatment of the material, however, is completely different.

The treatise on the Imperial Court Orchestra is a book of some 144 pages, followed by an alphabetical register of all musicians who were members during the period. The work goes into great detail. It starts with a historical survey of the orchestra. To quote from this section:

> An Institute of the Arts, which at the Imperial Court for a sequence of several centuries enjoyed the predilection of art-loving and gifted Regents, was obliged by its very nature and particularly at a time of the development of art, to incorporate within itself the most outstanding forces available, so as to exert a telling influence on the Court and on the land. One such institute of the arts, which in its prime was admired by all of Europe, and which, according to testimonials of its contemporaries, had no equal anywhere, was the Imperial Court Orchestra in Vienna, which counted among its most excellent sponsors the emperors Ferdinand III, Leopold I and Karl VI, who furthered the art not only because they had a liking for it, but because they were well-schooled cognoscenti and productive friends of the art themselves.

Next is a historical review of the progression of the court orchestra, which, at first, centered mainly on singers. In 1544, for instance, of a total of thirty-seven members, thirty-three were singers; these were supported by one conductor, one assistant conductor, one organist, and one servant. By 1549, the overall number had risen to forty-seven; by 1556, to fifty-six; by 1564, to eighty-three; and later, in 1619, reduced to sixty. "Around the middle of the seventeenth century," says Köchel, "came an important new element: opera, invented early in the century in Italy and finding its way to Vienna by this time, soon leading, in conjunction with the Ballet, to the most glamorous period of the Imperial Court Orchestra." It is mentioned in this context that grand opera was exclusively a matter of court entertainment.

During this heyday, the orchestra had to be augmented and had to become more efficient, so it had to be led by the best available talent. By 1705, there were 102 musicians employed; in 1711, 107; and in 1723, 134. The conductors were J. J. Fux and Antonio Caldara (1670–1736) in this period, from 1700 to 1723.

Less fruitful years were to follow, threatening the very existence of the orchestra. The last opera performance, in 1744, was to celebrate the wedding of Maria Theresia's sister Marianne to Prince Karl von Lothringen; a performance of Metastasio's "Ipermuestra" was held with music by Johann Adolph Hasse (1699–1783).

The decline in the years 1751 to 1772 under the conductorship of Reutter led to a reduction of numbers; in the end barely twenty musicians remained—there was not even an organist. The next phase sees the court orchestra concentrating on sacred music, and a contingent of fifty musicians became fairly stable.

The historical survey next points out that the conductors came from three countries: 1543–1618 from the Netherlands, 1619–1715 from Italy, and since 1715 from Germany.

Separate studies deal with singers and instrumentalists, listing their names and salaries. The singers were mostly male, including the contralto and soprano parts, sung by "falsetto" singers and castratos. These could not quite reach the pitch of boy sopranos and female voices. They were called "vocum miracula." The castratos were exclusively Italian. There were a few female singers as well: from 1718 to 1740, four; but later several more. The choir, from 1543 to 1558 consisting of twelve to twenty-four singers, rose to forty-four by 1740; then it gradually reduced again in numbers until by 1771 only five were left: one bass, two tenors, and two contraltos.

The instrumentalists, at peak, numbered six organists, twenty-three violins, one viola de gamba, four cellos, three double basses, one lute, two cornetts, four bassoons, five oboes, four trombones, one hunting horn, sixteen trumpets, and two timpanis. This was the contingent in 1721. (The cornett of the day must not be confused with the modern cornets. It was made of wood and had more affinity with woodwinds as we know them today but also some features linking it to modern brass instruments. The last known performer of the instrument died in 1746.)

The lute, a string instrument, "was plucked with the fingers . . . causing it to be constantly out of tune . . . unreliable. . . . A lutanist who reached the age of eighty would have spent sixty years of his life tuning his instrument," says Köchel. Other instruments mentioned here include the orbo, a bass lute used instead of the clavier in both opera and church performances; the dulcimer; and the viola da gamba.

Separate sections in the book are devoted to the training of young musicians: "in the case of specially gifted ones the emperor agreed to award special grants for journeys to Italy to study with Frescobaldi, Carissima and others"; salaries were paid to the members of the orchestra, in which it is mentioned that after rising till 1740 they "sank suddenly" and never rose again. Examples are given of those paid. Since 1807, three basic groups were established at 500, 600, and 800 Gulden per year, respectively, whereas the conductor was paid

1,500 Gulden and the total annual budget came to 30,000 Gulden. Retiring conductors also received parting gifts, up to 12,000 Gulden.

The historical review is followed by so-called supplements, which are longer than the review, because they contain in great detail the names and salaries of the singers and musicians throughout the period, followed by biographical notes about the conductors, assistant conductors, composers, and organists; the records of books and other materials used to document the period, apart from the official archive material.

The activity of the Court Orchestra is divided more or less on the basis of the monarch ruling; thus, the first period ("A") under Ferdinand I (1521–1564) lasts from 1543 to 1564; the final period covered in the work ("P") under Franz Josef I, who ruled from 1848, covers the period from 1847.

Twenty-five names are given of conductors. These include Arnoldus de Prugkh (1543–1545), Johann Joseph Fux (1715–1740), Antonio Salieri (1788–1824), and Joseph von Eybler (1824–1846). The last name to be mentioned is that of Johann Herbeck (1866–1867).

The first soprano singer whose name is included in the listing was male, in 1637, but the same year also sees the first mention of female performers: Margareta Catania and Lucia Rubini.

Many famous musicians are named in the relevant sections. Among the violinists we find, for instance, Ignaz Schuppanzigh; among the clarinettists, Anton and Johann Stadler, who figured prominently in connection with Mozart's compositions for this instrument.

Naturally Mozart's name is not omitted, but the entry about him is brief; a little more is said about Salieri. The final section of supplements is the record kept by the leader of the orchestra, Kilian Reinhardt, in 1727, which was presented by him in a neatly bound volume to Emperor Karl VI and in which the author listed all demands of sacred music made on the orchestra. In the first part this gives the dates of the various church events with obvious reference to the musical requirements of each; in the second part he lists the additional church events, recurring daily or by special requirement, relating to specific events during the period covered.

Köchel has no explanation for the creation of this record by Reinhardt, but it may have served to support a courteous petition for higher remuneration for the musicians by demonstrating the tremendous amount of time in performance and in rehearsal required of the musicians of the day. It must be borne in mind that with the constant employment of several composers and arrangers at any one time, it was the custom to present new compositions on each occasion.

Köchel's book was published in 1869—only two years after the end of the period discussed. Three years earlier, in 1866, saw publication of the other work mentioned earlier: this was the reprint of a lecture he had given at the Institute for Geography, of which he was an executive member. The writing style is very different here; the introduction is in fact a very beautiful piece of prose, quoted in chapter 18 introducing Köchel as a writer.

The earlier period, which is not part of Köchel's other study, is seen to cover many musicians of international fame, who were not Austrians or Germans but who were engaged by the imperial court. The most famous of these is the Dutch master Josquin Des Prés (ca. 1445–1521), whom Köchel calls one of the greatest musical geniuses of his time and who was followed in the position of Kapellmeister by one of his pupils, the German-born Heinrich Isaak (1450–1517). Another distinguished pupil mentioned was Nicolas Gombert or Gombertus, who became chief court musician in 1537. Numerous other names figure in Köchel's study, the most notable being that of Giovanni Pierluigi Palestrina (ca. 1525–1594), whose influence on the development of sacred music cannot be overemphasized and who, according to Köchel's lecture, was the greatest composer of the age of contrapuntal composition for unaccompanied chorus. (There is no suggestion that Palestrina was directly involved in the work of the Vienna Hofkapelle.)

Köchel frequently refers to the expert knowledge in the field of music displayed by the various monarchs under whose rule the court musicians functioned. A clear parallel is evident between the interest shown by an emperor and the size of the court orchestra/chorus. Special mention is made toward the end of the study of the role played by the female members of court. Empress Claudia, for instance, brought Vincenzia Mazzotti, described as the greatest virtuoso singer of her time, to the court in 1673, whereas Maria Theresia is said to have entertained, together with her sister Marianne, all listeners at court with her singing and playing of music. Köchel says, "In this way the beautiful women were and still are everywhere inclined to further what is beautiful, because they are ordained to spin and weave heavenly roses into earthly life." Thus ends Köchel's study.

III

THE
KÖCHELVERZEICHNIS

26

The Starting Point

I must commence here with two statements that, in a way, are contradictory. First, had Köchel never written his now famous register of Mozart's compositions, the other achievements of his life would still suffice to treat him as one of the "greats" of the nineteenth century. I hope that the preceding chapters have proved this point.

Second, however, had he done nothing else than write the *Register*, this in itself would be sufficient to make him famous and to preserve forever his name. My reason for leaving a detailed analysis and explanation of the "KV" to the end of this book is that I wanted to prove the first of these statements before dealing with this most important work of his, with which I wanted to conclude the history of his life and work. In this way I did not keep to the chronology of Köchel's opus; many of the matters discussed in preceding chapters were undertaken after the *Register* was completed.

As to the explanation of the *Register*, I wish to remark here that this is something that has never been done before, in spite of the fact that much has been written about it. Nobody ever attempted to explain the *Register* to those who are not likely ever to resort to it, to hold it in their own hands. As will be seen, there is much more here than a mere list of Mozart's compositions.

By the way, the generally adopted brief title of *Köchelverzeichnis* is naturally wrong; the Köchel name does not appear at all in the title. It should really be called the *Mozartverzeichnis*. The full title is seldom used.

Before analyzing the *Register*, it is important to realize the exact position of scientific knowledge at the time, regarding the musical output of Mozart. It must also be appreciated that he was not among the most popular, most performed composers at the time Köchel started his work.

Certain lists were already in existence, and some two-thirds of his known compositions had appeared in print, in some instances by a number of publishers, which in the days before copyright was quite customary but which added to the confusion. (I shall revert to this point later.) The same work may have been given a slightly different title by another publisher, or an inaccurate copy might have served as the basis of the publication, leading to duplications of records. As a result, the same composition may be listed twice or more often due to such discrepancies, and researchers faced the added difficulty of determining which of the available versions was the authentic one. (The very latest research indicates that sometimes more than one version was genuine: Mozart used the same composition in different guises for different purposes.)

Music printing itself was an expensive business, and usually it was cheaper to buy a handwritten copy than a printed one. These handwritten copies were not necessarily accurate. If every copyist made just one small mistake and if the original autograph was lost, there was again the added problem of determining which of the copies was closest to the original composition, even if there was no doubt that this work was by Mozart.

When the *Köchel Register* first appeared in 1862, more than seventy years after Mozart's death, at least one-third of his known compositions had still not appeared in print. According to Köchel, this applied to 240 compositions, but some of the editions to which he refers are not now recognized as such, and according to the latest guidelines, as published by Haberkamp, only 268 of the 626 Köchel numbers had appeared in print by 1862. By the time Breitkopf & Härtel published, with Köchel's valuable assistance, the first "complete edition" of his works, they were able to include 590 works. This was between 1876 and 1883. Of the 626 Köchel numbers, 581 were included. To this were added nine of those compositions originally listed in Köchel's appendix; of those, three were stated as "lost," five "incomplete," and one "doubtful" in its origin. Obviously, the lost ones were found, the incomplete fragments were considered worthy of inclusion, and the doubtful one received the seal of approval by the publishers.

Of the forty-five Köchel numbers not included in the first complete edition, twelve are transcripts, orchestrations, and so forth, based on other composers' works, ten are incomplete; four are not fully authenticated; six are parts of other compositions (which appeared in the edition); and thirteen were lost. All this demonstrates the rapid change of affairs even in such a relatively short time as between 1862 and 1883. The K numbers not included in the Gesamtausgabe (complete edition) are the following: 54, 62, 64, 90, 92, 103, 104, 105, 107, 140, 161, 176, 206, 223, 226, 227, 235, 241, 263, 288, 300, 324, 325, 340, 346, 362, 386, 405, 439, 443, 470, 489, 490, 514, 544, 552, 565, 566, 569, 572, 577, 591, 592, 611, and 615. And the numbers taken from the appendix and not included as K numbers by Köchel are appendix numbers 5, 9, 10, 21, 56, 72, 80, 91, and 191.

I have tried to reconstruct the knowledge about Mozart's compositions at the time Köchel commenced work on his register. There is an excellent book by Edward Holmes (1797–1859) entitled *The Life of Mozart,* which was first published in 1845 (i.e., six years before Köchel started his work) and which in an appendix lists "the works of Mozart." This list is divided into several sections. The first of these is a translation of Leopold Mozart's "Verzeichnis" of the twelve-year-old Mozart's compositions, to which I shall refer in greater detail in my analysis of the chronological order. Father Mozart's list, repeated in Holmes's book, contains the compositions "produced by Mozart between his Seventh and Twelfth Year," not in chronological order or in any logical groupings, sometimes combining "thirteen symphonies" or "fifteen Italian airs" under one number, although written at different times and in different places. More often a single work is given under one reference, sometimes stating the year of composition, but usually not. The length of the work is also given on occasion, as is the place of composition and/or publication, but all in all, nothing is systematic or consistent in this section. The incipits are also missing, which makes identification more difficult, but by and large these are the compositions that later received K numbers 6 to 49, with some omissions and some later ones included, up to 76.

The second section, which gives a breakdown by year and by month, is based on the theme register made by the composer himself of works composed between 9 February 1784 and his death. The first work here is the Piano Concerto in E flat (now known as K. 449), which is indeed the first entry Mozart made in his own register and which—according to Einstein—is the "beginning of a new series comprising no less than twelve great concertos written between 9 February 1784 and 4 December 1786, and constituting the high point of Mozart's instrumental composition."

The third section, surprisingly, is a "catalog of musical fragments and sketches"; whereas the fourth lists "compositions that, in addition to those mentioned, Mozart left complete." This last group should thus fill the gap between 1768 and 1784, a period of sixteen years and some four hundred or so compositions; these are listed in thirty-six sections with very few pointers as to the year of their creation and woefully short of detail to aid their comparison with later knowledge. For instance: "Thirty-two various church compositions—masses, litanies, offertories, motets, hymns, cantatas etc—and among them a requiem. Of these a Stabat Mater for three sopranos, consisting entirely of canons and an antiphona in four parts, which he wrote at Bologna in 1770, for reception into the Philharmonic Society of that city, deserves especial notice. The greatest work of all, is, however, the requiem." This is *not* the requiem written on Mozart's deathbed. I wonder whether it refers to the Mass in C minor (K. 139), which in Einstein's assessment is not a requiem mass, since on the occasion for which it was written, the funeral of Archbishop Sigismund, the funeral mass performed was the one by Haydn, also in C minor. But there is no other requiem mass by Mozart, except of course the unfinished one, K. 626!

All this is mentioned here to illustrate the utter confusion surrounding Mozart's works at the time of Köchel's activity. In the absence of opus numbers as used by most composers, with no dates appearing on many of the manuscripts and with a large number of these lost or scattered, the picture presented to the researcher was blurred to such an extent that it must have been hard to find a firm point from which to commence the task.

As to Holmes's book, Otto Jahn in his pioneering *Wolfgang Amadeus Mozart* pays tribute to the work (which, by the way, was the first account of Mozart's life and work in English). It made use of the Nissen biography, condensing all that was important and reliable in this work by the second husband of Mozart's widow, Konstanze. The book itself is indeed well worth reading even today, but the vague nature of the listing of Mozart's compositions only highlights the necessity of Köchel's subsequent work.

Looking for previous attempts to list Mozart's compositions, Köchel himself refers to the listing of the composer's sister, "Nannerl," together with corrections and dates added by father Leopold; to Dr. Josef Hauer, a medical practitioner in Öd, Niederösterreich, a friend of Schubert's, who had tried to combine previous listings by

Alois Fuchs and Leopold von Sonnleithner (both acquaintances of Köchel) into a register of Mozart's works and who thus "supplied the first significant material" (Köchel); and Karl Baumann, who assisted with the research in Frankfurt, presumably including neighboring Offenbach, seat of the André publishing house.

The relationship between Köchel and Hauer is well documented in seven surviving letters by Köchel to Hauer, five of which are from the relevant period. In the first of these, dated 10 August 1859, he addresses Hauer formally as "Hochverehrter [highly esteemed] Herr Doktor," an indication that they were not yet personally acquainted. The second letter of 20 October in the same year points to the fact that they had met and become friends, the address now being "Hochverehrter Freund" (friend), and Köchel refers to the pleasant day they had spent together. The meeting was arranged through the introduction of their mutual friend Dr. Franz Lorenz (the man whose pamphlet, to which I shall further refer later, had set Köchel on the road toward the *Register*), who appeared to be on most friendly terms with his fellow medical doctor, Hauer, as evidenced by a postscript he added to Köchel's fourth letter and in which he addresses his friend by the familiar *Du*.

With the fifth letter, Köchel sends Hauer a dedicated copy of the newly published *Register* in 1862. The inscription reads: "With patience and time, from rags is created a book!" He invites Hauer's criticism of the work by saying, "Please tell me in due course quite frankly what you like in this thing and what should be improved upon or supplemented so that we may have something accurate in front of us." (Hauer, by the way, lived from 1802 till 1876; his wide interests included the study of nature and the love of animals, fields that were also of great importance to Köchel. His father was an organist and composer.)

Other sources utilized included the Nissen biography with its appendix of works, based in part on the notes prepared by the abbot Maximilian Stadler (1748–1833), a friend of Mozart and of his wife, Konstanze. (Stadler also completed some of Mozarts unfinished compositions and helped the composer's widow in every possible way.) There was also Heinrich Henkel, who in 1841 published a register of those Mozart autographs that were then in the possession of court councilor André in Offenbach.

The brothers Johann, Johann Anton, Carl August, Julius, and Jean Baptiste André of Berlin and Offenbach made available to Köchel all manuscripts in their possession, of which they prepared an early list in 1833, the original of which is now in the British Library. Konstanze had sold all manuscripts she found in her husband's estate, about 120 in total, to the André company of music publishers for 500 Gulden.

The whereabouts of other originals were difficult to establish. They were scattered all over Europe, and it will never be known how many are still missing. When Köchel started on his task, musicologists generally assumed that there might be something like four hundred compositions in all. To publish a list of 626, apart from those Köchel considered to be unreliable or that remained uncompleted, is quite an achievement.

Köchel's work on the *Register* was to occupy about eleven years, during which he was spending large amounts of his own money to undertake journeys to many parts of Germany and to England, following up every lead that presented itself. Dr. Otto Biba, director of archives of the prestigious Vienna Gesellschaft der Musikfreunde (Society of the Friends of Music), writes in 1977 (the centenary year of Köchel's death) in the *Österreichische Musikzeitschrift*, "Köchel's achievement—surpassing all preliminary work—consisted of surveying all accessible manuscripts and examining earnestly the questions of chronology and genuineness. To this end he himself accumulated a large collection of first and early editions of Mozart's compositions, numerous of which he copied in his own hand with incredibly scrupulous accuracy. . . . Köchel's manuscript for printing which is in the archives of the Gesellschaft der Musikfreunde measures a pile of about sixteen centimeters in height with hundreds of closely written pages; even by its volume it demands our greatest respect for this undertaking." (I can vouch for the authenticity of this manuscript pile: I have held it in my own hands when I visited the archives in question.)

Fortunately for Köchel, Jahn had recently completed his definitive book on Mozart, and Köchel was able to lean heavily on the material collated by Jahn, who had plans of his own for a register but gave these up when he learned of Köchel's project. He proceeded to afford all possible help to Köchel; no wonder that Köchel dedicated the *Register* to Jahn "with sincere respect." This is what he said in his lengthy dedication:

> What name could adorn more worthily the introduction to these pages than that of a man, the close link to whose unsurpassed source of ma-

terial concerning the immortal composer, was one of the principal aims
of this work? Accept this, honored friend, as it is offered, with the full
compassion of one who feels compelled to express publicly his thanks
for such rich offerings.

When some time ago I submitted to you my well advanced work, it
turned out that you were on the point of starting upon the same task,
without one knowing of the endeavor of the other. However, as you
were in agreement with the plan and the part thereof accomplished by
me, you ceded to me a fullness of inestimable material that I cannot
sufficiently acknowledge. But this was not the full extent of your good-
ness: during the development of my task you never tired of rendering
your continuous attention and giving numerous hints. How much I
was aided by this is far for me to deny. But I must admit there were
times when I wished for less accuracy in your great work. For a researcher it is difficult to find a more pleasurable event than the discovery of something previously unknown; but several times I was keenly
disappointed and found it necessary to haul in the flag I had hoisted,
after finding on rescrutinizing your book, in some hidden corner a remark of yours which told me that you had already followed the same
scent before me. Then I had great difficulty in revising and coming to
a new conclusion.

But this is not the heart of the matter: to collect, sight, order the existing albeit scattered material so that one should easily locate, and in
its correct position, what is worth knowing; confidence inspiring relia-
bility and justification of data—this seemed to me the central issue in
such an undertaking. How far I have succeeded to reach this aim will
be evidenced by what follows; I strove toward this and perhaps can
take credit for having had the courage to attempt the first thrust in this
direction—with the risk of missing my aim! But whichever way things
may go, I can be certain of the assent of a few, and if I may number you,
my friend, among these, I could not consider as lost the time and effort
spent.

Salzburg, end of March 1862

This was not just a polite way of saying thank you for the help extended by Jahn. A feeling of mutual respect and friendship resulted
from the contact of the two men. Jahn was just as appreciative of this
friendship, as we know from the tribute he paid Köchel in the 1867
revised edition of his *Mozart*.

When I first examined Köchel's decision to start this work, I asked
myself, Why did he do it? He must have known that years of research would be required and large sums of his personal money

spent before he could hope to succeed. It should also be remembered that what he undertook to do was unique: no one before him had attempted to catalogue *all* works of a composer no longer among the living. The thematic registers published in 1846 (Mendelssohn), 1851 (Beethoven), and 1852 (Chopin) all dealt exclusively with the works of these composers that had appeared *in print*, whereas Köchel also incorporated the unpublished works by Mozart.

Köchel's love of Mozart was implanted by his father, and from childhood on he greatly honored the composer who for the first decades after his death was largely neglected by the musical establishment. Performances of his works were rare, his compositions were not readily available, and what was performed was not always the authentic version. By the time Mozart died, only 148 of his works had appeared in print (as shown in Deutsch's *Mozart Drucke*, published in 1931). By 1851, the time Köchel commenced his work on the *Register*, this figure had risen to 268 (according to Haberkamp's listing). But this is out of 626 works to be included by Köchel!

Some music lovers were deeply concerned about this sad position, and they feared that if something was not done soon, it may be too late—the remaining works would be scattered even more widely, and nobody would have the power and patience to search and find them.

One of these people was Dr. Franz Lorenz, a medical practitioner in Wienerneustadt who in 1851, as mentioned, had published anonymously a little brochure of some twenty-six pages, entitled "In Sachen Mozarts" (In Matters Concerning Mozart). It is generally considered and verified by Köchel himself in the foreword of the *Register* that the contents of this pamphlet were the immediate trigger for Köchel's work, started almost immediately upon reading it. Lorenz was a friend of Köchel's, and he likely had a lot more to say about his deep concern when the two men met. Let me quote some more from this brochure:

> A colorful disorder is the best description of the state of Mozart's compositions. Some have appeared in print, but many of these are unreliable; disfigured through frequent errors, alien insertions, ornamentations, curtailments; in numerous instances they contain the most outrageous mutilations, transformations, compilations of genuine and totally alien works; of the unprinted manuscripts, still a third of all his works, some lie hermetically sealed in Offenbach [this refers to the 120

or so manuscripts sold by Mozart's widow to the publishers André], slowly they decay, and this includes some of the most magnificent material, at second-hand dealers, collectors, admirers; transcripts traverse the world where the defective give birth to more defective copies until the original godly form is distorted into an unrecognizable caricature.

As a sad example of how far this evil had progressed, Lorenz cites the position of Mozart's masses. Thirty of these have been located, all carry Mozart's name, but more than half "have the mark of spuriousness upon their forehead." Seven have appeared in print, of which three are of doubtful authenticity, one is distorted, and one in two places is unbelievably mutilated (this last one having been published by Breitkopf of Leipzig). Thus, of the seven only one can be considered as totally genuine and complete.

Lorenz proceeds to talk about Mozart's early maturity:

By the time he was twelve he was not only in complete possession of theory and technique, in other words: master of his art, he was well acquainted with the most eminent classical composers and with their distinctive styles. . . . Because of this it will not be less difficult to survey the step by step development of Mozart and to bring this into a reliable chronological order of his compositions. . . .

Here, in the study and portrayal of the magnificent and not yet sufficiently brilliant period of Austrian musical composition there would be fruitful, almost virgin fields for a younger patriotic talent, equipped with the necessary knowledge and eagerness, who could wrest for himself high honor . . . and who could make good the severe sins of omission committed by our fathers. . . .

A lesson is to be learned from England which adopted the German Händel for itself . . . and found ways and means to protect his works for eternity by the process of printing. . . . What was achieved there by aliens for a foreigner and what Germany is about to do for one of her greatest sons, Bach, should we not be able to accomplish this for this exceptional man?

This, then, was the gauntlet picked up by the knight, Ritter von Köchel, who felt in himself the ability, eagerness, dedication, and patience required for this job and who did not shirk the responsibility of making what he calls "the first thrust" toward locating, sifting, sorting, and editing Mozart's life work.

Some of Köchel's later critics were of the opinion that he was the wrong man to do the job. Alfred Einstein, who was to revise the third edition of the KV; Otto Erich Deutsch, the eminent cataloguer of Schubert's compositions; Max Friedländer, singer and musicologist (about whom more will be said in chapter 30)—all point out Köchel's "inefficiency" or lack of musical schooling for the job. Certainly, he was not trained as a musicologist, but neither was Hauer, the medical doctor whose notes he used, nor Jahn, who had received some musical education but whose occupation was that of professor of philology and archeology at the University of Bonn. Count Waldersee, who was to supervise the second edition of the *Register,* was originally an army officer, and the list of "dilettants" in the field of musicology includes the politician and later finance minister of Austria, Carl Hermann Bitter, who wrote a Bach biography of note; the teacher Friedrich Chrysander, an acknowledged researcher into Händel's compositions and originator of the hundred-volume "complete edition"; Eduard Hanslick, who became one of the leading music critics of his time and who started his professional life as a doctor of law; Philipp Spitta, a theologian and Bach scholar; Ralph Georg Kiesewetter, a clerk in the Austrian court's military council who wrote an important treatise about the fifteenth- and sixteenth-century music of the Netherlands; his nephew August Wilhelm Ambros, a state attorney and self-taught composer who was the author of a major work on musical history, unfinished at the time of his death in 1876; the French politician Edouard Herriot who wrote a book on Beethoven. . . . The list is endless.

What Köchel may have lacked in musical education he made up by dedication, and what he did not know about Mozart's compositions by the time the *Register* was published was probably not worth knowing.

27

Köchel's Detective Work in Tracing and Authenticating Mozart's Compositions

I often wonder whether Köchel knew when he started work on the *Register* just how long it would take him to research all the material, how many trips would have to be undertaken, letters written, people encountered—not all of whom were friendly and helpful toward the project—and if he had known all this, whether he would still have embarked on his endeavor.

The challenge he met in his friend Dr. Franz Lorenz's pamphlet was to be taken up by a "young man"; yet Köchel was fifty-one at the time, and to be in the fifties in the 1850s was a lot older than today! More than eleven years of arduous labor followed, and it was an "old man" of sixty-two who handed over the completed manuscript.

What he had accomplished was unique; as mentioned, no one before him had attempted to organize a dead composer's total musical output. In fact, even his example failed to inspire others until well into the twentieth century: Hoboken published his Haydn register in 1957 and Deutsch the Schubert one in 1950; Kirkpatrick "organized" Domenico Scarlatti's works in 1953. (The format they used is remarkably similar to Köchel's, a tribute to his pioneering work.)

Sixty-one different manuscript sources are mentioned after the individual entries of the 626 Mozart compositions; and in addition are mentioned many works of which there were only copies to be traced. Whether Köchel actually saw all these manuscripts or whether in some instances he accepted the information received from Otto Jahn or others is not certain. (One manuscript was in the possession of Gustav André in New York at the time: Köchel certainly did not travel to the United States, but it is conceivable that he obtained sighting of this through other members of the André family of publishers. The work in question, Symphony in E flat, now known as K. 18, was later considered a copy made by Mozart of another composer's work.)

Nor do we know the exact number of shorter and longer journeys undertaken in the process of the research work. The sources mentioned cover twenty-three different locations, including Paris, Prague, Munich, Berlin, Frankfurt, Hamburg, Darmstadt, Stuttgart, St. Petersburg, and Leipzig. There was also London, where we know that Köchel visited to find the manuscripts listed as belonging to J. B. Cramer, Mr. Ella, Mr. Caulfield, Mr. Plowden, Mr. Hamilton, Mr. Schmidt, and the British Museum. The most important of these are probably the six string quartets dedicated to Joseph Haydn: K. 387, K. 421, K. 428, K. 458, K. 464, and K. 465. These all belonged to Plowden, who also owned the manuscript of the later quartet K. 499.

What is known about Köchel's findings naturally only covers the positive results of his search. To these must be added the uncounted wasted journeys, just as tiresome and because of the final frustration probably even more so, when he located manuscripts believed to be genuine but on closer investigation and scrutiny found to be fraudulent.

I shall be dealing in chapter 30 with some of the mistakes Köchel made in his assessment, particularly where he accepted a composition to be genuine Mozart and where later researchers discovered reasons strong enough to discredit Köchel's findings, although many of these can also not be considered "final." Here I wish to stress only that the vast majority of his first judgments leading to his list of 626 compositions, which by his own strict criteria were considered genuine, original, and complete, were correct. True, today's experts talk in terms of about eight hundred Mozart works, and because thirty-two of the original list are not now included in this number, there must have been approximately two hundred compositions not spotted by Köchel—not found, at any rate, in time to be included in his *Register,* perhaps incomplete or uncertain to such an extent that they were relegated by Köchel to the appendix section. I have no wish to analyze these omissions; it would be unfair to condemn Köchel's work partly because some manuscripts had not as yet been located or because with his caution he treated a genuine Mozart work as "doubtful" and did not, therefore, include it in the list.

It must also be remembered that the task he had set himself included the placing in chronological order and the finding of first and other early editions of each composition. This meant additional investigative work, and again, as will be explained in chapter 29 on the chronology of Mozart's works, in the vast majority of cases his judgment proved to be correct, or very nearly so.

Köchel's "Anmerkungen" (remarks) after each composition give us some clues about the research and verification process. Taking the very first composition entered, the "Menuett für Klavier," K. 1, he says, "On the autograph is the following note: 'Undersigned certifies that this piece was composed by her brother and written down by himself in his fifth year, signed by Frau von Berthold-Sonnenberg née Mozart' (Nannerl, the sister who traveled with Mozart and their father and performed jointly for royalty and nobility in many parts of Europe)."

Later researchers, by the way, found four Mozart compositions considered to predate this one, the very first of which, an "Andante für Klavier," is believed to have been written at the end of January or early February 1761. Also, for some reason (probably on Leopold Mozart's instruction), almost all of Nannerl's references to age are one year off: what she calls "fifth year" should therefore become sixth.

K. 6 and K. 7 were the first works of Mozart to have a printed edition. There is a long dedication of these sonatas to Princess Victoire, daughter of the king of France. Two interesting points emerge here: the works are by "J. G. Wolfgang Mozart," the G standing for *Gottlieb*, the German for Amadeus. And the sonatas are referred to as "Oevre premier," or first work of the composer—which they were certainly not!

French is also the language in which six sonatas, K. 10 to K. 15, are dedicated to the "Queen of England, Sophie Charlotte," born Princess Mecklenburg-Strelitz, the wife of King George III.

The story related by Köchel in connection with K. 16, a symphony written when Mozart was ill and dictated to sister Nannerl, is that he said to her, "Remind me to give something decent for the hunting horn to do."

In connection with K. 88, an aria for soprano that Köchel put into the year 1770, when Mozart was fourteen, Köchel says, "Only after repeated scrutiny did I recognize in the manuscript No. 1276 in the Royal Court and State Library of Munich an undoubted autograph. This Aria is not mentioned anywhere; perhaps it was one of those intended for the Soirées of Count Firmian in Milano"—the others being K. 77 to K. 79. "He was prevailed upon to write these, as mentioned by himself, to demonstrate his ability to compose dramatic material."

About the oratorio "La Betulia liberata," K. 118, Köchel writes, "this is totally in the Italian style. . . . Mozart received in 1771 in Padua a commission to write an oratorio and I surmise that it was the Betulia . . . although this was first performed only in 1786 . . . for which performance Mozart wrote a new introductory chorus which however belongs to the 1780s."

To explain the approximate date of the composition of the Minuet in E flat, K. 122, Köchel refers to a few lines written by Leopold Mozart on the autograph requesting his wife to dispatch a copy of his violin manual to H. Brinsechi in Bolsano, as requested of him by "P. Martino." This indicates that the autograph was sent from Italy to Salzburg, and, as in 1770–1771 Mozart father and son were in close contact with Martino (better known as Padre Martini [1706–1784], composer and one of Mozart's tutors); this fact enables Köchel to put an approximate date to this composition.

Analyzing the instrumentation of Divertimento in B flat, K. 186, Köchel finds close parallel with that listed under K. 166, which is of "assured date." He therefore puts it into the same period at the end of the compositions whose dates are certain.

To justify inclusion and date of K. 238, Piano Concerto in B flat, Köchel refers to two letters. One of these, written by Mozart from Mannheim on 14 February 1778 to his father, mentions that Rosa Cannabich had performed his Concerto "ex B flat," an earlier mention being in a letter he wrote from Augsburg on 24 October 1777: "then I played my Concerto ex B flat." Köchel puts the composition of the work into 1776, and this date has been generally accepted.

In a letter written from Vienna to his father on 2 April 1782, Mozart says, "I request the dispatch of my Concerto in C [written] for the Countess of Litzow." This must have referred to K. 246, says Köchel, as it was known that a Countess Lützow had lived in Salzburg during the relevant period (1776) and seemed to have been a pupil of Mozart's. (The letter *ü* is often given as *i* by Austrians.)

K. 250, the "Haffner Serenade," was composed for the nuptials of the Salzburg townsman F. X. Späth and Elisa Haffner, daughter of the wealthy wholesale merchant and mayor of Salzburg Sigmund Haffner, described as an admirable, patriotic, and generous man.

The wedding took place on 22 July 1776, hence the 1776 date for the composition.

The two concertos for flute, K. 313 and K. 314, are "probably those" mentioned by Mozart together with three flute quartets written for H. Dejean, who reportedly paid 96 Gulden for these works, as Mozart says to his father in a letter from Mannheim on 14 February 1778.

The work known as K. 345, choruses and intermezzi to the heroic drama "Thamos, King of Egypt," written by Baron von Gebler, vice chancellor of the k.k. Bohemian Court Chancellery, were occasioned by the appearance of a theatrical company under the direction of Böhm and Schikaneder in Salzburg. Köchel explains that the period of composition (1779–1780) is verified by the style of writing, the quality of paper of the original score, and the assured treatment of the orchestral parts. (By the way, this was the first occasion when Mozart worked with Emanuel Schikaneder, who was to write the libretto of *The Magic Flute*, composed in 1791 for Schikaneder's company.)

About the Scene and Aria for Soprano "Misera dove son?" "Ah non so io, che parlos" (K. 369), Köchel writes, "On the autograph is a remark by another [female?] hand: 'A la comtesse de Paumgarten Veuveé (née Lerchenfeld). It was this aria that was sung by J. V. Adamberger, Mozart's leading tenor [!] in Mozart's concert in Vienna on 22 March 1783. . . . Mozart refers to it [on 15 September 1781] as 'the Aria for the Baumgarten.'"

The story behind the Andante and Allegretto for Piano and Violin, K. 404, is this: In 1782 Mozart started to write a sonata in C major for his wife, Konstanze; a two-part andante, which should probably have been followed by variations, exists, as does the beginning of a final movement that André concluded with a few bars and then published the trifle as a sonatina. The compositions Mozart intended for his wife were all strangely doomed; they are all affectionately dedicated, but all remained incomplete.

The Symphony Minuet, K. 409, seems to have been written for the "academies" (concerts) given by Mozart in Vienna in 1782, as in the whole decade of the 1780s it was customary to incorporate such compositions as insertions in the concerts.

Three of Mozart's piano concertos, K. 413, K. 414, and K. 415— known as Nos. 11, 12, and 13—were offered at a joint subscription price of 4 ducats per copy in a newspaper advertisement placed by the composer in the *Wiener Zeitung* on 15 January 1783: "Herr

Kapellmeister [conductor], Mozart hereby announces to the highly esteemed public the appearance of these three newly composed concertos. These three concertos which may be performed with large orchestra including wind instruments or 'a quattro' [i.e., with two violins, one viola, and one violoncello] will only be available at the beginning of April and only to those, neatly copied and overseen by himself, who have subscribed for same." Regarding these same concertos, Mozart wrote to his father on 23 December 1782, "The concertos are an in-between of 'too difficult' and 'too easy'; they are most brilliant, pleasant to the ear, but naturally without sinking into emptiness. Here and there they afford satisfaction to the connoisseur, but in such a way that the dilettanti must be satisfied without knowing why." As can be seen, says Köchel, Mozart knew exactly what he wanted! And Köchel knew almost exactly when they were composed. It belongs to this story to know that the advertisement was not successful, but Deutsch informs that they were later (in 1785) published by Artaria.

K. 423 and K. 424 are the two duos for violin and viola. Both were composed during a visit to Salzburg in 1783 for Michael Haydn (1737–1806), who had received a commission from the archbishop to write two such works but was unable to do so due to his illness. They are written with unmistakable fondness, and Michael Haydn held them in high regard and kept the original score as a worthy memento throughout his life.

The "Linz" Symphony, as we know it today, No. 36 or K. 425, "must have been composed before 1784. . . . According to H. F. Niemeczek [the first Mozart biographer] it was dedicated by Mozart to the count of Thun; this can be taken as determining factor that this is the symphony composed in Linz because it is known that count Thun offered kind hospitality to Mozart in Linz and that therefore it is very likely that he dedicated to him his symphony composed in Thun's house."

Most of the later entries in the *Register* refer to works listed by Mozart in his own register, making it unnecessary for Köchel to use his deductive ability in verifying or putting a date to the composition. But the examples given here are a small fraction of those where Köchel was obliged to use the most varied types of information, coupled with his own powers of deduction to arrive at the approximate date of a composition.

28

The Thematic Order of Mozart's Works

Mozart's musical output was possibly the most versatile of all composers. One of Köchel's tasks was to categorize his works, and in so doing, he created a separate part in the *Register* that precedes the chronological list. The title page of this section calls this

Übersicht   Survey
der vollständigen Compositionen   of the completed compositions
nach Gattung und Zahl   by category and number

There are twenty-three groups of works listed, always followed by the number of works contained in the group:

I.	Masses, Requiems	20
II.	Litanies, Vespers	8
III.	Offertories, Kyrie, Te Deum, Veni, Regina Coeli, Hymns	40
IV.	Organ Sonatas	17
V.	Cantatas with Orchestral Accompaniment	10
VI.	Operas, Theatrical Serenades, and Such	23
VII.	Arias, Trios, Quartets, Choruses with Orchestral Accompaniment	66
VIII.	Songs with Piano Accompaniment	41
IX.	Canons for Two to Twelve Voices	23
X.	Piano Sonatas and Fantasias	22
XI.	Variations for Piano	16
XII.	Individual Pieces, Minuets, Rondos, Allegros and Similar for Piano	23
XIII.	Piano Works for Four Hands or Two Pianos without Accompaniment	11
XIV.	Sonatas and Variations for Piano and Violin	45
XV.	Piano Trios, Quartets, Quintets	11
XVI.	String Duets and Trios	6

XVII.   String Quartets [Including Those] with One Added
        Wind Instrument   32
XVIII. String Quintets   9
XIX.   Symphonies   49
XX.   Divertimenti, Serenades, Cassations   33
XXI.   Orchestral Pieces: Marches, Symphonic Movements   27
XXII.   Dances for Orchestra   39
XXIII. Concertos   55
        —making a total of 626 works.

On the pages following this initial summary, we find each of the works mentioned, group by group, preceded by its "Köchel number," stating the tempo, key signature, and beat, followed by the first two or three bars of music, with text where applicable.

The logic of the classification appears to be to take first the religious compositions. These represent the first three sections. The sonatas for organ, which follow, were usually performed in a church—where else would there be an organ? The cantatas, being compositions for solo voices and chorus with orchestral accompaniment, provide the transition from church-based music to secular works. There follows the group of operas and so forth; in fact, Groups V to IX are all based on the human voice.

Groups X to XV use the piano as their link; next come the strings (XVI–XVIII), followed by works for the full orchestra (XIX–XXII), leaving the concertos for solo instrument with orchestral accompaniment last (XXIII).

This thematic grouping, which was later also to be used for the first collected edition of Mozart's compositions, was not challenged or altered by subsequent revisers Waldersee and Einstein, who were to be responsible for the second and third editions of the *Köchelverzeichnis*, respectively, although the contents and numbers became somewhat different, and Einstein decided to put the thematic list after the chronological details. The sixth edition shows several changes in the thematic grouping by rearranging and adding a few groups.

The original *Köchelverzeichnis* provides no explanation of the thematic grouping, and the list gives no detailed information about the compositions, as this would obviously duplicate what comes in the section of chronology, the main body of the work. As mentioned before, however, an article by Köchel appeared in the second volume of *Mitteilungen der Gesellschaft für Salzburger Landeskunde* (Notifications of the Society for Geography in Salzburg) for 1861–1862, which is in fact a reprint of a lecture he gave to the members of the society in May 1862, soon after he concluded his work on the *Register*. It must have been a difficult task for Köchel to condense into a short lecture the results of some eleven years of research, yet he was able even to furnish some examples in detail to justify the inclusion of some of those Mozart compositions others may have omitted from the list. For instance in Group V, Cantatas, he says, "Here are also included four Oratorios by Händel: Acis and Galatea, Messiah, Alexander's Feast and the Ode for St. Cecilia's Day, newly orchestrated by Mozart in 1788–1790 on the instigation of Baron von Swieten. . . . The Cantata Davidde penitente was compiled by Mozart from parts of his unfinished Mass in C minor with the addition of two new Arias."

Interestingly, in this compilation Köchel lists the first part of the sacred play in three parts, "Die Schuldigkeit des ersten Gebots" (The Obligation of the First Commandment), composed by Mozart at the age of ten, among the operas, referring to it under the title "Das fürnehmste Gebot" (The Most Important Commandment) and mentioning that Michael Haydn composed the second and (Anton Cajetan) Adlgasser (1728–1777) the third part of the work. The text was by Ignaz Weiser (1701–1785), whose initials are mentioned by Köchel, but he says in his "Remarks" that the initials given on the title page, "J.A.W.," also fit Johann Adam Wieland (1710–1774), concluding, "Certainty as to the author of the text could not be achieved." Weiser's first initial is *I* rather than *J*, but these two letters are often interchanged. Otto Erich Deutsch (1883–1967) (a Mozart biographer and the man who constructed the Schubert register) is emphatic in stating Weiser's name as the author of the text.

The correct full title was "Die Schuldigkeit des ersten und fürnehmsten Gebottes" (note the different spelling); hence the two shortened versions of the title, different from each other. It belongs to the story of this work that the manuscript was acquired in 1841 by Prince Albert and that Queen Victoria deposited it in 1863 in the Royal Library at Windsor Castle, where it is to this day.

This being sacred rather than worldly music, its place should perhaps more correctly have been in Group V with the oratorios and so on, but Köchel may have felt it more important to show this early attempt at quasi-operatic composition in that context; both the above work (K. 35) and the music to "Apollo et Hyacinthus" (K. 38) precede the operas *Bastien and Bastienne* (K. 50) and *La Finta semplice* (K. 51), written at age twelve, by one and two years, respectively.

The reference to the uncompleted requiem gives a condensed version of what Köchel knew about the commissioning of this work, to be supplemented two years later by the additional and most reliable information about this last Mozart composition (discussed in chapter 32).

Group XIX lists Mozart's symphonies. In his lecture Köchel mentions forty-nine of these, yet we usually refer to the last symphony written, the "Jupiter," as being No. 41. In his book on Mozart symphonies, published in 1986 by BBC Publications, Stanley Sadie, the distinguished musicologist and editor of *Grove's Dictionary of Music and Musicians*, asks, "How many symphonies did Mozart write?" He says that this question

> can be answered in several different ways. Several early ones, probably, are lost—of two "rediscovered" in recent years one is authentic, one almost certainly not. . . . The old "complete edition" numbered them up to 41 in the first place, including however two (Nos. 2 and 3, K. 17 and K. 18) that we now know to be spurious, and another (No. 37, K. 444) of which only the slow introduction is Mozart's.
>
> The supplements to that edition include six further symphonies from the years 1767–1772, numbered 42–47, and indeed numbers up to 55 have been assigned to other works, some of them of dubious authenticity, that might be regarded as Mozart symphonies. . . . One could say that Mozart wrote something like sixty [!] symphonies, but any such figure is somewhat arbitrary. We can however say that, of works composed as symphonies in the first place, there are forty-eight surviving (though there are doubts about the authenticity of four of them) as well as a few that are lost.

This, then, is a typical example of the general mess surrounding Mozart's compositions. Similar examples could be furnished in almost every section. Köchel's undoubted merit is that he was the first person who tried to create order amid these chaotic conditions, and he most certainly regarded his work as no more than a starting point from which others could and should pursue their research. Let me quote from his extensive foreword to the book:

> No one can be more convinced than the author as to how much of what is submitted here had to remain fragmented because no further sources opened up, and that the publication of this piece of writing will give occasion to entice some of the unknown from its hiding place; thus an urgent request is made here to all proprietors of autographs, rare edi-

tions and copies, particularly as concerns those numbers that show a gap in the records, to contribute through friendly advice to the author or publisher, in the interest of all music lovers, to a task to which this individual, on his first attempt, cannot have been equal.

And, as already mentioned, in the dedication to fellow Mozart researcher Otto Jahn, Köchel writes, "Perhaps I can take credit for having had the courage to attempt the first thrust in this direction—with the risk of missing my aim."

Köchel gave us an insight into his methodical approach to the task, as shown by the following further extract from the foreword:

> The survey by number and category of the composition should not just disclose Mozart's overall activity to us, but to significantly help through the compilation of homogeneous material the locating of the thematic beginnings. The emphasis of the whole work naturally rests in the subsequent chronological register of the completed compositions. Before all, the main scrutiny had to be directed at establishing that the compositions included should be genuine. Although with all significant compositions, and generally speaking numerically, the authenticity is completely assured through existing manuscripts, through Mozart's own register and through editions made under his own supervision, yet by the nature of the matter, this could not be achieved everywhere. . . . Even where the slightest cause for doubt remained, the composition was demoted into the section of doubtful or falsely attributed works, without consideration for how long it had been regarded as authentic or included in otherwise creditable collected editions.

The thematic register—or survey, as Köchel calls it—makes it very easy to locate any of the 626 compositions listed. It is enough to know what type of work one is looking for; the key signature or the opening bars will help find it. Obviously, for further details, including a longer quotation, one must look in the chronological sequence, but by stating the Köchel number, the cross reference is further facilitated.

Possibly the other tasks Köchel had set himself with the register—locating all compositions, establishing their authenticity, and putting them into chronological order—are more important than the thematic survey. But there is no better way to appreciate the versatility of Mozart's musical output than to look through this awe-inspiring record.

29

The Chronological Order of Mozart's Works

The chronological register constitutes the main body of Köchel's analytical work on Mozart's compositions, and as his register, the famous *Köchelverzeichnis*, stands foremost among Köchel's varied contributions to scientific research, it is essential to deal with this sequence in great detail. We have already looked at the "starting point"—that is, the scope of knowledge as it existed before Köchel; at his research work to locate as many as possible of the manuscripts, early editions, and copies of missing autographs and to confirm their authenticity "where there was no doubt"; also at his thematic grouping of what he considered genuine Mozart compositions.

Far more difficult than all this was to try and establish the correct chronological order—in other words, to place in the order of their composition the 626 works which he believed to be genuine. Why was this so difficult? Having outlined the scope of his intended task in the foreword of the *Köchelverzeichnis,* he proceeds:

One can only wonder that it took seventy years before a similar thought first appeared. During this long period regretfully a large number of living and lifeless aids for such a compilation were lost. Mozart's contemporaries, with the exception of a few elderly ones, who were children in his lifetime, were for ever silenced; autographs wandered from hand to hand—sometimes into iron fists—much has been scattered whilst more than one third of all compositions have never appeared in print, so that it is most surprising that the list of lost and missing compositions is not longer.

Apart from this, already in Mozart's lifetime, greed, in its peculiar way, took hold of his spiritual possessions causing deficient editions or reprints to appear, concoctions to be published under the name of Mozart, arbitrary transcripts to be made in ignorance of the original work; in a word, the public at large, not withstanding its opinion to know its Mozart, remained in ignorance of the total scope of his artistic activity. To counter this mistake was one more reason for the decision to undertake this task, thus discharging an old debt to the master, so often praised, yet never properly understood in his innermost being. . . .

Finally, there was the influence of the thought that this register may serve as a preliminary exercise for a future collected edition of Mozart's works.

This indeed turned out to be the case, as we know, although not without Köchel's further enthusiastic canvassing in the right places or without leaning heavily on his anonymous financial contribution. About the criteria of inclusion, Köchel says in the foreword that

genuine compositions had also to be original: transcripts which lacked information about the original are listed in the "Appendix." The compositions included in the chronological register are complete works; but the definition of completeness has been interpreted in a broadened sense so that operas, masses and such items generally which consist of several movements or parts, were included if not all parts, but some of these existed; thus individual kyrie, movements of symphonies, piano allegros or rondos and similar. Even some of those individual parts, fugues, arias, kyrie were included as complete where the significant matter was by Mozart and the exposition completed by other masters, such as Abbot Stadler, Süssmayr, Sechter and others. . . . With all such compositions there is a precise indication as to how much of them is by Mozart.

Looking at the actual sequence in which compositions are listed, it is again essential to see what was in Köchel's mind. Knowing that in the absence of exact dates, particularly where no manuscripts were found and in the period before Mozart himself started to list his compositions (9 February 1784), a degree of guesswork would have to come into play. He decided that

it would be appropriate to divide the productive periods of Mozart into five fairly naturally defined periods from which there were characteristic compositions of chronologically assured dates. These are:

I. period 1761–67 Boyish attempts (Several symphonies, concertos, piano compositions)

II. period 1768–73 Mozart the youth (*La Finta semplice, Mitridate, Ascanio, Il Sogno die Scipione,* Litanies, Masses)

III. period 1774–80 The young man (*La Finta giardiniera, Il Re pastore,* Misericordias)

IV. period 1781–84 The mature man (*Idomeneo, Il Seraglio*)

V. period 1785–91 The prime period (Haydn quartets, *Figaro, Don Giovanni, Cosi fan tutte, Magic Flute, Titus,* Jupiter symphony, Requiem)

In each of these periods it was also possible to determine its beginning, middle and conclusion and to fit a given composition into one of these sections. . . .

It must be emphasized that with those compositions whose exact timing could not be determined, more than a higher or lower degree of likelihood could no longer be attained in our time. . . . Mozart himself, where he made his record at a later date, could often provide from memory no more than the month, and not seldom only the year of origination, in the end not even that; how could it be justified to ask more of epigones than what the master himself was able to do? . . .

Providentially for the purpose of chronology, the complete prime period is firmly determined through Mozart's own register; and for the time before 1784 this applies . . . to his most significant works: operas, masses, litanies, arias, quartets, quintets, symphonies, concertos—at least as regards the year.

To demonstrate to the reader by numbers how much credence should be given to the pursuant "chronological register," a statistical survey and the method applied is stated below.

In the chronological register in total 626 complete compositions of Mozart are listed, of these

after 1784 (Mozart's own register)	179
before 1784	447
giving a total of	626

Of these the following number may be considered reliable as regards their date:

after 1784	170
before 1784	176
making a total of	346
against those of uncertain dates:	280

This gives a ratio of about 9 to 8 in favor of the time assured compositions, i.e. more than half of the total. Of the 280 of uncertain dates, all of which belong to the period before 1784, there is great likelihood as to their year of composition for about half this number, leaving about a quarter of all compositions where a greater risk had to be taken to incorporate them in a particular year.

But even in these instances there is no danger for the reader to be misled because all those compositions whose date is uncertain are preceded by a warning asterisk * and in the pursuing text the degree of likelihood and the reasons for entering them in that place are briefly stated. . . . The time assured works have always been placed at the beginning of each year and are followed by those of uncertain dates with their sign of warning.

As mentioned before, Köchel has been much criticized by future revisers of his work, most of all by Alfred Einstein, who edited the third edition of the *Register* and who took it upon himself to renumber the Mozart compositions (but whose findings were also not foolproof!). I carried out a comparative study to see how "wrong" Köchel had been with his inclusion of compositions and with his chronology. Leaving aside those works not included in his 626 accepted numbers, some of which were later found and authenticated or which appeared in the appendix because of Köchel's doubts as to their authenticity and were later given the seal of approval by researchers, there is a total of thirty-two compositions (i.e., approximately 5 percent of the total number) that are today not considered to deserve their place in the *Register*. These are Nos. 17, 18, 55 to 61, 92, 93, 140, 142, 154a (!), 177, 187, 197, 198, 221, 226, 227, 235, 268, 291, 324 to 327, 340, 342, 350, and 510. (Ten of these were omitted from the second edition published in 1905, to which Köchel himself had supplied important notes.)

On the matter of chronology, looking at the year of inclusion, 135 are now thought to be listed in the wrong place, a little less than one in four, which is almost exactly what Köchel said when he assessed his own sequence of numbers! Roughly sixty-nine of these are also in the wrong "artistic period" as described earlier, but usually only marginally so. They are Nos. 46, 67 to 69, 76, 91, 101, 102, 106, 119, 146, 152 to 154, 178, 189, 199 to 203, 205, 206, 223, 228 to 234, 236, 237, 279 to 283, 290, 293, 312, 341, 346 to 349, 351, 352, 355 to 362, 381, 387, 390 to 392, 395, 406, 410 to 411, 429, 434, 445, and 514. However, in fact only *26* compositions out of 626 are five or more years out of place, and I shall discuss later some of these "mistakes" made by Köchel. As a percentage, this number is not significant, either—some 4 percent of all works listed. In summary, therefore, he was right, or nearly right, *in over 90 percent* of his entries!

Wolfgang Hildesheimer, in his *Mozart* (published in 1977 and translated into English by Marion Faber in 1982), sums this up in the following way:

> The Köchel Catalogue lists 626 works. It will always remain provisional in that it does not contain what is lost, it justly questions what has been rediscovered, and from edition to edition it jockeys what is dubious from the main catalogue to the appendix and back again. In addition it is synthetic, for it is not the composer's own catalogue of works. Mozart . . . did not start keeping a catalogue until very late, with the E flat piano concerto, K. 449. Mozart started his catalogue . . . because of his sudden hastening understanding of his own importance; he entered only what he thought was up to his standard. . . . He also made no entries for miscellaneous pieces he thought unimportant. The Köchel catalogue, on the other hand, is a scholarly work, giving a number for every discarded sketch, every beginning, even if it is only 3 bars long; it includes what was abandoned, attempted, lost.

What aids were available to Köchel, what previous lists existed to facilitate his work? Most important, there was Mozart's own register of compositions, a unique record in its format for any composer before or after, limited however to the last eight years of his activity. There is also a diary known as "Nannerl's Tagebuch" (Nannerl's Diary), covering the journey to France, England, and the Netherlands in 1763 to 1765, which Mozart's sister Maria Anna, born in 1751, kept, on father Leopold's behest. This contains a childish but complete record of events, noting the many Merkwürdigkeiten (curiosities or noteworthy events) of the journey and incorporating a list of compositions written by brother Wolfgang. To these father Leopold added some comments in his own hand to signify whether a work mentioned was actually written or just copied by his son as part of his musical education. The record is woefully incomplete, and we will never know whether some of the compositions were left out intentionally because Leopold Mozart may have felt they did not merit inclusion, or purely by mistake.

Similar comments must apply to another list compiled by Leopold himself in 1768, entitled "Verzeichnis alles desjenigen, was dieser 12-jährige Knab seit seinem 7-ten Jahre componiert und in originali kann aufgezeigt werden" (Register of All Such Items as Have Been Composed by This Boy Aged Twelve since His Seventh Year and Can Be Shown in Its Original). This latter list, compiled to demonstrate Wolfgang's true creative ability at a time when allegations were made in Vienna that he did not himself compose the opera *La finta semplice*, leading to the cancellation of its performance, was for some reason ignored by Köchel. He makes no mention of it in the *Register*, although all thirty-six compositions listed therein are included in Köchel's number sequence, starting with Nos. 6 and 7, sonatas for piano and violin, dedicated to Mme. Victoire de France, and incorporating numbers up to 76 (which proves how many of the early works must have been omitted from father Mozart's list). Five of the items, all symphonies, are relegated by Köchel into the appendix under Nos. 214 and 220 to 223, labeled as "doubtful." Köchel's remark applying to these works says that they are included in the old Breitkopf & Härtel list based on manuscripts once in the publisher's possession; these are now largely lost and only the opening bars remain. In later revised editions of the *Köchelverzeichnis*, these symphonies reappear as genuine Mozart compositions.

The original of Leopold Mozart's register is in the Manuscript Section of the British Library, but it was first in the possession of Nannerl Mozart. When she handed it on 4 August 1799 to Breitkopf & Härtel, she inserted from memory the years of composition that had not been recorded by her father. These are therefore not "safe"; moreover, there was no record of the opening bars of the pieces, which adds to the difficulty of identification. Bearing in mind that Breitkopf & Härtel were to publish the *Köchelverzeichnis* in 1862, it is quite possible that the contents of the register were known to Köchel but ignored by him because of these uncertainties.

Regretfully, no register of any kind was kept by anyone for 1769 to 1784, a period encompassing approximately four hundred of the Köchel numbers—a time span in which he was, numerically speaking, most creative and when his irregular habits, need for money, and travels all contributed to the scattering of manuscripts. When in February 1784 he decided to keep a register of all his compositions, this was, in Köchel's words, an attempt "to emulate the father of whom he said 'Nach Gott kommt gleich der Papa' [Papa comes right after God]. But it is only natural that with the best will the spirited genius in the heat of creation forgot the prosaic registration of the date, first sometimes, then frequently; in trying to repair the omission later he stated just the month or the year and even to this end his memory did not serve him well."

After giving the dates of André's publication of the two printed versions of Mozart's own register, Köchel continues: "We take this opportunity to remark upon a few minor errors therein. It says there under No. 105 '6 Variations' instead of 9, No. 132 twice refers to 'legerer' in place of 'Leirer' (or Leyerer in the old style of writing)." Köchel then describes the shape and system of the book, which is today also the property of the Manuscript Section of the British Museum. It lists a total of 145 compositions, quoting the opening bars of music; details of the instruments; the dedication; and, in the case of operas, the cast, date of the first performance, and so on. It covers the period from 9 February 1784 until 15 November 1791 (Mozart died on 5 December 1791). Sadly, at the end of the book remain fourteen blank pages, ruled off in preparation for future entries. Köchel continues:

> The date stands next to each composition; whether Mozart intended to note the beginning or the end of a composition can no longer be determined; with the operas (Mozart Reg. Nos. 32, 37, 67, 118, 141, 142) it is certain that he wished to signify the completion, as the dates of the first performances are known. But not seldom only the month is stated, as in Nos. 26, 27, 83, 102, 107, 109, 110, 113 to 122 and 140. It is more than likely that Mozart got into arrears with his listings and from memory was able to determine only the month, not the day. . . .
> Into the period 1789–90 fall frequent instances of ill-humor over his pecuniary circumstances, his health etc. which were bound to distract him from his previous routine. A. André . . . advises that in the case of several compositions the heading of the autograph does not correspond to Mozart's register; thus the autograph of the Piano Quartet in G minor (K. 478) has the heading "Vienna li 16 d'ottobre 1785" whereas the same piece appears in the Register under No. 27 as having been composed "in the month of July 1785." [The October date is now thought to be the correct one.] It is also correctly mentioned by André . . . that Mozart incorporated in his register here and there compositions that were written earlier and altered later, among others the Quartet Fugue in C minor (K. 622) under No. 144 which is a transcription of a concerto for bassethorn, the autograph of which still exists in part.
> Finally, Mozart also combined several compositions of different dates under one entry, e.g. the canon "O du eselhafter Martin" (K. 560) (Oh, you asinine Martin) which is in the register under No. 95 with seven other canons as having been composed on 2 September 1788,

whereas it probably belongs into the year 1785, coined for the singer Peyerl. [The current edition of the *Köchelverzeichnis* again gives September 1788 as the date of this canon.]

To this "register of sins" committed by the master we can add some of omission which consist in the fact that a considerable number of compositions which definitely fall into the period 1784–1791 are not included in his register, these are [K. Nos.] 448, 461–3, 506–8, 514, 532, 579, 609, 624, 625 and 626 of the pursuant chronological list.

Two of these, Nos. 448, Sonata for Two Pianos, and 514, Rondo for Horn and Orchestra, are now thought to have been composed in 1781 and 1782, respectively (i.e., prior to the start of Mozart's own register). And K. 510, which is not mentioned here by Köchel as one of the "omissions" and which has no corresponding number in Mozart's own register, has the following story attached to it, as mentioned in the *Köchelverzeichnis*.

During his stay in Prague in 1787, Mozart promised Count Johann Pachta to write some contredances for the society balls, but he failed to fulfill his promise. Eventually he was invited to dinner by the count, but his invitation was for one hour before the customary start of the meal. When Mozart arrived, he was handed music paper and writing materials and asked to compose the promised dances immediately as they were required for the following day. Mozart sat down and completed four of the dances before dinner, including their complete orchestration. Otto Jahn believed this story, and Köchel saw no reason for doubt, but Nottebohm (another leading musicologist) challenged the validity of the works entered under K. 510, and current classifications support his belief that they are spurious on the basis of the manuscript's handwriting, which is not in character with the composer's usual style. The story may of course relate rather to K. 509, which appears in Mozart's own register and was composed in Prague. Köchel continues:

Of these last mentioned numbers there are mostly autographs, in other instances very firm clues. Whether Mozart intentionally omitted these compositions because they seemed less significant to him or whether it was just an oversight will never be determined. The last number, 626, the Requiem, was of course not completed in all its parts; we could not, however, exclude from the list the magnificent torso of this work. But these minor offences committed by the master . . . become insignificant when set against the certainty pledged with the majority of the data.

Toward the end of Köchel's register there are two numbers—624, Cadenzas to Piano Concerto, and 625, Comical Duet "Nun liebes Weibchen" (Well, Dear Little Wife)—that are not listed by Mozart in his own register. Why not? Einstein implies that the duet, based on a composition by Benedict Schack (1758–1826), preceded the *Magic Flute* (K. 620) and gives it No. 592a—that is, between the orchestration of Händel's "Ode to Saint Cecilia" and the Quintet for Strings in D major, Nos. 592 and 593, respectively. If we accept Einstein's view, why did Mozart omit this work from his register? Einstein also puzzles me in numbering the Cadenzas 626a—*after* the Requiem— but the cadenzas were finished, whereas the Requiem was left uncompleted and by all accounts was still worked on when Mozart was on his deathbed. This should mean that the cadenzas were written *before* No. 626 and not after! Current research proves that the duet was composed toward the end of August 1790, justifying its earlier position in the sequence, but the cadenzas were composed "some time between 1767 and 1791," which means there is no firm chronological place for them in the register. As to Mozart's failure to record these two compositions in his own register, the probable explanation is that he did not "rate" them, as they were based on other composers' works. The cadenzas were for piano concertos written by others, including Johann Schröter (1750–1788).

If it was "wrong" of Köchel to try and "improve" on Mozart's own record by adding a few numbers at the end and some more for earlier "missed" entries, it must be even more wrong to change the Köchel numbers, as attempted by subsequent revisers, particularly by Einstein. An example of the mounting confusion caused by these attempts is given by Dr. Helmut Riessberger in his article in the *Wiener Zeitung* on 18 October 1984. He refers to the Sonata in A major, K. 331. This is renumbered by Einstein (in the third edition of the *Köchelverzeichnis*) as "300 i," but it is also known as Sonata No. 11 in the Breitkopf & Härtel edition. Moreover, as if this were not enough, it has a rare "opus" number, being No. 2 of opus 6 given by its first publisher, Artaria.

Examining the structure of the chronological register, it is important to mention the scope of its material. It extends from page 27 to page 494 of the book, a total of 467 printed pages. By comparison the thematic part covers only 20 pages.

Looking at any page of the register, the top left-hand corner gives the year of composition; the top right shows the Köchel number(s) mentioned on that page.

In dealing with a composition, first comes its number, as given by Köchel, next the title of the work, the voices or instruments for which it was written, and then the date of its composition. If this date is considered doubtful, an asterisk appears in front of the year. Next comes a two-part musical quotation with the usual Italian indication of the mode and speed of playing, the clef, measure, sharps or flats if applicable, and the volume of sound to be produced. At the end of each line of musical quotation, or incipit (which varies but usually consists of three to six bars), the number of bars of the movement, or in the case of single-movement pieces, the whole composition is noted.

Underneath the musical quotation comes the heading "Autograph" with all that is known about the original manuscript, including its location at the time of writing. Unfortunately, only too often do we find the one-word answer "unbekannt" (unknown).

Next comes "Ausgaben" (editions), often followed by "keine" (none), but where Köchel was able to trace printed editions, these are stated in full. As with all other information in Köchel's book, there are obvious omissions in this respect. Otto Erich Deutsch says in *Mozart-Drucke* (published in 1931 in conjunction with Cecil B. Oldman), "Ludwig von Köchel's attempt to list the Mozart editions in his famous work and to determine the most important ones of these, had to show a very incomplete result . . . it remained a random listing without the scent for what is important, in spite of his ambition which made him concentrate on those editions made under Mozart's own scrutiny and which he also used for assessing the authenticity of a work." But having thus criticized Köchel, Deutsch concludes with a request to all music libraries to resort their stock in the sequence of Köchel numbers, this being the "natural chronological order" of Mozart's compositions.

Köchel's successors did not fare better. After the appearance of the sixth edition, Paul van Reijen, in a fifteen-page article published in the *Bulletin* of the Mozarteum in 1982, takes the editors to task for the inconsistent way in which they referred to literary sources throughout the *Register*. As an example, Gridlestone's edition of piano concertos (published in 1939 under the title "Mozart et ses concertos pour piano") is referred to in six different ways and Alec Hyatt King's "Mozart in Retrospect" in seven different ways, whereas abbreviations used throughout the *Register* are also stated to vary. My own feelings about this matter are that as long as the information provided is not misleading as a result of such inconsistencies, what difference does it make?

The scholar who wants to delve into the field of "assured" early editions of Mozart may read the comprehensive two-volume work by Gertraut Haberkamp, *Die Erstdrucke der Werke von Wolfgang Amadeus Mozart* (First Editions of the Works of Wolfgang Amadeus Mozart), published by Tutzing in 1986. It will be found here that the early editions listed (i.e., those preceding the "Collected Edition" by Breitkopf & Härtel prepared on Köchel's initiative and with his participation until his death) make a total of 374 of the recognized Köchel numbers. In contrast, the first edition of the *Köchelverzeichnis* listed 387 of Mozart's works—a very small discrepancy in numbers! Haberkamp also mentions that 131 works only were published in print in the composer's lifetime; this compares with 148 listed in this way in Deutsch's *Mozart-Drucke*—a very similar discrepancy. Haberkamp explains this divergence between the numbers by referring to "untraceable editions" that, although mentioned by Köchel, are doubtful in their existence. And Max Friedländer (to be mentioned in greater detail in chapter 30 about the "Wiegenlied" lullaby) says in his book *Das deutsche Lied im 18. Jahrhundert* (German Song in the Eighteenth Century), "the worthy Köchel unfortunately leaves us in the lurch when it comes to establishing the first edition of a work."

Reverting to the *Köchel Register,* "Ausgaben" is sometimes followed by "Abschriften" (copies), and again, the reader is reminded that in Mozart's time it was cheaper to prepare handwritten copies than printed editions of a work. Köchel's decisions often had to be based on such copies as he was able to trace, where manuscripts were not available.

The last heading under each composition is "Anmerkung" (comment, remark), and this gives the "story" of the composition, its origination and commission, the tracing by Köchel and others to establish its authenticity, plus any other remarks Köchel saw necessary to include. Some of the remarks are the briefest possible, while others extend to pages of information. About K. 50, *Bastien und Bastienne,* for instance, Köchel writes, "This operette was performed in Vienna's Landstrasse in a garden house belonging to the Messmer family, good friends of Mozart's, in his presence in 1768. J. A. Helfert's view is that the name Messmer does not refer to the hypnotist Messmer (after whom the expression to mesmerize is named), but to medical doctor Anton Messmer who had a house at No. 94 Landstrasse."

This is part of what Köchel writes about K. 294, Recitative and Aria for Soprano: "Composed for Aloysia Weber, with whom Mozart was in love at the time. About this aria Mozart reports in a letter dated 28.1.1778: 'As an exercise I made this aria . . . so beautifully composed by Bach, for the reason that . . . I wanted to attempt whether disregarding it I am able to create an Aria which is totally different from the one by Bach. . . . I composed it and decided to make it suitable for the Weber. . . . This has now become her best Aria which earns her merit wherever she goes.'"

The original manuscript of Köchel's book at the Vienna Gesellschaft der Musikfreunde includes hundreds of pages of music carefully copied by Köchel in his own hand from early manuscripts, copies, and first editions, intended for inclusion in the book (and later for the collected edition). A so-called "Handexemplar" of the Köchel manuscript also exists. When I first approached Breitkopf & Härtel about information relating to the *Köchelverzeichnis*, I was told that all their records had been destroyed during World War II. In the meantime, they were able to repurchase in an auction the original Handexemplar. There is also a record in the Sächsischen Staatsarchive of some of the letters written by the publishers to Köchel, but unfortunately none of Köchel's letters to Breitkopf & Härtel survive.

30

The "Wiegenlied" and Other "Spurious" Compositions

By the time Köchel started to work on the *Register*, many "Mozart" compositions were in circulation that on closer scrutiny turned out to be the work of others. In some instances, all that could be firmly established was the fact that Mozart was not their composer. One of the sections of the appendix of the *Register* gives details of Köchel's judgment of such spurious works, but with all the care in the world, a number of mistakes crept into his list of "genuine" compositions. Here are a few examples.

The two symphonies listed under Nos. 17 and 18 were included on the basis of manuscripts held by Carl August André, of which Köchel said, "They are probably copies with some markings by Mozart." In connection with the piano sonatas, K. 55 to K. 61, he says: "To determine their time of origination all evidence is missing except that of conception which seems to indicate approximately the year in which they are included" (1768).

The Symphony in F major, K. 98, was included "on the authority of Aloys Fuchs and Ludwig Gall who considered it genuine."

K. 140, the Missa Brevis in G, "was considered genuine by several music lovers and chorus directors who thought the style Mozart-like." Otto Jahn, however, whose judgment Köchel usually accepted, thought this work spurious. The work must subsequently have been lost for a long time because the first known public performance took place as part of the bicentenary birth year celebrations of Mozart in 1956 in Salzburg. The *Österreichische Musikzeitschrift*'s Sonderheft (special edition) commemorating the events of the year, in a chapter entitled "Die Kirchenmusik im Mozart-Jahr" (Church Music in the Mozart Year) writes as follows:

A special event of the Mozart year was the premiere of the Missa Brevis in G, K. 140. . . . This work by the young Mozart had a peculiar fate: The Mozart biographer Otto Jahn considered the mass as not genuine, whilst Lorenz and Köchel maintained their belief in its authenticity. The Mozart year 1956 now provided the proofs of its genuineness: The music archives of the cathedral in Salzburg contain those compositions that were written by the master under his obligation of his service in the Salzburg court music. . . . The Missa Brevis in G, K. 140, copied by the same hand, is bound in one volume with the well-known K. 194 (Missa Brevis in D). . . . Apart from this, the cathedral's conductor Joseph Messner found an additional separate copy . . . originating from the estate of widow Konstanze . . . which names Mozart as its composer. Mozart researcher Dr. Walter Senn found in a South German Stift voice parts to this Mass in G, containing additions and corrections in Mozart's own hand.

I would have thought all this was sufficient proof for authenticity, but the current sixth edition of the *Köchelverzeichnis,* published in 1964, lists the work only in the appendix section in spite of giving a summary of these proofs and without evidence to the contrary! Perhaps a case for reassessment for the next revised edition?

The Tantum Ergo, K. 197, was thought by Jahn to be a Mozart composition, and he refers back to Aloys Fuchs for support, but the score that reached the archives of the Mozarteum in Salzburg through the estate of Mozart's son does not include the timpani part to which Fuchs refers. The offertorium "Sub tuum Praesidium," K. 198, is included on the basis of a copy found at Stift Göttweig, of which Köchel says, "Melody and part writing make it impossible to mistake this little known work. . . . Prof. Schafhäutl in Munich is justified in considering it genuine." So did Einstein in the 1937 (third) edition of the *Köchelverzeichnis,* and even in the 1958 fourth edition, it is still shown among the genuine works, albeit under an earlier number.

All the above are now treated as "spurious," but perhaps the biggest "lapse" concerns K. 350, long considered the most famous of all Mozart compositions, the lullaby "Schlafe mein Prinzchen" (Sleep Little Prince of Mine)—or does it? Köchel says merely that "there is no indication of the time of composition . . . mentioned by O. Jahn." It also figures in the Nissen biography of Mozart (it will be remembered that Nissen was married to Mozart's widow).

Köchel gives the author of the text as "Claudius"; this must refer to Mathias Claudius (1740–1815), also known as Asmus or the "Wandsbeck Messenger," who is indeed responsible for the text of several lullabies, all simply called "Wiegenlied," but I was unable to trace one with words even remotely similar to those of the "Mozart" song. By Köchel's standards, this must count as a careless omission.

Later researchers attribute the words to "Gotter." Friedrich Wilhelm Gotter (1746–1797) wrote poems and plays, and the "Wiegenlied" appears in the fifth act of his *Esther,* one of three plays published under the collective title *Schauspiele* (Plays) in 1795—four years after Mozart's death. Max Friedländer (1852–1934), German singer and writer on music, "exposed" this fact in two articles written in 1892 and 1897, respectively, and, quite logically, he deduced that if the text was written after Mozart's death, Mozart could not be the composer of the song.

I wonder whether Friedländer, or anyone else who believed his version, took the trouble of reading Gotter's *Esther?* Because of the importance of the song in question, I did. This work is a farcical rendering of the biblical Esther story. The "Wiegenlied" is fitted into the story in a most peculiar way. When King Ahasuerus is unable to find sleep, he calls for the slave Fatmé, who makes no previous or subsequent appearance in the play, to come and sing for him. She sings the "Wiegenlied," which in style does not resemble the text of the play and is an obvious "insertion," almost a "party piece" for Fatmé. The poem does not appear in Gotter's previously published volume of poems. Being a lullaby, the text is such as to lull a child to sleep; Ahasuerus certainly remains fully awake, but, to add to the farcical effect, his physician soon snores most audibly.

The joint publication with two other plays in 1795 is no proof as to when the play was written, a fact well realized by Friedländer. In fact, he refers to a letter in G. Waitz's *Caroline* published in Leipzig in 1871 and dating "from October 1789" (i.e., more than two years before Mozart's death), which says, "Gotter created a proud Vasthi [a reference to another of the plays in Schauspiele and thematically preceding *Esther*] and a humble Esther of which he gave a reading in Weimar." We know from Rudolf Schlösser's biography of Gotter that this reading was in the house of the Duchess Anna Amalie in front of guests assembled for the occasion, probably a birthday party, and that the play was never performed on stage, at least not until 1894, the date of the biography. (*Vasthi* had one performance in a private theater in Weimar on 24 October 1800 to honor the birthday of the duchess, who was always well disposed toward Gotter.)

Friedländer examines the possibility that the poem may have been an insertion in the play and may have been written by another poet. He says that "this possibility cannot be ruled out due to Gotter's desire to produce a convivial play where such minor matters would be of no consequence."

As to the musical side of the matter, Friedländer first of all casts doubt on Mozart's version by relating the "suspect" circumstances in which "a copy of a copy" was handed by Nissen to the publishers André thirty-seven years after Mozart's death. But as we know, many other Mozart compositions came from the same source and in similar circumstances and are nevertheless regarded as genuine.

In the first of his two articles, Friedländer does not yet refer to the version by Bernhard Flies, which he found later and which today enjoys the recognition of experts as the genuine original composition. Instead, he concentrates on the music by J. Friedrich A. Fleischmann (1776–1798), which is very similar to the "Mozart," though not identical. Apparently there was artistic contact between Fleischmann and Gotter, whose *Geisterinsel* (Island of Ghosts, a rewrite of Shakespeare's *Tempest*) he had set to music, whereas we know of no contact between Gotter and Flies. According to Friedländer, the "Wiegenlied" is supposed to have been composed in 1796, yet Gotter's play was published in 1795 and its "reading" took place in 1789, posing the question, what song did Fatmé sing on that occasion?

When Friedländer, in his second article published in 1897, refers to the song by "Bernhard" Flies, of which he found a rare printed version published by Böheim of Berlin (a firm that ceased to publish music in 1798) and later an autograph in the library of the Berlin Music Academy, he confirms that no date appears on either, but he "assumes" that the year of Flies's composition was 1796—the same year as the Fleischmann version. The *New Grove Dictionary of Music and Musicians* (1980) says that Fleischmann's version "may have served as its [i.e., Flies's] model," whereas Friedländer believed it was the other way around. This source also advises that a variant of the song was used by Wenzel Matiegka ("Mädchen schlumm're noch nicht"—Maiden Don't Slumber Yet) for variations in the last movement of his Notturno Op. 21, which Schubert (!) later arranged as a guitar quartet.

As to Bernhard Flies, not much is known about him; even his first name is in doubt: Gerber's encyclopedia gives this "medical doctor's" names as Carl Eduard and his birth year as 1770 or 1771. A few other works by him are listed, including an operetta, but none of these survived, and there is no record of publication or performance of any of them. Thus, the obscure Flies, if he composed this song at all, would almost count as a "one tune composer," whereas Fleischmann has much more to commend him.

Not every expert accepted Friedländer's conclusions; the distinguished head of the Salzburg Mozarteum, Johann Evangelist Engl, for instance, was adamant as late as 1915 that the song was composed by Mozart.

I asked myself, was there a connection between Gotter and Mozart? Alfred Einstein gave a lecture at the University of Wisconsin in 1941, a reprint of which appeared in *Monatshefte für Deutschen Unterricht* (Monthly Publications for German Language Instruction) entitled "Mozart und Shakespeare's *Tempest*." He said:

> On 31 October 1791, a few weeks before Mozart's death, the poet Gottfried August Bürger wrote to his pupil and friend August Wilhelm Schlegel: "Gotter has written a magnificent free imitation of Shakespeare's *Tempest* under the title *Die Zauberinsel* [The Magic Island] . . . Mozart composes the music." . . . Gotter's name was not unknown to Mozart . . . he admired his "Medea" . . . Gotter was much performed in Vienna . . . he planned a visit to the city . . .
>
> Gotter was the poet of the Wiegenlied which for a long time was considered a composition by Mozart . . . had he been its composer he would have needed to be in close contact with Gotter because although the song, an insertion in Gotter's biblical travesty "Esther" originated in 1789, it was published only in 1795. Mozart would thus have to have obtained it from Gotter or from someone in his immediate circle. . . .
>
> Court Councilor Schlichtegroll, the first Mozart biographer, was since 1787 teacher at the grammar school at Gotha where Gotter lived, proof that Mozart's name must have been well-known there.

Einstein then explains in his lecture that the *Geisterinsel,* as the Gotter play was eventually called, was most similar to Mozart's *Magic Flute* and that it was this similarity that suddenly made Gotter realize that Mozart would be the ideal composer for the work. Alas, Mozart died before this could be done, and it was Fleischmann who eventually received the "exclusive" commission to write the music, an exclusivity quickly forgotten after Fleischmann's death when further versions were written by Johann Friedrich Reichardt and Johann Rudolf Zumsteeg. Of Fleischmann's music, only the overture survives, which was published by André as Op. 7. Fleischmann was a great follower of Mozart dating from the time when, as a twelve-year-old schoolboy in Mannheim, he became acquainted with the master's music during Mozart's visit to that town. He later wrote arrangements for eight wind instruments of several of Mozart's operas.

Einstein has nothing to say about Flies and his possible connection with Gotter, which makes me wonder what he really thought about the "Wiegenlied"'s true composer.

To summarize the position, let us look again at Friedländer's articles. He asks himself whether the "Mozart" composition can be treated as "genuine without doubt" and replies in the negative. As proof, he mentions the absence of an original manuscript and a published version in Mozart's lifetime. But if these two points were relevant in determining the validity of all Mozart compositions, the register of 626 works would be considerably curtailed; in fact, Köchel's work would have been superfluous! Friedländer obviously did not think much of Köchel's work. He says, "In the same admirable catalogue by Köchel there are no less than sixty-three compositions shown as being by Mozart but found to be spurious. I think we may assume that the Wiegenlied is one of those cuckoo's eggs laid into Mozart's nest."

Even if this were entirely true, it would still mean that only some 10 percent of all entries in Köchel's register are wrong. If this was thought to be the case in 1892, at the time of the current edition of the *Köchelverzeichnis* (1964), we find that this applies to only thirty-two of the original Köchel entries.

Friedländer also looked at the possibility that the "Wiegenlied" was an "insertion" in the play *Esther* and says that its origin may lie in a folk song. He even draws attention to three with similar beginnings: "Schlaf, Kindchen, schlaf," "Schlaf mein klein Kindchen" and "Schlafe mein Söhnchen, schlaf ein." Unfortunately, he gives no details of the music or full text of these.

I find it puzzling that the flimsy evidence offered by Friedländer should have satisfied the experts and that as a result of his articles Köchel's original judgment to treat the "Wiegenlied" as a Mozart composition should have been ruled out ever since. Friedländer's details certainly make it a "dubious" work, but similar doubts must relate to the other explanations offered, yet Flies's name has appeared unchallenged in all subsequent listings as the song's composer.

The various musical versions circulating are almost identical. The opening bars of the "Flies" are different from the "Mozart" version, and in one place there is an E flat instead of an E. Similar slight variations occur in the texts, but by and large they are very similar.

Friedländer wants us to believe that several composers picked up the text from an unperformed play within a year or two of its publication to set it to music. Is it not much more likely that Gotter (who knew of Mozart and considered him for setting to music one of his plays) came across the "Wiegenlied," complete with music, quite possibly written by Mozart years before, and decided to insert it in his play? It must also be borne in mind that whereas a connection, however loose, between Gotter and Mozart is established, as is the one between Mozart and Fleischmann, there is nothing to link Bernhard Flies with Gotter, with Mozart, or with anyone else!

31

The Appendix

A list of 626 compositions is longer than can be expected of a composer who died at the age of thirty-six. When the length of some of these works (operas, masses, symphonies, concertos, sonatas, etc.) is also taken into consideration, this is indeed a monumental output of music. Even more surprising, therefore, is the fact that Köchel had a total of 921 items to deal with. In addition to those listed in the main (chronological) body of the *Register,* he examined another 295 works that for one reason or another were to be excluded but that—because of their affinity to Mozart—had to find their place in the book. They took their place in the Anhang (appendix), which is in five parts:

  I. Lost Compositions (Nos. 1–11a)
 II. Uncompleted Compositions (12–109)
III. Transcriptions (110–184)
 IV. Doubtful Compositions (185–231)
  V. Falsely Attributed Compositions (232–294)

As mentioned before, there has been a lot of two-way movement in later editions of the *Köchelverzeichnis* between the main register and the appendix, the reasons for which are obvious: "lost" compositions were later found; doubtful ones authenticated; falsely attributed ones turned out to be genuine after all, whereas some of those treated by Köchel as genuine later became "doubtful" or were found to be totally spurious.

A "lost" composition was included here only if there was definite proof of its previous existence, and those listed in this section were therefore all genuine Mozart compositions of which no manuscript or copy was found by Köchel. There is, for instance, No. 2 of this section, the Aria "Misero tu non sei" from Metastasio's *Demetrio*, composed on 26 January 1770 in Milan. This is evidenced by Mozart's letter to his sister written that day in which he tells her, "Just before writing this letter I completed an aria from Demetrio which starts like this: 'Misero tu non sei/tu spieghi il tuo dolore.'" We therefore know that the aria was written, but a manuscript or copy has never turned up.

Of No. 9, Sinfonia concertante for flute, oboe, hunting horn, and bassoon, composed in 1778 in Paris, Köchel says, based on a letter by Mozart written on 1 May 1778, that the work had been intended for his Mannheim and Paris friends, the instrumentalists Wendling, Ramm, Punto, and Ritter, for a "concert spirituel" in Paris, but due to "intrigues" it was not performed there. Mozart sold the autograph to LeGros and unfortunately retained no copy for himself. The original is lost. (The concert spirituel was a musical institution founded in Paris by Anne Danicau Philidor in 1725 for the production of initially sacred, later also secular, works; these concerts were held right up to 1791, the year of Mozart's death. LeGros (1730–1793) was originally trained as a singer but had become too stout for the stage, and from 1777 to 1791, he managed the concert spirituel. A later version of the events says that LeGros would have been responsible for the first performance and how much Mozart regretted that this did not take place, bearing in mind how difficult it would be to reassemble four such excellent soloists.)

Some of the lost compositions of this section were later rediscovered and have found their rightful place, where appropriate, in subsequent editions of the *Register.*

Köchel's criteria for "uncompleted" works have been stated: where the most important parts of a composition were written by Mozart, as in the case of the Requiem, this was incorporated as a complete item. (Einstein, who was to be responsible for the third edition of the *Köchelverzeichnis,* took a different attitude: he included all fragmentary works in the chronological order together with the completed compositions without differentiating between them.)

The section listing "transcriptions" refers to those compositions of which the original example was given a "Köchel number" and where Köchel felt that the arrangement for a different combination of instruments or voices did not merit a second listing. (Transcriptions of other composers' works are included in the main register.)

In the section of "doubtful" compositions, the opening bars are printed for easy identification. Some examples from this list include two Masses for Four Singing Voices with organ accompaniment listed under (appendix) Nos. 185 and 186. According to Köchel these come from a set of seventeen published by J. Novello in London as Mozart compositions, but only ten are considered genuine, five definitely falsely attributed, and these two doubtful.

Similarly, of the canons published by Breitkopf & Härtel, ten are for voices with or without accompaniment, listed here by Köchel as Nos. 189 to 198 and considered by him as doubtful. One of these, No. 190, is in fact identical with K. 228 in the main register, but this item has now moved from its original place in 1775 to No. 515b in 1787.

The story attached to the two sonata movements, Allegro and Andante, No. 203 in the appendix, is that they are

> copied from an autograph exercise book into which Mozart entered each day the musical exercises set by his father. This book also contains Mozart's first attempts at composition. . . . One such piece is the above mentioned Allegro, written in unsure hand . . . it is quite possible that this is a composition by young Wolfgang, but it must remain doubtful. . . . The Andante does not figure in this book. . . . To assume here a Sonata by Wolfgang Amadeus Mozart is really unjustified.

But looking at later editions of the *Köchelverzeichnis,* I find that the two movements have now become 5a and 5b of the main register. Also, because they first appear in this way in Waldersee's second edition in 1906, which made much use of Köchel's own notes handed to the publishers between 1862 and 1877, it is quite likely that he had changed his mind regarding the authenticity of these movements.

Of four string quartets, appendix Nos. 210 to 213, Köchel says, "Aloys Fuchs [who prepared the earliest list of Mozart's works] received these in the form of copies from Salzburg, he includes them as genuine. However, they are no longer accessible, totally unknown, and thus lack credibility."

Ten symphonies figure here under Nos. 214 to 223, all emanating from the old Breitkopf & Härtel handwritten catalog. "Only their opening bars are now known," says Köchel, but in the current (1964) revision of the *Register,* some of them were "promoted" to the regular list. This is not necessarily justified, as the following example will prove. Numbers 215 and 218 are now shown as K. 66c and K. 66d, but their autographs, copies, and publications are all "unbekannt" (unknown), and all we have is the following remark: "It is pure, but perhaps not unfounded, supposition of Einstein's that these symphonies were composed for the planned journey to Italy. On 16 January 1770, Mozart performs three symphonies in Mantua . . . and it is most unlikely that he again used the symphonies of the big journey, rather that he wrote some new ones." Surely, with no further information available even now, it is more justified to list these works, as Köchel has done, among the "doubtful" compositions!

And so to the section of "falsely attributed" or spurious compositions. You may ask, why should anyone write a piece of music and then, instead of reaping the benefits of recognition, pass it off as the work of another person? The answer is that it was obviously easier to get a work performed if it bore the name of a well-known author, and the most important thing for a composer is that his music should be *heard*. Add to this the fact that most performances were from handwritten rather than from published scores, enabling the real composer to sell for gain the copies of his music bearing Mozart's name, and you have plenty of explanation for the motivation of unknown or little-known persons to pass off their work as that of the master.

The mass listed as No. 232 here is one of those published by Novello in London. Köchel says, "The manuscript is hardly in Mozart's hand . . . the treatment of the instruments, particularly of the bassoon, totally deviates from Mozart's usual way in his Salzburg masses.—All experts consider this as falsely attributed."

And of Mass No. 233 he says, "We are sufficiently knowledgeable from Mozart's letters that he wrote no Mass except the one in C minor during the relevant period. The widow also declared to Chorus Master Jähndl in Salzburg that this mass was a composition by Süssmayr."

J. Novello's editor explained with regard to the "Requiem brevis," No. 237 here, that this was based on a German manuscript in the possession of the Rev. C. J. Latrobe (an English clergyman, composer, and friend of Haydn, who lived 1757–1836) and that "he has more reason for now believing it to be a genuine composition of Mozart, although probably a very early production." But it is a fact, says Köchel, that "Mozart composed no Requiem, early or late, apart from the uncompleted final composition."

Then there are the songs. More than thirty of these are listed here (246–277) as having appeared in various collected editions or even singly, the collections being a mixture of genuine and spurious material. One such edition, purporting to be a "complete collection" under the title "All Songs and Tunes at the Forte-Piano by Conductor Wolfgang Amadeus Mozart" published by Rellstab in Berlin, contains but five genuine Mozart songs among the thirty-three included! Breitkopf & Härtel's handwritten catalog lists sixty-three songs, sometimes mentioning the real composer, as later established, but even where this is not so, the spurious ones are recognizable by their un-Mozart-like content. Among the names thus given as composers of "Mozart" songs we find Lorenz, Schneider, Müller, and Dalberg.

Of the aforementioned songs, one only, No. 276, is now considered genuine and identical with K. 148, although reordered chronologically as 125h, written "in the freemasonly sentiment." The text is by Friedrich Lenz, and the song was composed in 1772 in Salzburg.

Six further songs, Nos. 278 to 283, are shown by their publisher to be "by Mozart" without any further details being given. Köchel declares, "Certainly not Wolfgang Amadeus Mozart by their treatment!" And the "Twelve Variations for Piano on an Andantino," No. 287, on a theme by Dittersdorf, have been proved to be by Anton Eberl (1765–1807).

But Köchel reserves his final venom for No. 291, a sonata for piano, violin, and cello. This was published by Artaria in Vienna as Op. 41, by Magasin de Musique in Braunschweig as Op. 63, and by J. André in Offenbach as Op. 60. Köchel describes it as "a miserable, slovenly scribble, absolutely unworthy of the name of Mozart, lacking in spirit and invention with the mistakes of composition associated with a novice."

The appendix is followed in the book by a few "corrections" and one addition. This is to be slotted in after K. 154 and is known as K. 154a "Zwei kleine Praeludien für Clavier (oder Orgel)" (Two Short Preludes for Piano or Organ) allegedly composed in 1772 and marked with one of Köchel's asterisks to denote the uncertain date, which he based on the style of writing of the manuscript. Ironically, this work is not now considered to be by Mozart, but by giving it an "a" number, Köchel created a precedent that was, unfortunately, pursued by subsequent editors, leading to the present confusion of the numbering system.

Finally, there is a listing of all song titles, including those of arias, canons, and the like, in alphabetical order and with Köchel number references for easy location in the main register.

And so ends the first edition of the famous *Köchelverzeichnis*.

32

The Mystery Surrounding
Mozart's Requiem

When Peter Shaffer wrote his play *Amadeus,* he included in it a tremendous story of intrigue and murder, unfortunately untrue. He must be excused on the grounds of "poetic license," and perhaps he chose Mozart's middle name for his title to demonstrate his conscious deviation from the facts of the matter. After all, nobody ever referred to Mozart by that middle name, which in itself is wrong. On his birth registry entry, his name is given as "Joannes Chrysost Wolfgangus *Theophilus,*" and this last name was later translated into the German "Gottlieb," from there into the Italian "Amadeus," which in turn became "Amadeo" and from about 1777 "Amadé."

Mozart himself usually signed his name just "Mozart," "Mzt," or "Wolfgang Amad Mozart," and this *Amad* once or twice came out as "Adam"—the most notable place for this error being on his marriage registry entry at the Parish Church of St. Stephen, Vienna, on 4 August 1782. One biographer at least, Heinrich Eduard Jacob, in his *Mozart* of 1956 thinks this was no mistake but a conscious attempt to indicate Mozart's leading role of humankind! This is what he says:

> But was it really an error? None of the great biographers, but a little known outsider, Alexander Haidecki, found that on important documents, notably on his marriage registry entry in the Vienna St. Stephan's Church the name appears not as Wolfgang Amad. Mozart, but as Wolfgang Adam Mozart. . . . It is unlikely to be a spelling mistake, must therefore mean something different. But what? We enter here upon a mysterious world. Was it a "rococo joke"? Was it a musi-

cal trick to reverse the consonants, as if they were tones, performing a sort of "Krebskanon" [lobster canon—i.e., reverse canon]? The game assumes bourgeois proportions and assumes a deeper sense: Konstanze was married for nine years not to Amadeus, but to "Adam": to the first man, to the human being itself. Childish prank, music and deep meaning were all united here, as so often in Mozart.

Reverting to the way others addressed Mozart, we find that according to the trumpeter Andreas Schachtner, a friend of the Mozart family, the four-year-old Mozart was called "Wolfgangerl"; later "Wolferl" and "Klein-Wolfgang" appear, but never "Wolfi," as in Shaffer's *Amadeus*. As an adult it all reverts back to "Mozart." Even his widow, Konstanze, in a letter to her son Karl says, "Should you still find anything on Mozart, not just things written by him, but what others wrote about him, please send it all to Father Nissen [Konstanze's second husband and the first Mozart biographer]; he is seeking such things day and night . . . such a defender of Mozart as Nissen will be hard to find."

Having diverged here into the question of Mozart's middle name, how about the first, "Wolfgang"? This was the only one chosen by his mother, Maria Anna née Pertl, who came from St. Gilgen on the Wolfgang See (Wolfgang Lake).

To revert now to Shaffer's *Amadeus:* We now know that Salieri did not murder Mozart, but, additionally, the "mystery" about the commissioning of the Requiem, which Shaffer with absolute invention ascribes to Salieri, or someone coming on his behalf, is a mystery no longer. Nor is there any doubt as to how much of the Requiem is by Mozart himself and how much was written by others; the identity of these is well documented.

(Lest the reader form a false impression about my views on the play *Amadeus*, I wish to emphasize that I considered it a wonderful experience, both on stage and in the cinema, and that it has, in my opinion, contributed, at least in the film version, to make Mozart's music accessible to a larger public.)

My reason for dealing with this matter is to prove that long before the "remarkable discovery" by such eminent Mozart biographers as Alfred Einstein (1944), Otto Erich Deutsch (1964), and H. C. Robbins Landon (1988), Ludwig von Köchel gave the full facts in an article published under his name in Vienna on 26 November *1864* in the weekly publication *Recensionen und Mitteilungen über Theater und*

Musik (Reviews and Announcements about the Theater and Music), volume 10(48), of which I have a reprint. The article is neither concealed, starting, as it does, on the front page of the publication, nor obscure in its title: "Mozart's Requiem. Nachlese zu den Forschungen über dessen Entstehen" (Mozart's Requiem: Survey of the Research of Its Origin). Here follows a translation of Köchel's article:

After long and sharp literary and nonliterary skirmishes the historical facts of the origin of Mozart's Requiem emerged by and by, as shown in O. Jahn's "Mozart" Vol. IV from p. 565 and especially on pages 775–790. This still left unresolved some of the issues of interest to the researcher. In this connection through the courtesy of Ritter I. von Pfusterschmied in Vienna we came upon two documents and it has been kindly permitted for me to make use of same. The first is this statement by the subsequent Court Conductor Josef Eybler (†1846):

"Undersigned herewith acknowledges that the widow Constanza Mozart commissioned him to finish the Requiem started by her late husband; he declares that he will complete same by the middle of Lent and assures her at the same time that there will be no copy made nor will it be allowed to fall into other hands than those of the widow. Vienna, 21st December 1791. Joseph Eybler."

In this way there is definite proof of at least one of the "several masters" who according to Süssmayr (in his letter to the publishers Härtel on 8 February 1800—L.v.K.) were commissioned by Mozart's widow to complete the Requiem, and who were unable to accomplish this task. Süssmayr made no mention of any names.

This reference induced me to take to hand again the original manuscript of the Requiem from the Court Library, but on this occasion with particular regard for those sections which were inserted by alien hands. It is well known that when the original manuscript was found it was noted and decidedly stated by the abbot Stadler that in the autographed score plans of the Dies Irae, Tuba Mirum, Rex Tremendae, Recordare and Confutatis the vocal part and some indication of the orchestration originates with Mozart; these parts were thus separated in the edition by André by stating that ". . . they were in Mozart's own hand and copied by Stadler," whereas the orchestration made by other hands and introduced into the design were circled by pencil. This instrumentation by an "alien hand" I find after careful comparison with other autographed scores to be in the hand of Josef Eybler. The same also applies to the two bars of the vocal part of the Lacrymosa. (See O. Jahn's "Mozart" p. 696, Note 30. L.v.K.)

The instrumentation does not extend beyond the Confutatis and is usually restricted to the string quartet, only in the Dies Irae and the

Confutatis are winds included. One notices the anxiety in the rhythms of the accompaniment in these attempts at orchestration, in the distribution of the harmonies, etc., and one comes to understand that this attempt was eventually abandoned because of the insufficient ability (of Eybler) after which the completion (of the work) was, without further regard for the first attempt, handed over to the much more authoritative Mozart pupil F. Süssmayr. It is likely that the abbé Stadler and Eybler who were both friends of Mozart and concerned about his musical estate, were given the plan of the score of the Requiem by the widow, perhaps also to help preserve the "secret" of the completion of the work.

The second document is entitled: "The true and detailed history of the Requiem by W. A. Mozart. From its inception in the year 1791 until this present year of 1839. By Anton Herzog, regional school director and director of the choir, Wienerneustadt." The manuscript in question was to appear in print, but it never came to that.

Robbins Landon says in *1791: Mozart's Last Year* an endorsement at the bottom of the document constitutes an imperial veto of its publication. Bearing in mind that count Walsegg, the principal protagonist of the story to be told here died in 1827 (i.e., twelve years before the document from which Köchel quotes was written), this imperial veto is somewhat surprising. Köchel continues:

The author of the document was a teacher at Klam in the nineties of last century [i.e., the eighteenth century] at a school under the patronage of the Count of Walsegg who ordered the Requiem; as a musician he participated in the count's largely improvised orchestra and in particular in the first performance of the Requiem. The information in this "History" merits integral and overall credibility and, being characteristic of the person placing the order, moreover because of various circumstances relating to its first performance and subsequent publication, deserves deeper appreciation. Leaving aside the introduction and those parts not based on the author's own observations, we allow the historical presentation in his own words and supplement these merely by a few remarks of our own.

After this introduction, Köchel hands over to Anton Herzog:

Count Franz von Walsegg, owner of the estates of Schottwien, Klam, Stuppach, Pottschach and Ziegersberg in Austria under the [River] Enns, in the region below the Vienna Woods, lived since his marriage to Anna von Flammberg in his castle at Stuppach as a tender husband

and true father of his vassals. He was a passionate lover of music and of the theatre; for this reason on Tuesdays and Thursdays of every week for a full three hours quartets were played and on Sundays theatre performances held at which the Count and the Countess, together with her maiden sister participated, as did all officials, the numerous members of the household, each assuming parts in accordance with their abilities. For the purpose of the quartets the count employed two excellent artists, Johann Benard on the violin and Louis Prevost on the cello. In string quartets the Count played the cello part, in flute quartets the flute, I usually played second violin or viola.

So as to avoid a shortage of new quartets with such frequent performances the Count not only acquired all such works that had been published, but maintained a contact with many composers, but "always without mention of his name," these delivered their compositions of which he reserved his sole ownership and for which he paid them well. Specifically, Hoffmeister delivered a number of flute quartets in which the flute part was easily manageable and the other three parts uncommonly difficult to play so that the players had to work real hard giving the Count cause for laughter.

The scores having arrived by a secret route the Count usually copied them in his own hand and then allowed the separate parts to be rewritten from the score. We never saw the original score. When these quartets were performed we were asked (by the Count) to guess their composer. Usually we suggested the work was by the Count himself because he occasionally composed some bagatelles; he smiled and was glad to have mystified us; we laughed over his belief of our assumed gullibility. In this way we continued our mutual deception for years. I believe it essential to explain these circumstances in advance to allow for a better judgment of the "mysterious" inception of the Requiem.

On 14 February 1791 death snatched from the Count his beloved wife in full flower of her life. To honor her memory he arranged through his business manager Dr. Johann Sortschan to order an expensive memorial stone and from Mozart a Requiem of which, as was his custom, he reserved sole ownership.

After receiving the score of the Requiem he copied same in his accustomed way note by note in his own hand and gave the copy sheet by sheet to his violinist Benard to write out the individual parts. I often sat for hours next to Benard while he was engaged upon this task and pursued the progress of this excellent work with increasing interest; at this time the whole procedure (i.e., the order placed with Mozart—L.v.K.) of the Requiem was well-known to me through senior official Leutgeb who had to deal with the payments (to Mozart and later to his widow) from the gypsum depot (belonging to the estate) in Vienna.

When all parts were written out arrangements were immediately made to prepare for the first performance of the Requiem. But because not all musicians required could be found in the Stuppach area it was decided that the first performance of the Requiem should be in Wienerneustadt. The selection of the musicians was conducted in such a way that the solo and most important parts were given to the best musicians that could be found; thus it came about that the soprano Ferenz from Neustadt and the bass Turner from Gloggnitz were employed for the solo vocal parts.

The rehearsal took place in the choir loft of the Cistercian Abbey Church in Wienerneustadt in the evening of 12 December 1793, and on 14 December a Memorial Requiem Mass was celebrated in the same church at which this famous Requiem had its first performance for its intended purpose. (This account differs from that by Krüchten in "Cäcilia" IV. 306 and VI. 221 whereby the rehearsal of the Requiem was held in the house of the physicist Obermayr with Obermayr's daughter singing the soprano part both at the rehearsal and at the church performance. Krüchten who erroneously puts this first performance in the year 1791 also appears to have made mistakes concerning the information given by Obermayr. Altogether, the eye witness Herzog who was so closely involved in the performance merits more credence.—L.v.K.)

Count Walsegg conducted the performance. On 14 February 1794, the anniversary of the Countess's death, a performance of the Requiem was given in the church standing under the count's patronage at Maria Schutz on the Semmering [mountain]; but after this date no further use was made by the Count of the work apart from making a transcript for string quintet, the score of which was for several years under my supervision. The score of the Requiem, allegedly in Süssmayr's hand (in the main, though the Requiem and Kyrie are in Mozart's hand—L.v.K.), has not been seen by me or anyone else except the Count, nor did anyone know what the Count did with the manuscript and with other original scores in his possession. The score handed to me by the Count for the coaching of the singers was in his own hand and I would still instantly recognize same. I have never seen the score obtained from the k. & k. Court Library but believe this to be the one in the hand of the Count of Walsegg as it has not been found among his musical legacy after his death. (Here the author is mistaken: The Count's copy was after his death in the possession of the Countess Sternberg, Count Walsegg's sister, and was entitled "Requiem composto dal Conte Walsegg."—L.v.K.)

It may be imagined what impression it made on the Count to learn that the score which belonged to him appeared in print in Leipzig. At first he contemplated taking serious steps against Mozart's widow but eventually his kindheartedness led to an amicable solution. By the way, he was never correctly advised how far Mozart's (own) work extended (although through the abbé Stadler's negotiations he must have been acquainted as to the extent of Mozart's participation in the Requiem; but he did not wish to admit the borrowed prestige toward his own people.—L.v.K.), he thought up to the Agnus Dei. This emerges from the following circumstances: When later I arranged to have the parts copied from the score published in Leipzig I asked the Count to let me have the organ part of his Requiem as in the printed version this did not show the figured basses and I wanted to save myself the trouble of working these out; he then told me I would be unable to use the organ part in its entirety because he had a different Agnus Dei. I proved him wrong as I was familiar with every note of his Requiem. His claim to having a different Agnus Dei in his score to the one in the Leipzig edition he substantiated by saying that being Mozart's pupil, he had sent his work to Vienna for Mozart's scrutiny on a page by page basis. He claimed that shortly before Mozart's death he sent him his Benedictus for this very purpose.

When after Mozart's death the score of the Requiem up to the Agnus Dei was found it was assumed to be Mozart's composition, their respective handwriting being so very similar. The Count then supposedly completed the Requiem by the addition of the Agnus Dei. Süssmayr substituted this by his own composition and this was the supposed cause of (the Count's score including) a different Agnus Dei from the Leipzig score.

Here ends the quotation of Herzog's account of the events. Köchel continues:

In this way deceptions were attempted in the camp of the Count of Walsegg; totally different motives were the cause of the supporters of Mozart's widow for withholding and altering the true facts. The result was total confusion of public opinion until, after feuding for nearly forty years, and following the death of most participants, bit by bit the truth emerged.

Thus ends Köchel's article. The "mystery" of the sponsor and of the completion of the composition of the Requiem was thus totally resolved by him through the publication of the above article, and the only mystery remaining is why no one had taken notice of this published article at any time between 1864 and 1944!

Robbins Landon in his aforementioned book quotes from a longer version of the Herzog statement; it would appear that Köchel abbreviated this for the purpose of his article, or it might have been curtailed by the editor. Nevertheless, all relevant details are identical and were available in 1864 through Köchel's disclosure.

As to Köchel's views on the Requiem, these were best summed up in the stanza of the Mozart Canzonen that I repeat here, in my own translation:

At close of day the dying sun descends
In glory and a golden web unfurls,
Transmutes the placid countryside
Before the dusk with strings of countless pearls.
In light, eternal genius ascends
To reach the splendrous edifice and stride
With solemn pride.
For Mozart the last trumpet sounds.
His Requiem, in measured fugal tone,
In ghostly flight ascends the timeless throne,
To breach at last life's utmost bounds.
Your Requiem, you sang it for your death,
Stays unfinished upon your final breath.

33

Köchel as Motivator of the First "Complete Mozart Edition"

In looking at Köchel's life and work and in trying to separate the two from each other for the purpose of this book, I came up against a dilemma in connection with the publication of the collected edition of Mozart's compositions. This venture became such an obsession with Köchel, who felt that the nonexistence of a comprehensive edition was a reflection on the musical establishment of his native Austria (in which he had carved out a permanent place for himself), that he took this omission almost as a personal insult.

The reader will remember that the pamphlet by Dr. Franz Lorenz that triggered Köchel's work on the register of Mozart's compositions referred to the collected editions of Händel's works in England and Bach's compositions in Germany. Köchel himself raised the possibility of a Mozart edition in the foreword of the *Register*. It is very likely, therefore, that this plan existed in his head even before he commenced looking for manuscripts and early editions and that he treated the *Register* as a mere stepping stone to this more important venture.

From the age of fifty in 1850, his life became attached to this project, and he was merely biding his time waiting for the right opportunity to put forward his suggestions. There can be no doubt that without his work in tracing Mozart's compositions and putting them in order, no such publication would have been possible. It is also an obvious fact that his research continued after the publication of the first edition of the *Köchelverzeichnis* in 1862, even while he was engaged in other important activities—for instance, the compilation of the register of Johann Joseph Fux's compositions published in 1872.

The opportune moment arrived in 1874 when the German music and book publishing house Breitkopf & Härtel published a collected edition of Mozart's operas. As a brief aside, Breitkopf & Härtel, whose name comes up repeatedly in this book, can trace its history to 1542 when a printer named Heinrich Eichbuchler first obtained his license. The first Breitkopf was Bernhard Christoph in 1719; the partnership with Gottfried Christoph Härtel came about in 1796. The company, apart from pioneering music typesetting in 1754 and publishing many of the works of Mozart, Haydn, Clementi, Dussek, Brahms, and Wagner, made first publications of thirty-five original Beethoven compositions, including the Fifth and Sixth Symphonies and the opera *Fidelio*. It also initiated the famous musical periodical *Allgemeine Musikalische Zeitung* and established a piano manufactory. It is still active today as a publisher of music and books.

What happened next is best explained by Köchel himself through the text of the second codicil of his last will and testament, dated 12 April 1874 (given in full in chapter 12). I repeat the most relevant part only:

> To bring about a complete edition of the works of Mozart has occupied my thoughts for many years. When the music publishers Breitkopf & Härtel of Leipzig published Mozart's great operas in a uniform critically revised edition, I drew their attention to the possibility of linking this with a total edition of all of Mozart's works. . . . I declared that I could give a guarantee for 10,000 Thalers if the matter could really be brought about, but I did not name the supporter as I really meant my own person.

The codicil also contained full provisions to ensure that Köchel's heirs maintained payment of the necessary installments to the publishers even after his death.

When the publishers in April 1876 announced the complete edition and invited subscriptions for same, they said in their brochure, "Only through the highly motivated support of an 'unnamed person' has it become possible for us to approach this venture which by its whole concept is remote from customary publishing economics." Breitkopf & Härtel estimated that the total production cost "per copy" would amount to 350 Reichsthaler, or 525 Gulden (more than $75 at the time). The subscription price was 1,500 Gulden, or $225, and this worked out at 30 pfennigs (i.e., less than $0.25) per sheet of music. The price was maintained for some time after the issue was made, and it was also possible to purchase separately all the works published. These numbered 533 complete works, plus 57 in a "supplement" containing uncompleted and unverified compositions (which were nevertheless attributed to Mozart) and a few completed works that had surfaced after the edition of twenty-three volumes had gone to print. (The supplementary volume contained the Requiem.) The edition is nowadays called the "AMA," for Alte Mozart Ausgabe (Old Mozart Edition), to differentiate it from the more recently published new edition.

At the time Köchel had commenced work in 1851 on the *Register*, a total of only 387 Mozart compositions had appeared in print. To be more accurate, this was the number of works for which Köchel stated that there had been a publication, but the present view, as evidenced in the book by Haberkamp, is that only 268 such editions existed. It is a direct result of his tireless work that this number was more than doubled to 590 works by the time the AMA was printed. (As mentioned earlier, 581 of these come from the 626 K numbers, a further 9 from the appendix.)

As noted, Köchel's contribution was arranged in such a way that the sum was to be paid over a five-year period, from 1876 to 1881, in installments "on behalf of an admirer of Mozart through Dr. Ludwig Ritter von Köchel" (i.e., anonymously), and even the publishers, as evidenced by the extract quoted from their brochure, did not realize until after Köchel's death in 1877 that this "admirer" was none other than Köchel himself. The provision made in the second codicil of his testament to continue the payments was duly discharged after his death by his administrators. Although the complete edition was finished only by 1886, Köchel had the satisfaction of seeing the first volume of this work in 1876, the year before he died.

Köchel organized the patronage of a number of crowned heads of Europe for the Mozart edition, and he undertook to act as "honorary inspector"—a task he was unable to fulfill for later volumes as he died before the second volume appeared in print.

The edition also had the financial support of the International Mozart Foundation in Salzburg and the individual assistance of such famous persons in the musical world as composer Johannes Brahms (1833–1897); his friend and inspiration, the Hungarian violinist-composer Joseph Joachim (1831–1907); musical writer and friend of Mendelssohn and Schumann, Gustav Nottebohm (1817–1882); music librarian and editor Franz Espagne (1828–1878); composer-conductor

Carl Reinecke (1824–1910); composer-conductor Dr. Julius Rietz (1812–1877); pianist-teacher-composer Ernst Rudorff (1840–1916); musicologist Philipp Spitta (1841–1894), described as "a bastion of German musicology"; pianist-composer Otto Goldschmidt (1829–1907); court conductor, pianist, composer and music historian Dr. Franz Wüllner (1832–1902); and Count Paul Waldersee (1831–1906), who in 1905 was to be in charge of the second edition of the *Köchelverzeichnis*. None of these individuals knew about Köchel's financial contribution to the venture.

When Breitkopf & Härtel, in the 1889 reprinted first edition of the *Köchelverzeichnis* (not to be confused with the revised second edition), referred to the "complete edition," they had this to say about the origination of same:

> Only through the loyal, unselfish cooperation of an imposing number of musicians and musicologists . . . was it possible to complete this endeavor in the spirit in which it was undertaken. Naturally, since the spring of 1875, when the decision for this enterprise was taken, many have passed away whose name remains closely linked with this edition; even before the start of its realization, on 4 August 1875, the principal of our publishing house, Dr. jur. Hermann Härtel died, but from his sickbed he made known his support for the Mozart edition; in the first year after the start of publication, on 3 June 1877, came the death of Dr. Ludwig Ritter von Köchel who through his chronological systematic register of all compositions by Wolfgang Amadeus Mozart laid the foundation to this edition and who anonymously aided same with a substantial donation.

The twenty-three sections in which the collective edition appeared are identical with those of Köchel's thematic grouping. A twenty-fourth volume has been added "as a supplement that offers uncompleted, unauthenticated and newly discovered works. . . . One-third of these works have never been published." As mentioned, this was also Köchel's view, but the latest studies indicate that the number of published works before the Breitkopf edition numbered only 268 works. "The total edition is still offered at its subscription price of 1,000 Marks. At the same time, individual volumes are also offered for subscription for the first time . . . to offer musicians of lesser means the opportunity to acquire the desired portion of the work and thus to participate in this memorial to Wolfgang Amadeus Mozart." The date under this announcement is September 1889. A complete list follows, citing on more than sixteen pages all those Mozart compositions that can also be bought individually, with the price, and always preceded by their Köchel number.

An important tribute to Köchel's contribution comes from Count Waldersee. In a study published in 1879 by Breitkopf & Härtel, entitled *Die Gesamtausgabe der Werke Mozart's* (The Complete Edition of the Works of Mozart), he writes:

> It was chiefly two men who through their research contributed significantly to the practicality of the plan to bring about a complete edition of the works of Mozart: Otto Jahn through his biography and Ludwig von Köchel through the chronological thematic register of Mozart's works. . . . The Köchel-Catalog, the result of eminent diligence, is in close cohesion with Jahn's work to which it (constantly) refers. . . . Our new edition follows Köchel closely in its arrangement of works; each opus carries the same number as in the catalog.

While Köchel's specific work toward the "complete edition" was not extensive and his death came long before the publication of the twenty-four volumes was completed, the project had nevertheless been part of his life for more than twenty-five years. He himself certainly looked upon the beginning of this achievement with more satisfaction than at anything else he had accomplished in his life.

34

The *Köchelverzeichnis* after Köchel's Death

When I started work on this book I tried to purchase a copy of the 1862 first edition of the *Köchelverzeichnis* but soon found that very few of these exist today, and their proprietors are most unwilling to part with their copies. I advertised to try and get one on loan, but this brought no better response. Fortunately, the British Library has several copies. Even more fortunate is the fact that when the first edition was sold out, a new one was prepared, and this procedure has been followed ever since so that any music lover or student, any library or music school, is able to have a *Köchelverzeichnis* on its shelves.

Officially the second edition is the one that came out in 1905 in time for the 150th Mozart birthday year of 1906, edited (as noted previously) by Count Paul Waldersee (1831–1906), an amateur musicologist who knew Köchel well and who was able to utilize some of the supplementary discoveries made by Köchel after the publication of the original edition.

But this second edition was preceded by at least one reprint of the original one in 1889. This has a Nachtrag (supplement) in which the publishers, Breitkopf & Härtel, announce full details of the new collected edition of Mozart's compositions. Apart from listing on fourteen pages the appropriate Köchel number and the volume in which each composition is included, mention is made where possible of the owner of the original manuscript.

Apart from this supplement, the 1889 edition is identical with the 1862 one. By 1905 a number of changes became necessary, as new valuable source material had become available. For instance, the Mozart letters published by Ludwig Nohl in 1864 were unknown to

Köchel; he took most relevant data from Nissen's biography. Waldersee tells us that the versions by Nissen and Nohl of these same letters deviate from each other.

Indeed, the first "revision" of the *Köchelverzeichnis* comes from Köchel's own new findings published in his article entitled "Nachträge und Berichtigungen zu v. Köchels Verzeichnis der Werke Mozarts" (Supplements and Corrections to v. Köchel's Register of the Works of Mozart) on 20 July 1864—two years after publication of the first edition—in the prestigious *Allgemeine Musikalische Zeitung*. Before giving details of his new discoveries, Köchel says:

> The expectation mentioned in the Register, that its appearance would bring to light some of the concealed and lost [items] has been scarcely fulfilled since then. It was particularly the compositions from Paris in the year 1778 . . . all these works, so far lost without trace, stubbornly eluded all research for them. It seemed advisable, therefore, to undertake a personal voyage of discovery to Paris, which was subsequently extended to London and to the Rhine. Although I found many things I was not looking for, I could again not find what I was seeking. . . . In spite of all endeavor not even a trace of a shadow of the missing compositions showed itself . . . I did not find what I was looking for and the only glimmer of hope I brought back with me is that perhaps one of the excellent men whom I made aware of this situation will propitiously remember it.—Contrariwise, what I found without looking for it was a not inconsiderable number of Mozart autographs previously unknown to me, whose detailed examination was permitted with commendable willingness in Paris, as in London and at the Rhine. . . .
>
> My two friends, Leop[old] von Sonnleithner and Ferd[inand] Pohl, will permit me to utilize their remarks (in the Vienna Recensionen and in this musical journal) and to amalgamate these with my own. . . .
>
> I hope the supplements which follow here will occasion communications whereby the gaps of the Register will reduce in the interest of the cause, even if it cannot be expected that all of these will ever be filled.

The details that follow are mainly additions to existing entries, such as first editions, locations and proprietors of manuscripts, names of librettists previously omitted, details of first performances, and so on. There are also details of one composition previously omitted, now listed as No. 315a "8 Minuette mit Trio für Clavier" (Eight Minuets with Trios for Pianoforte), of which the incipits are given. Köchel places the composition in 1778 based on the style of handwriting. (In the current, 1964 edition of the *Köchelverzeichnis*, this work is numbered 315g, and its likely date of composition is given as early 1779.) Most of Köchel's corrections and supplements were included in later editions of the *Register*. Of these, K. 291 is now known to be Mozart's copy of a work by Michael Haydn, and this has been "relegated" to the appendix under No. A52. On the other hand, the partially completed symphony (*Köchelverzeichnis* appendix No. 56) is now in the main register under No. 315f as part of the new regime to incorporate uncompleted works in the main register.

Waldersee made use of all this material. He also incorporated the numerous notes Köchel added to the original manuscript, which was in the possession of Breitkopf & Härtel, and he made good use of the collected edition of Mozart's works published between 1876 and 1886, of the third edition of Jahn's *Mozart*, published in 1889, twenty years after Jahn's death, and of *Mozartiana* by Nottebohm, published in 1880.

The main system of numbering has been retained; the newly included items have been slotted between existing numbers by using the letters *a* and *b* after a given number. There was also some movement to and from the appendix in the light of new research. In all, ten Köchel numbers had to be eliminated from the main chronological register: 54, 140, 206, 226, 227, 235, 342, 350 (about which my opinion is different), 362, and 514, whereas eleven new ones are included: 9a, 9b, 25a, 65a, 89a, 154a (which already appears as an added number in the first edition—only to be excluded in the latest one!), 271a, 315a, 468a, 511a, and 535a. In addition, there are twenty new entries in the appendix section.

Another important addition is the inclusion of Victor Reusch's biography of Ludwig von Köchel, the first to appear and, short as it is, forming the basis for future entries in encyclopedias and other textbook articles. (Reusch's name, by the way, is not mentioned.)

The edition officially known as the third, published in 1937 and edited by Alfred Einstein (1880–1952), a cousin of the famous physicist, is a different matter entirely. Many documents previously missing had come to the fore, manuscripts had been found where their existence was previously not known, and letters by Mozart and members of his family were discovered, furnishing researchers with valuable data regarding compositions.

Einstein was, in contrast to Köchel and Waldersee, a trained musicologist. He felt that the only way in which he could still use the title of "chronological register" was to change the sequence of the numbers allotted by Köchel and to reorder the compositions in their "correct" sequence. Fortunately, the scientific motivation displayed by him did not ignore the practical fact that during the preceding seventy-five years, Mozart's compositions had been so closely linked to their first Köchel numbers, so many had appeared in print with those numbers, musicians had them in their repertoires and with the advent of gramophone records, music lovers who played no instrument at all also recognized them under these numbers, that it was no longer possible to give new individual numbers in contradiction to those already in wide use.

Einstein changed the order in which the compositions are entered with their full details, but he retained the original K. numbers. He interposed the newly discovered and authenticated works and the fragments of compositions (previously in the annex) by adding the letters of the alphabet in lowercase after the numbers, a system already started by Waldersee. In fact, Köchel himself, as mentioned, did this with 154a, added to the notes of the first edition. But whereas Waldersee only inserted a handful of items, Einstein, in trying to create a totally reliable chronological order, shuffled everything around and created a list of numbers that at first glance is most confusing. For instance, K. 180 is now 173c, K. 183 becomes 173dB, 202 is 186b, and so on. The "new" number is based on Köchel as well, so 173c comes after 173 and is preceded by 173a (K. 205, later to become 167A!) and 173b (K. 290, later 167AB). Most confusing to anyone, I am sure.

One reason for this newly created confusion was that whereas Köchel had put all compositions of uncertain date at the end of the time-assured ones each year, marking them with a warning asterisk to draw attention to this fact, Einstein made his chronological order an unquestioned one, with no vague open-endedness. He still used Köchel's asterisks to denote uncertainty of date, but not at the end of a given year, rather at the point where he thought the composition fitted into the date sequence. By using a parallel system of original Köchel numbers (which he dared not change) and his own "correct" ones, the resulting jumble is perhaps even more confusing, particularly to the uninitiated.

When it comes to differentiating between genuine and doubtful compositions, Einstein's view was often different from that of Köchel or Waldersee, and he made numerous changes on this basis, many correctly and some, as it turned out, incorrectly. The information provided after each entry has been augmented by the newly found facts and suppositions, producing a wealth of additional material and enlarging the size of the volume by some 50 percent. (The chronological section alone has risen from 467 to 824 pages.)

Alec Hyatt King, musicologist and one of the leading Mozart experts until his death in 1994, said of Einstein's edition in his "Das neue Köchelverzeichnis":

> This was the result of seven years work during which he brought to light many lost autographs and some early copies of lost works . . . his principles of selection were rather inconsistent . . . a chronological order of impressive exactitude into which . . . he introduced nearly a hundred fragments previously relegated to the appendix. . . . The first person to dispel any illusion of finality . . . was Einstein himself. . . . He published copious additions and corrections with further notes . . . reprinted in 1947 as an appendix to the re-issue of the whole 1937 edition.

Einstein's lengthy foreword to the third edition was handed to the publishers in April 1936, but the volume appeared only a year later. This necessitated a "Supplement," to which Einstein wrote in his introductory notes, "By the time this work appeared I had collected a number of corrections and addenda which in the years that followed was further augmented through research and through the participation of friendly helpers." The supplement was not published in Germany, where the laws of the Third Reich by now forbade the very mention of the Jewish Einstein's name. It appeared in sections in the American publication *Musical Review* in 1940–1945 and in 1947 was incorporated in a new edition of the *Köchelverzeichnis* published by J. W. Edwards of Ann Arbor, Michigan. This edition, like the 1889 one, has no official number in the sequence of known editions.

Einstein was highly critical in his assessment of Köchel's work. He says:

> I can dispense with exercising comprehensive criticism of Köchel's achievement. This criticism will be found by the expert or user by comparison between the third edition and the first and second edition and he may draw his own conclusions. Köchel, to say this much, was not a sufficient musician; in organizing Mozart's works he proceeded purely from the archivist's point of view; it signifies only his honesty if he did

not touch on matters that were beyond his comprehension. . . . He always becomes uncertain when Jahn leaves him in the lurch. . . . But his
diligence, enthusiasm and idealism led him far beyond a simple compilation of the work of his predecessors. Anyone who had the opportunity to tread on his path of research knows with what care he pursued every lead . . . the incompleteness of his book is caused by the lack
of resources of his era, a period of time in which musicians' autographs
and first editions were not yet taken particularly seriously.

Here we have a mixture of praise and rebuttal, all in a somewhat
condescending fashion; Einstein recognizes that the resources available to Köchel were not the same that he was able to use, but he says
that Köchel could supplement his lack of technical knowledge only
by his "diligence and enthusiasm."

One definite advantage Einstein had over his predecessors (and,
as it turned out, over his successors as well) was that "just in time
and before it was too late it was possible, mainly through the efforts
of the custodian of the Berlin Royal Library, Franz Espagne, and the
donation of the necessary sum by the Berlin manufacturer Landsberger, to assemble the majority of those manuscripts [of Mozart's
compositions] still in the possession of [the publisher] André into
the Royal Library and to preserve them there for the benefit of the
German nation." This happened in 1873 and related to 138 manuscripts, by which the total of autographs in the library was increased
to 224 complete works apart from those of incomplete works and
sketches. The acquisition included the operas *Idomeneo* and *Cosi fan
tutte*, fifteen of the symphonies, and ten string quartets. Further and
later acquisitions by the library included *Re pastore, Seraglio*, and *Die
Zauberflöte*. To find all these manuscripts under one roof certainly
made Einstein's work that much easier.

Einstein refers to the usual "peripheral clues" in determining date
and authenticity: the type of paper and the style of handwriting. For
the latter he was aided by a 1919 book by L. F. Schiedermair, *W. A.
Mozarts Handschrift in zeitlich geordneten Nachbildungen* (W. A.
Mozart's Handwriting in Chronologically Arranged Reproduc-
tions), which illustrates the development of Mozart's handwriting
throughout his productive years with examples of each period from
1766 to 1791. Reference is also made to the lists of Mozart publications made during the composer's lifetime and published by O. E.
Deutsch and Cecil B. Oldman in London under the title *Mozart-
Drucke*.

After World War II, which led to the division of Germany, Breit-kopf & Härtel's head office building in Leipzig was taken under state control by the new East German government, and the publishing house continued functioning as a "VEB" (Volkseigener Betrieb, or people-owned concern). It produced two reprints of Einstein's third edition of 1937, without incorporating his supplementary details of the (unnumbered) American edition of 1947. These reprints were called the fourth and fifth edition, respectively, although they contained nothing new.

Meanwhile, the independent Breitkopf & Härtel management reconstituted itself in Wiesbaden, West Germany, and in 1964 published a sixth edition on the basis of revisions made by Franz Giegling, Zurich; Alexander Weinmann, Vienna; and Gerd Sievers, Wiesbaden. Further reprints led to the official seventh and eighth editions, which are identical with the sixth. Of the eight official editions, only four are truly different in substance: Köchel, Waldersee, Einstein, and Giegling/Weinmann/Sievers.

By 1964, further revisions had become necessary. The new foreword relates the sensational happenings around the appearance of the third edition under the name of the Jewish Alfred Einstein in 1937 Nazi Germany. It appears that legislators first tried to prevent publication, then to suppress any reference to the author. It required the personal intervention of the president of the Reichs Musikkammer, Dr. Peter Raabe, to ensure publication of the work, which stated the name of the revisor, but even so it was forbidden to publicize this in any way.

A decision for the new edition was made soon after the Wiesbaden company was formed. Einstein had emigrated to the United States and died there in 1952, so the firm obtained his notes, together with the right of their publication, from his widow. After several false starts, 1958 saw the final commission of the new edition.

A new scattering of autographs had taken place during and after the war, and 120 manuscripts—including such works as *Seraglio, The Marriage of Figaro* (third and fourth acts), *Die Zauberflöte*, and a number of the "mature" piano concertos—were lost from the Berlin library. More reliance had therefore to be given to "authentic" copies of these lost originals. (Fortunately, the lost manuscripts were later rediscovered in Kraków.)

The new revisers also maintained the established system of numbering and the general layout of the *Register*. By now, by also including newly found manuscripts and making the fragmentary authentic compositions part of the main register, the number of works included in this edition is 839, but the magic final number given by Köchel, "626" for the Requiem, is still the last number. This contradiction is the result of adding letters in lowercase (per Köchel, Waldersee, and Einstein) and then in capitals (sixth edition) between the numbers allotted before, thus creating some very odd-looking reference numbers. As a result, the chronological section currently runs to 743 pages, a slight reduction from the third edition, and the total book consists of well over 1,000 pages.

A new system has been applied in the appendix, but the reader will forgive me if I dispense with an explanation of the alterations made here, particularly as they relate mostly to compositions that are probably not by Mozart.The thematic order has also been somewhat revised, whether for better or worse is most subjective and will therefore not be detailed here, either.

In comparing the sixth edition with the previous ones, Hyatt King praises the new heading for "first editions," previously often concealed amidst "early editions." He also commends the inclusion of all known cadenzas written for the piano concertos and the convincing alterations made to the system of numbering vis-à-vis the Einstein (third) edition.

On the negative side, Hyatt King draws attention to the unclear references to autographs and libraries, to mistakes made with names and editions and other inconsistencies, and in particular to the compilers' apparent ignorance regarding the relocation of the famous Paul Hirsch music library, which was moved from Cambridge to the British Museum (now British Library) in 1946, a fact consistently and curiously ignored in this 1964 edition.

However, he concludes his analytical article published in *Die Musikforschung* in 1965 by saying, "It would be unfair to deny that the new edition of the *Köchelverzeichnis*, in spite of these deficiencies, is a most important work which for the next decade at least will constitute the main support for all Mozart research."

Nearly four decades later, a newly revised edition is now in preparation. The Herbert Gussman Professor of Cornell University, in Ithaca, New York, Neal Zaslaw, was commissioned with this work in 1993 by Breitkopf & Härtel. Originally it intended to publish the new edition in 2000, but it now seems that it will appear some time later. In an article recently published in *Newsletter of the*

Mozart Society of America, Neal Zaslaw explains that the new edition will be called *Der neue Köchel* (The New Köchel), to avoid adding to the chaotic state of the previous editions.

It also appears, much to my gratification, that the dual numbering system first introduced by Einstein will be dispensed with. Some sixty of the original Köchel listings will be relegated into the appendix, together with everything that seems doubtful; works that appear in the wrong place in the chronological order will have an asterisk to indicate this fact. The new *Köchelverzeichnis* will contain much that has previously been left out to conceal the divergent views of musicologists. The world of music may await its publication with justifiably excited anticipation.

In 1965, just one year after the publication of the sixth edition, Breitkopf & Härtel of Wiesbaden also published an abbreviated form of the *Köchelverzeichnis* called *Der Kleine Köchel* (The Little Köchel). This seems to have been an instant publishing success, as by 1971 seven editions had appeared! The compiler was Hellmuth von Hase. The book, in less than one hundred pages, is an excellent summary of what appeared in the sixth edition and should enable most interested readers to become acquainted with the main aspects of the *Register.*

Der Kleine Köchel's introduction gives a potted history of Mozart registers, starting with Leopold Mozart's listing of the twelve-year-old composer's works, mentioning Mozart's own register kept between 1784 and 1791, the Stadler/Nissen list of autographs in the possession of Mozart's widow, Konstanze, André's register of the manuscripts he had acquired, Aloys Fuchs's register, and Otto Jahn's book leading to Köchel's endeavor. Surprisingly, perhaps, the publishers declare that

> from the evidence in front [of us] it is not apparent whether Köchel commenced his work on his own initiative or on the behest of the publishing house. His spirit of enterprise and the role he later played as real motivator of the great critically supervised collected edition of Mozart's works let us assume that he created his famous work of his own volition and that he offered it to the publishers upon completion. Even though the first edition, for which he was responsible, is regarded as substantially incomplete when compared with today's position—Köchel linked the sourcing of Mozart's work so intensively with his name that the *Köchelverzeichnis* has come to occupy worldwide recognition which then enabled it to preserve its place within the field of Mozart research through the subsequent improved editions. . . .

   Dr. Ludwig Alois Ferdinand Ritter von Köchel was the first to solve
this comprehensive task as meritoriously as was possible on the basis
of source material and scientific perception of his time.

It thus seems that those in charge today have no idea how the project of the *Köchelverzeichnis* first came about; on the basis of the correspondence between Köchel and Hauer, I can assuredly say that
Köchel had been in constant touch with Breitkopf & Härtel and did
not approach the publisher "after" completing his work.

   There follows a paragraph or two of biographical data on Köchel,
then an account of future editions of the *Köchelverzeichnis* through
Waldersee "with no decisive alterations" because "to touch upon the
contents of the work in a fundamental way he regarded as an au-
dacity"; to Einstein's third edition, which "most decisively altered
the chronological order." Reference is also made here to the important contribution to Mozart research by the appearance of the
Wyzewa–Saint-Foix book (discussed later) and the influence this
had on Einstein.

   The aim of the condensed *Kleine Köchel* is explained like this:

> It should enable its user to establish the title of a work known to him
> by its Köchel number or to identify its Köchel number on the basis of
> the title known to him. . . . Whereas the Kleine Köchel is no substitute
> for the Köchelverzeichnis it does give details of the exact title, ensem-
> ble (for which it was written), Köchel number, year of origination (sci-
> entifically proved or assumed), special name and category number
> (e.g., "Jupiter symphony No. 41") and the opening bars of the first
> movement of those compositions where their titles and key signature
> are identical (e.g., "Symphony in G major") in a special appendix.

   The main part of the book is in two sections. The first lists in the order of Köchel numbers (1–626b) all Mozart compositions in the sequence of the sixth edition of the *Köchelverzeichnis;* this is followed by
Nos. 1 to 245 of its appendix.

   The second section gives a thematic listing of the works based on
twenty-seven sections plus one for miscellaneous compositions.
This is followed by the appendix, containing those 279 compositions
for which it was felt necessary to show the opening bars to avoid
confusion.

   In addition to the aforementioned "authorized" editions of the
Köchelverzeichnis, the total number of which is by now almost as con-

fusing as the number of Mozart compositions they contain, there is a completely separate work by Karl Franz Müller under the title *Wolfgang Amadeus Mozart: Gesamtkatalog seiner Werke, "Köchel Verzeichnis"* (Collective Catalogue of His Works), published in 1951 by Paul Kaltschmied of Vienna. In the introduction, Dr. Erik Werba says:

> To publish the register of the works of Mozart in a new order has for years been the favorite wish of the composer/musician Karl Franz Müller. . . . It is worthy of the interest of the admirers of Mozart. . . . In the circle of those who are meritorious concerning the works of Mozart we really know of no one worthier than Ritter von Köchel . . . the "K" of whose name is known by everyone who has something to do with music. . . .
>
> K. F. Müller's daring attempt to revise again what has already been revised by Waldersee and Einstein is justified as it was undertaken mainly because of the newly found Mozart works. . . . At last a register will be commercially available.

This last remark indicates that before the appearance of the sixth edition, copies of the *Köchelverzeichnis* were almost unobtainable.

In his own foreword, Müller emphasizes that "the altered numbering of the 1937 edition by Einstein has made it more difficult to locate a given work . . . I therefore decided to revert to the order of the first [1862] edition. This resulted in the necessity to create a special new group of the works newly discovered since Köchel and Waldersee and to attach this to the end of K. 626 with the new numbers 1–76. . . . This achieved a chronological sequence of the newly found works without disturbing the main part of the Köchel register."

To demonstrate the book's affinity with the "official" editions, shortened versions of the original dedication by Köchel to Jahn, Köchel's first foreword, and the Köchel biography from the second edition are included. There follow reprints of Leopold Mozart's "Verzeichnis" of the twelve-year-old Mozart's compositions and of Mozart's own register of works between 1784 and 1791, with the full text of the entries, but without the musical quotations that accompanied them.

In broad outline the book then follows the established format. The text is updated where necessary but abbreviated where considered possible, and there are no incipits of music after the entries.

Interestingly, the canons, K. 231 and K. 233, are shown here with their original vulgar texts written by Mozart himself: "Leck mich im Arsch" (Kiss My Arse) and "Leck mir den Arsch fein recht schön" (Kiss My Arse Nice and Clean), which in the first edition of the *Köchelverzeichnis* are shown with the initials of these titles, followed by the "polite" ones given by Breitkopf & Härtel: "Lasst froh uns sein" (Let Us Be Merry) and "Nichts labt mich mehr" (Nothing Nourishes Me More). Einstein had also included these vulgarities by Mozart in the third edition of the *Köchelverzeichnis*, adding the following comments: "As the *Köchelverzeichnis* is of documentary purpose we have no scruples in restoring here . . . the original words by Mozart. This coarseness is essential for the effect of these canons."

A complete and detailed analysis is provided to show how the successive editions differed from one another, and at the end there is an extra register giving the key signatures of symphonies and other works where this was thought essential for easier locational finding of a work.

In all, Müller's version is a much smaller, quite handy, inexpensive volume, but it lacks some important aspects, in particular the incipits of music.

I mentioned earlier that Müller gave the newly found works the numbers 1 through 76. It should be mentioned here that sixty-four of those compositions were listed in the sixth edition and were not included in the original *Köchelverzeichnis*, not in the main section nor in the appendix, of which twenty-three are listed as "fragments" or "sketches," doubtful, or uncompleted. Some of these are movements of planned compositions. The total of newly found complete works therefore number forty-one, of which it can be said that they were "overlooked" by Köchel.

One of the most important studies relating to Mozart's works this century comes from the French authors T. de Wyzewa and G. de Saint-Foix. Their *W.-A. Mozart* first appeared in Paris in 1912, and revised editions were published later. The book, in five volumes, is like a combination of Jahn and Köchel in relating the life and work of the composer and establishing a new classification ("nouveau classement") of Mozart's compositions. The authors' attitude to Köchel is summed up in the foreword, in which they refer to

an admirable monument of conscience and zeal published in 1862 by the Austrian "naturalist" [!] Ludwig Köchel. Piece by piece all works by Mozart are listed here together with an indication of the type of paper and format of the autographs and of the various editions thereof. But unfortunately it is sufficient for us to cast our eyes on some of those pieces not dated by the master to observe the very arbitrary fashion, nearly always mistaken, in which these are fitted into this book of Köchel's.

Such strong words entitle us to look for "perfection" in the Wyzewa–Saint-Foix classification, but having compared the listing of the original 1912 edition with that of the 1946 revised one, a large number of discrepancies is evident. Suffice it for me to say that whereas the first list ends with No. 582, the revised one includes 646 numbers, and the last number in each case refers to the Requiem, K. 626, which thus first becomes No. 582 and later No. 646. Again, I wish to emphasize that my remarks should not be misunderstood: I appreciate the significant value of the new entries in this work, but I find it wrong that the authors should expose Köchel almost as a joker, a charlatan, whereas their work was also anything but faultless.

Einstein, by the way, was almost envious of the freedom enjoyed by the Frenchmen as regards the renumbering of Mozart's compositions; he felt he was bound by the original Köchel sequence, a restriction that did not apply to these compilers. He said, "They did not shirk from the endeavor to declare war upon the old data and tried to establish almost the exact day and hour in which each work was composed. Their book is, without the wish to do so, unwittingly directed against Köchel. . . . I do not need to say how much I owe to its content, even though in decisive questions I often find myself in contradiction with their findings."

I already referred to some of the developments in the twentieth century in the Mozart research achieved by others. Some musicologists nowadays say that the *Köchelverzeichnis* has been "overtaken" by the results of this research. This is implied by Howard Chandler Robbins Landon, the well-known musicologist who specializes in Haydn and Mozart, in an article published on 9 March 1990 in the Vienna daily *Die Presse*. According to Robbins Landon, a new Mozart compendium scheduled to be published in 1990, with the participation of twenty-five noted writers on music would create a sort of substitute for the *Köchelverzeichnis* as, in many respects, it overtakes Köchel. When it actually appeared, twenty-two writers participated, among them Otto Biba, Albi Rosenthal, and Alec Hyatt King. My judgment is that the compendium is a good supplement to the KV, but in no way its substitute.

The same article also mentions the important work by Gertraut Haberkamp, *Die Erstdrucke der Werke von Wolfgang Amadeus Mozart* (First Editions of the Works of Wolfgang Amadeus Mozart), which challenges Köchel's listings of first and important editions and which, indeed, is today accepted as the benchmark regarding first editions.

Two comparatively recent scientific methods have been employed in the aid of chronology. "Schriftchronologie," pioneered by Ludwig Ferdinand Schiedermair (*W. A. Mozart's Handschrift in zeitlich geordneten Nachbildungen*, 1919) and developed by Wolfgang Plath (*Chronologie der Handschrift W. A. Mozarts*, 1962), uses the principle of the changing style of musical handwriting as its guide for placing compositions in their proper order. Second are the watermarks and paper studies carried out by Alan Tyson and published in book form in 1987 under the title *Mozart Studies of the Autograph Scores*. Tyson says:

> This book consists of articles (and, in two cases talks) on aspects of Mozart and his autographs . . . written . . . between 1975 and 1986.
>
> . . . How and where did Mozart's music paper receive its staff-ruling (Rastrierung)? Neither question can be completely answered at present . . . some of it was ruled by hand and some by machine . . . staff-ruling machines cannot have been uncommon, but it appears that we do not have a picture of one, or a detailed description of one, dating from the late 18th century.
>
> The question of "where" Mozart's music paper was ruled has also not been fully answered yet. The obvious possibilities are these: at the place where the paper was made . . . at the music shops in Vienna . . . or in Mozart's home. . . . I believe that the paper was most commonly ruled at the music shops or at any rate in Vienna (and perhaps in Salzburg).
>
> It will probably not have escaped attention that as a general rule Mozart used ten-staff paper in Salzburg and twelve-staff paper during the Vienna years. I think I have discovered an explanation for this: it appears that Mozart could not buy twelve-staff machine-ruled paper in Salzburg. . . . Occasionally he returned from a visit to Vienna or a trip to Milan with some twelve-staff paper, which he then saved for Salzburg compositions that required a lot of staves, as for example, the Regina Coeli, K. No. 108 (74d) of May 1771 which is on Viennese paper, or the Litaniae de venerabili altaris sacramento, K. No. 125 of March 1772, on paper from the second Italian journey. . . .
>
> Immediately after his return to Salzburg from his third and last Italian journey in March 1773, Mozart began regularly to use paper of a

size he had scarcely ever employed before. This is the size that Köchel calls *Klein-Querformat* (small oblong format). At least five types can be identified. . . . Mozart must have liked this small paper, for he continued to use it in the next six years. . . .

K. No. 369, a soprano aria, is on ten-staff paper and is dated "Monaco (Munich) li 8 di marzo 1781." And K. No. 371, a rondo for horn, is on paper with the same watermark, but with 12 staves; it is dated "Vienne ce 21 mars 1781," only 13 days later. Did Mozart therefore sometimes carry unruled paper around with him and have it ruled locally?

It is the assumption that as a general rule compositions on the same paper-type are likely to have been written—or at any rate to have been begun—within the same period of time.

One objection to dating scores by their paper-types will no doubt always be made: "But surely Mozart could have been using old paper?" Certainly he did so from time to time—but not, in my experience, often—and then in most cases he used only single leaves (not normally bifolia). . . .

It appears to be the case that Mozart bought paper in comparatively small quantities and used it up before buying more . . . in some instances Mozart took a long time to complete a work. . . .

I claim—on the evidence of its paper—that the Piano Sonata in B flat K. No. 333 (315c) was not written in Paris in 1778 (the traditional view, although already challenged by Plath) [the Schriftchronologie expert], but was written in or around Linz about November 1783.

Most dating involves assigning a date to a complete work, although as I have suggested, both paper-studies and "Schriftchronologie" can occasionally offer different dates for the beginning and for the end of a piece.

It will be observed that none of these experts dispute Köchel's merit in creating a fundament, a real starting point where they may commence their research. And Köchel himself, in his well-known modesty, knew and prophesied that this would happen. What is more, he welcomed it.

And so the story of Mozart registers goes on and on. The bicentenary year of 1991 saw a wealth of new Mozart books appear, including one, I am told, about his teeth and the dental work done on them! The chronological order of his compositions has been altered many times, and there is no finality in this respect. The existence of lost and uncertain compositions will also continue, as will the incidents of "new and sensational" discoveries of manuscripts, letters, and forgeries.

Of one thing, perhaps, we can be sure: As long as Mozart's music continues to be performed and long after most of the persons who criticized Köchel's modest pioneering work are totally forgotten, we can expect to hear the announcer say, "by Wolfgang Amadeus Mozart, Köchel number. . . ."

Appendix A

Chronological List of Books and Articles by Ludwig Ritter von Köchel

Verzeichnis der Kirchenkompositionen von Johann Joseph Fux welche sich im Musikarchive des Stiftes Göttweih befinden (1834) (Register of Sacred Music by J. J. Fux, Located in the Music Archive of Göttweih)

"Theodor Kotschy" (published in *Allgemeine Zeitung* 40, Augsburg, 1844)

Die Mineralien des Herzogtums Salzburg (Gerold Sohn, Vienna, 1859) (The Minerals of the Duchy of Salzburg)

Über den Umfang der musikalischen Produktivität Wolfgang Amadé Mozarts (Salzburg, 1862) (Regarding the Scope of the Musical Output by W. A. Mozart)

Chronologisch-thematisches Verzeichniss sämmtlicher Tonwerke Wolfgang Amadé Mozarts (Breitkopf & Härtel, Leipzig, 1862) (Chronological and Thematic Register of All Compositions by W. A. Mozart)

"*Nachträge*" (published in *Allgemeine Musik Zeitung*, 1864) (Supplements). This incorporates some corrections to the Register.

"Mozarts *Requiem*" (in *Recensionen und Mitteilungen über Theater und Musik*, Vienna, 1864)

Drei und achtzig neu aufgefundene Original Briefe Ludwig van Beethovens an den Erzherzog Rudolf (Beck & Hölder, Vienna, 1865) (Eighty-three Newly Discovered Letters by L. v. Beethoven to Archduke Rudolf)

Die literarische Tätigkeit des Carl Ehrenbrecht Freiherrn von Moll (1865) (The Literary Activity of C. E. Baron von Moll)

Die Pflege der Musik am österreichischen Hofe vom Schlusse des XV. bis zur Mitte des XVIII. Jahrhunderts (privately published, 1866) (The Practice of Music at the Austrian Court from the End of the Fifteenth to the Middle of the Eighteenth Century)

Die meteorologischen Verhältnisse des Landes mit der Flora des Herzogtums (Society for Geography, Salzburg, 1866 and 1868) (The Meteorological Influences of the Land on the Flora of the Duchy)

"Nachruf an J. Freiherrn von Spaun" (privately published, Vienna, 1866) (Obituary of Baron J. von Spaun)

"Vier Briefe Beethovens an den Grafen Brunswick" (published in *Musik und Bildende Kunst* XIII, No. 34, Vienna, 1867) (Four Letters by Beethoven to Count Brunswick)

Thematisches Verzeichnis der im Stifte Kremsmünster vorhandenen Compositionen von Johann Joseph Fux (1867) (Thematic Register of the Compositions by J. J. Fux in Stift Kremsmünster)

"Zur Biographie Wolfgang Amadé Mozarts" (published in *Jahrbuch für Landeskunde von Niederösterreich*, 1868) (To the Biography of W. A. Mozart)

Die Kaiserliche Hofmusikkapelle in Wien von 1543–1867 (Becksche Universitätsbuchhandlung, Vienna, 1869) (The Imperial Court Orchestra in Vienna)

Umrisse des Lebens und Wirkens des Dr August Neilreich (k.k. Zoological and Botanical Society, Vienna, 1871) (Outlines of the Life and Work of Dr. A. Neilreich)

Gedichte (privately published, 1872) (Poems)

Johann Joseph Fux, Hofcompositor und Hofkapellmeister der Kaiser Leopold I., Joseph I. und Karl VI. von 1689–1740 (Hölder, 1872 or 1873) (J. J. Fux, Court Composer and Conductor of Emperors Leopold I, Joseph I, and Karl VI)

Appendix B

Mozart's Compositions as First Published in Köchel's *Register* in 1862

K. 1	Minuet and Trio for Piano (in G)
K. 2	Minuet for Piano (in F)
K. 3	Allegro for Piano (in B flat)
K. 4	Minuet for Piano (in F)
K. 5	Minuet for Piano (in F)
K. 6	Sonata for Piano and Violin (in C)
K. 7	Sonata for Piano and Violin (in D)
K. 8	Sonata for Piano and Violin (in B flat)
K. 9	Sonata for Piano and Violin (in G)
K. 10	Sonata for Piano and Violin (in B flat)
K. 11	Sonata for Piano and Violin (in G)
K. 12	Sonata for Piano and Violin (in A)
K. 13	Sonata for Piano and Violin (in F)
K. 14	Sonata for Piano and Violin (in C)
K. 15	Sonata for Piano and Violin (in B flat)
K. 16	Symphony (in E flat)
K. 17	Symphony (in B flat)
K. 18	Symphony (in E flat)
K. 19	Symphony (in D)
K. 20	Madrigal "God Is Our Refuge"
K. 21	Aria for Tenor "Va, dal furor portata"
K. 22	Symphony (in B flat)
K. 23	Aria for Soprano "Conservati fedele"
K. 24	Eight Variations on an Allegretto for Piano (in G)
K. 25	Seven Variations on "Willem van Nassau" for Piano (in D)
K. 26	Sonata for Piano and Violin (in E flat)
K. 27	Sonata for Piano and Violin (in G)
K. 28	Sonata for Piano and Violin (in C)

K. 29 Sonata for Piano and Violin (in D)
K. 30 Sonata for Piano and Violin (in F)
K. 31 Sonata for Piano and Violin (in B flat)
K. 32 Galimathias musicum (for Strings and Wind instruments)
K. 33 Kyrie (in F)
K. 34 Offertorium pro Festo Sti. Benedicti "Scande coeli limina"
K. 35 Die Schuldigkeit des ersten Gebothes (Geistliches Singspiel)
K. 36 Recitative and Aria for Tenor "Orchè il dover" "Tali e cotanti sono"
K. 37 Concerto for Piano (in F)
K. 38 Apollo et Hyacinthus (Latin comedy)
K. 39 Concerto for Piano (in B flat)
K. 40 Concerto for Piano (in D)
K. 41 Concerto for Piano (in G)
K. 42 Grabmusik (Passions-Cantata)
K. 43 Symphony (in F)
K. 44 Motet "Ex adipe frumenti"
K. 45 Symphony (in D)
K. 46 Quintet
K. 47 Offertorium "Veni Sancte Spiritus" (for Four Voices and Instruments)
K. 48 Symphony (in D)
K. 49 Missa brevis (in G)
K. 50 *Bastien et Bastienne,* Deutsche Operette
K. 51 *La Finta semplice,* opera buffa
K. 52 Song "Daphne, deine Rosenwangen"
K. 53 Song "Freude, Königin der Weisen"
K. 54 Six Variations for Piano on an Allegretto (in F)
K. 55 Sonata for Piano and Violin (in F)
K. 56 Sonata for Piano and Violin (in C)
K. 57 Sonata for Piano and Violin (in F)
K. 58 Sonata for Piano and Violin (in E flat)
K. 59 Sonata for Piano and Violin (in C minor)
K. 60 Sonata for Piano and Violin (in E minor)
K. 61 Sonata for Piano and Violin (in A)
K. 62 Cassation (in D)
K. 63 Cassation (in G)
K. 64 Minuet (in D)
K. 65 Missa brevis (in D minor)
K. 66 Missa ("Dominicus") (in C)
K. 67 Sonata (in E flat)
K. 68 Sonata (in B flat)
K. 69 Sonata (in D)

K. 70	Licenza, Recitative, and Aria for Soprano "A Berenice" "Sol nascente"
K. 71	Aria for Tenor "Ah, piú tremar non voglio"
K. 72	Offertorium pro Festo Sti. Joannis Baptistae
K. 73	Symphony (in C)
K. 74	Symphony (in G)
K. 75	Symphony (in F)
K. 76	Symphony (in F)
K. 77	Recitative and Aria for Soprano "Misero me" "Misero pargoletto"
K. 78	Aria for Soprano "Per pietà, bell'idol mio"
K. 79	Aria for Soprano "O temerario Arbace"
K. 80	Quartet (for Strings, in G)
K. 81	Symphony (in D)
K. 82	Aria for Soprano "Se ardire esperanza"
K. 83	Aria for Soprano "Se tutti i mali miei"
K. 84	Symphony (in D)
K. 85	Miserere
K. 86	Antiphon "Quaerite primum regnum Dei"
K. 87	*Mitridate, Rè di Ponto*, opera
K. 88	Aria for Soprano "Fra cento affanni"
K. 89	Kyrie for Five Sopranos
K. 90	Kyrie (in D minor)
K. 91	Kyrie (in D)
K. 92	Salve Regina
K. 93	Psalm "De profundis clamavi"
K. 94	Minuet for Piano (in D)
K. 95	Symphony (in D)
K. 96	Symphony (in C)
K. 97	Symphony (in D)
K. 98	Symphony (in F)
K. 99	Cassation (in B flat)
K. 100	Serenade (in D)
K. 101	Serenade (in F)
K. 102	(Final?) Movement of a Symphony (in C)
K. 103	Nineteen Minuets with and without Trio
K. 104	Six Minuets with Trio
K. 105	Six Minuets with Trio
K. 106	Three Contradanses
K. 107	Three Sonatas after J. S. Bach arranged as Concertos by Mozart
K. 108	Regina Coeli
K. 109	Litaniae de B.M.V. (Lauretanae)
K. 110	Symphony (in G)
K. 111	"Ascanio in Alba," theatrical serenade

K. 112	Symphony (in F)
K. 113	Divertimento (in F)
K. 114	Symphony (in A)
K. 115	Missa brevis (in C)
K. 116	Missa brevis (in F)
K. 117	Offertorium "Benedictus sit Deus" "Introibo" "Jubilate"
K. 118	"La Betulia liberata," oratorio
K. 119	Aria for Soprano "Der Liebe himmlisches Gefühl"
K. 120	Finale of a Symphony (in D)
K. 121	Last Allegro of a Symphony (in D)
K. 122	Minuet (in E flat)
K. 123	Contredanse for Orchestra (in B flat)
K. 124	Symphony (in G)
K. 125	Litaniae de venerabili
K. 126	"Il sogno di Scipione," dramatic serenade
K. 127	Regina Coeli (in B flat)
K. 128	Symphony (in C)
K. 129	Symphony (in G)
K. 130	Symphony (in F)
K. 131	Divertimento (in D)
K. 132	Symphony (in E flat)
K. 133	Symphony (in D)
K. 134	Symphony (in A)
K. 135	"Lucio Silla," dramma per musica
K. 136	Divertimento (in D)
K. 137	Divertimento (in B flat)
K. 138	Divertimento (in F)
K. 139	Missa (in C minor)
K. 140	Missa brevis
K. 141	Te Deum
K. 142	Tantum ergo
K. 143	Aria for Soprano "Ergo interest an quis" "Quaere superna"
K. 144	Sonata (in D)
K. 145	Sonata (in F)
K. 146	Aria for Soprano "Kommet her ihr frechen Sünder"
K. 147	Song "Wie unglücklich bin ich nicht"
K. 148	Song "O heiliges Band"
K. 149	Song "Ich hab es längst gesagt"
K. 150	Song "Was ich in Gedanken"
K. 151	Song "Ich trachte nicht nach solchen Dingen"
K. 152	Canzonetta "Ridente la calma"
K. 153	Fugue for Piano (in E flat)
K. 154	Fugue for Piano (in G minor)

K. 155	Quartet (for Strings, in D)
K. 156	Quartet (for Strings, in G)
K. 157	Quartet (for Strings, in C)
K. 158	Quartet (for Strings, in F)
K. 159	Quartet (for Strings, in B flat)
K. 160	Quartet (for Strings, in E flat)
K. 161	Symphony (in D)
K. 162	Symphony (in C)
K. 163	Final Movement of Symphony (in D, K. 161)
K. 164	Six Minuets with Trio
K. 165	Motet for Soprano "Exsultate, jubilate"
K. 166	Divertimento (in E flat)
K. 167	Missa ("Trinitatis")
K. 168	Quartet (for Strings, in F)
K. 169	Quartet (for Strings, in A)
K. 170	Quartet (for Strings, in C)
K. 171	Quartet (for Strings, in E flat)
K. 172	Quartet (for Strings, in B flat)
K. 173	Quartet (for Strings, in D minor)
K. 174	Quintet (for Strings, in B flat)
K. 175	Concerto for Piano (in D)
K. 176	Sixteen Minuets with Trio
K. 177	Offertorium sub exposito venerabili
K. 178	Aria for Soprano "Ah, spiegarti, o Dio"
K. 179	Twelve Variations for Piano (in C)
K. 180	Six Variations for Piano (in G)
K. 181	Symphony (in D)
K. 182	Symphony (in B flat)
K. 183	Symphony (in G minor)
K. 184	Symphony (in E flat)
K. 185	Serenade (in D)
K. 186	Divertimento (in B flat)
K. 187	Ten Pieces (for Winds and Timpani, in C)
K. 188	Divertimento (in C)
K. 189	March (in D)
K. 190	Concertone for Two Violins (in C)
K. 191	Concerto for Bassoon
K. 192	Missa brevis (in F)
K. 193	"Dixit" et "Magnificat"
K. 194	Missa brevis (in D)
K. 195	Litaniae Lauretanae
K. 196	*La Finta giardiniera,* opera buffa
K. 197	Tantum ergo

K. 198	Offertorium "Sub tuum praesidium"
K. 199	Symphony (in G)
K. 200	Symphony (in C)
K. 201	Symphony (in A)
K. 202	Symphony (in D)
K. 203	Serenade (in D)
K. 204	Serenade (in D)
K. 205	Divertimento (in D)
K. 206	March
K. 207	Concerto for Violin (in B flat)
K. 208	"Il Rè pastore," dramatic cantata
K. 209	Aria for Tenor "Si mostra la sorte"
K. 210	Aria for Tenor "Con ossequio, con rispetto"
K. 211	Concerto for Violin (in D)
K. 212	Sonata (in B flat)
K. 213	Divertimento (in F)
K. 214	March (in C)
K. 215	March (in D)
K. 216	Concerto for Violin (in G)
K. 217	Aria for Soprano "Voi avete un cor fedele"
K. 218	Concerto for Violin (in D)
K. 219	Concerto for Violin (in A)
K. 220	Missa brevis (in C)
K. 221	Kyrie (in C)
K. 222	Offertorium de Tempore "Misericordias Domini" (in D minor)
K. 223	Osanna (in C)
K. 224	Sonata (in F)
K. 225	Sonata (in A)
K. 226	Canon "O Schwestern traut dem Amor nicht"
K. 227	Canon "O wunderschön ist Gottes Erde"
K. 228	Canon "Ach zu kurz ist unsers Lebens Lauf"
K. 229	Canon "Sie ist dahin"
K. 230	Canon "Selig, selig alle"
K. 231	Canon "Lasst froh uns sein" ("L.m.i.A.")
K. 232	Canon "Wer nicht liebt Wein und Weiber" ("Lieber Freistädtler")
K. 233	Canon "Nichts labt uns mehr" ("L.m.d.a.r.s.")
K. 234	Canon "Essen, Trinken, das erhält" ("Bei der Hitz im Sommer ess ich")
K. 235	Canon for Piano
K. 236	Andantino for Piano
K. 237	March (in D)
K. 238	Concerto for Piano (in B flat)
K. 239	Serenade (in D)

K. 240   Divertimento (in B flat)
K. 241   Sonata (in G)
K. 242   Concerto for Three Pianos
K. 243   Litania de Venerabili
K. 244   Sonata (in F)
K. 245   Sonata (in D)
K. 246   Concerto for Piano (in C) (Lützow)
K. 247   Divertimento (in F)
K. 248   March (in F)
K. 249   March (in D, Haffner)
K. 250   Serenade (in D, Haffner)
K. 251   Divertimento (in D)
K. 252   Divertimento (in E flat)
K. 253   Divertimento (in F)
K. 254   Trio for Piano, Violin, and Violoncello (in B flat)
K. 255   Recitative and Aria for Alto "Ombra felice," "Io ti lascio quest' ad-dio"
K. 256   Aria for Tenor "Clarice, cara mia sposa"
K. 257   Missa (Credo Mass, in C)
K. 258   Missa brevis ("Spatzen" Mass, in C)
K. 259   Missa brevis ("Orgelsolo," in C)
K. 260   Offertorium "Venite populi, venite"
K. 261   Adagio (in E, probably for the Violin Concerto K. 219)
K. 262   Missa (in C)
K. 263   Sonata (in C)
K. 264   Nine Variations for Piano "Lison dormait"
K. 265   Twelve Variations for Piano "Ah, vous dirai-je, Maman"
K. 266   Trio for Two Violins and Bass (in B flat)
K. 267   Four Contredanses
K. 268   Concerto for Violin (in E flat)
K. 269   Rondo concertante for Violin (and Orchestra, in B flat)
K. 270   Divertimento (in B flat)
K. 271   Concerto for Piano (in E flat)
K. 272   Recitative and Aria for Soprano "Ah, lo previdi" "Ah, t'invola agli occhi miei"
K. 273   Gradual "Sancta Maria, mater Dei"
K. 274   Sonata (in G)
K. 275   Missa brevis (in B flat)
K. 276   Regina Coeli
K. 277   Offertorium "Alma Dei Creatoris" (in F)
K. 278   Sonata (in C)
K. 279   Sonata for Piano (in C)
K. 280   Sonata for Piano (in F)

K. 281   Sonata for Piano (in B flat)
K. 282   Sonata for Piano (in E flat)
K. 283   Sonata for Piano (in G)
K. 284   Sonata for Piano (in D)
K. 285   Quartet for Flute, Violin, Viola, and Violoncello (in D)
K. 286   Notturno for Four Orchestras (in D)
K. 287   Divertimento (in B flat)
K. 288   Divertimento (in F)
K. 289   Divertimento (in E flat)
K. 290   March (in D)
K. 291   Introduction and Fugue
K. 292   Sonata for Bassoon and Violoncello
K. 293   Concerto for Oboe (in F)
K. 294   Recitative and Aria for Soprano "Alcandro, lo confesso" "Non sò dondo viene"
K. 295   Aria for Tenor "Se al labbro mio non credi" "Il cor dolente"
K. 296   Sonata for Piano and Violin (in C)
K. 297   Symphony (Paris, in D)
K. 298   Quartet for Flute, Violin, Viola, and Violoncello (in A)
K. 299   Concerto for Flute and Harp (in C)
K. 300   Gavotte (in B flat)
K. 301   Sonata for Piano and Violin (in G)
K. 302   Sonata for Piano and Violin (in E flat)
K. 303   Sonata for Piano and Violin (in C)
K. 304   Sonata for Piano and Violin (in E minor)
K. 305   Sonata for Piano and Violin (in A)
K. 306   Sonata for Piano and Violin (in D)
K. 307   Song "Oiseaux, si tous les ans"
K. 308   Song "Dans un bois solitaire"
K. 309   Sonata for Piano (in D)
K. 310   Sonata for Piano (in A minor)
K. 311   Sonata for Piano (in D)
K. 312   Allegro of a Piano Sonata (in G minor)
K. 313   Concerto for Flute (in G)
K. 314   Concerto for Flute
K. 315   Andante for Flute (in C)
K. 316   Recitative and Aria for Soprano "Popoli di Tessaglia" "Io non chiedo, eterni"
K. 317   Missa (Coronation, in C)
K. 318   Symphony (Overture, in G)
K. 319   Symphony (in B flat)
K. 320   Serenade (in D)
K. 321   Vesperae de Dominica

K. 322   Kyrie (in E flat)
K. 323   Kyrie (in C)
K. 324   Hymn "Salus infirmorum"
K. 325   Hymn "Sancta Maria ora pro nobis"
K. 326   Hymn "Justum deduxit Dominus"
K. 327   Hymn "Adoramus te"
K. 328   Sonata (in C)
K. 329   Sonata (in C)
K. 330   Sonata for Piano (in C)
K. 331   Sonata for Piano (in A)
K. 332   Sonata for Piano (in F)
K. 333   Sonata for Piano (in B flat)
K. 334   Divertimento (in D)
K. 335   Two Marches (in D)
K. 336   Sonata (in C)
K. 337   Missa solemnis (in C)
K. 338   Symphony (in C)
K. 339   Vesperae solennes de Confessore
K. 340   Kyrie
K. 341   Kyrie (in D minor)
K. 342   Offertorium "Benedicite Angeli"
K. 343   Two German Church Songs
K. 344   *Zaide,* opera
K. 345   Choruses and Music to "Thamos König in Aegypten"
K. 346   Terzetto "Luci care, luci belle"
K. 347   Canon "Lasst uns ziehn"
K. 348   Canon "V'amo di core teneramente"
K. 349   Song "Was frag ich viel nach Geld und Gut"
K. 350   Song (Wiegenlied) "Schlafe mein Prinzchen, nur ein"
K. 351   Song "Komm, liebe Zither"
K. 352   Eight Variations for Piano
K. 353   Twelve Variations for Piano on "La belle Françoise"
K. 354   Twelve Variations for Piano on "Je suis Lindor"
K. 355   Minuet for Piano
K. 356   Adagio for Harmonica
K. 357   Piano Sonata for Four Hands (in G)
K. 358   Piano Sonata for Four Hands (in B flat)
K. 359   Twelve Variations for Piano and Violin "La Bergère Silimène"
K. 360   Six Variations for Piano and Violin "Hélas, j'ai perdu mon amant"
K. 361   Serenade (for Winds, in B flat)
K. 362   March
K. 363   Three Minuets
K. 364   Sinfonia concertante for Violin and Viola (in E flat)

K. 365   Concerto for Two Pianos (in E flat)
K. 366   *Idomeneo, Rè di Creta,* opera seria
K. 367   Ballet Music to "Idomeneo"
K. 368   Recitative and Aria for Soprano "Ma, che vi fece, o stelle" "Sperai vicino il lido"
K. 369   Scena and Aria for Soprano "Misera, dove son?" "Ah non so io, che parlo"
K. 370   Quartet for Oboe, Violin, Viola, and Violoncello (in F)
K. 371   Concert-Rondo for Horn (in E flat)
K. 372   Allegro of a Sonata for Piano and Violin (in B flat)
K. 373   Rondo for Violin (in C)
K. 374   Recitative and Aria for Soprano "A questo seno deh vieni" "Orchè il cielo a me ti rende"
K. 375   Serenade (for Winds, in E flat)
K. 376   Sonata for Piano and Violin (in F)
K. 377   Sonata for Piano and Violin (in F)
K. 378   Sonata for Piano and Violin (in B flat)
K. 379   Sonata for Piano and Violin (in G)
K. 380   Sonata for Piano and Violin (in E flat)
K. 381   Piano Sonata for four hands (in D)
K. 382   Concert-Rondo for Piano (in D)
K. 383   Aria for Soprano "Nehmt meinen Dank, ihr holden Gönner"
K. 384   *"Die Entführung aus dem Serail,"* Komisches Singspiel
K. 385   Symphony (Haffner, in D)
K. 386   Concert-Rondo for Piano (in A)
K. 387   Quartet (for Strings, in G)
K. 388   Serenade for Winds (in C minor)
K. 389   Duet for Two Tenors "Welch angstliches Beben"
K. 390   Song "Ich würd' auf meinem Pfad"
K. 391   Song "Sei du mein Trost"
K. 392   Song "Verdankt sei es dem Glanz"
K. 393   Solfeggi for Voice
K. 394   Fantasia and Fugue for Piano (in C)
K. 395   Little Fantasia for Piano (in C)
K. 396   Fantasia for Piano (in C minor)
K. 397   Fantasia for Piano (in D minor)
K. 398   Five Variations for Piano "Salve tu Domine"
K. 399   Suite for Piano (in C)
K. 400   First Movement of a Sonata for Piano (in B flat)
K. 401   Fugue for Piano for Four or Two Hands (in G minor)
K. 402   Sonata for Piano and Violin
K. 403   Sonata for Piano and Violin (in C)
K. 404   Andante and Allegretto for Piano and Violin (in C)

K. 405   Five Fugues by J. S. Bach arranged for String Quartet
K. 406   Quintet (for Strings, in C minor)
K. 407   Quintet for Horn and Strings (in E flat)
K. 408   Three Marches
K. 409   Minuet to a Symphony (in C)
K. 410   Little Adagio for Two Basset Horns and Bassoon
K. 411   Adagio for Two Clarinets and Three Basset Horns
K. 412   Concerto for Horn (in D)
K. 413   Concerto for Piano (in F)
K. 414   Concerto for Piano (in A)
K. 415   Concerto for Piano (in C)
K. 416   Scena and Aria for Soprano "Mia speranza adorata" "Ah non sai, qual pena"
K. 417   Concerto for Horn (in E flat)
K. 418   Aria for Soprano "Vorrei spiegarvi oh Dio" "Ahi Conte, partite"
K. 419   Aria for Soprano "Nò, nò, che non sei capace"
K. 420   Aria for Tenor "Per pietà, non ricercate"
K. 421   Quartet (for Strings, in D minor)
K. 422   *L'Oca del Cairo,* opera buffa
K. 423   Duo for Violin and Viola (in G)
K. 424   Duo for Violin and Viola (in B flat)
K. 425   Symphony (Linz, in C)
K. 426   Fugue for Two Pianos (in C minor)
K. 427   Missa (in C minor)
K. 428   Quartet (for Strings, in E flat)
K. 429   Cantata "Dir, Seele des Weltalls, o Sonne"
K. 430   *Lo Sposo deluso,* opera buffa
K. 431   Recitative and Aria for Tenor "Misero! o sogno!" "Aura, che intorno"
K. 432   Recitative and Aria for Bass "Cosi dunque tradisci" "Aspri rimorsi atroci"
K. 433   Aria for Bass "Männer suchen stets zu naschen"
K. 434   Terzetto "Del gran regno delle Amazoni"
K. 435   Aria for Tenor "Müsst ich auch durch tausend"
K. 436   Terzetto for Two Sopranos and Bass "Ecco quel fiero istante"
K. 437   Terzetto for Two Sopranos and Bass "Mi lagnerò tacendo"
K. 438   Terzetto for Three Voices "Se lontan ben tu sei"
K. 439   Terzetto for Two Sopranos and Bass "Due pupille amabili"
K. 440   Aria for Soprano "In te spero, o sposo"
K. 441   Terzetto "Liebes Mandl, wo is's Bandel?"
K. 442   Trio for Piano, Violin, and Violoncello (in D minor)
K. 443   Fugue (for Three Instruments)
K. 444   Symphony (in G)

K. 445   March (in D)
K. 446   Music for a Pantomime
K. 447   Concerto for Horn (in E flat)
K. 448   Sonata for Two Pianos (in D)
K. 449   Concerto for Piano (in E flat)
K. 450   Concerto for Piano (in B flat)
K. 451   Concerto for Piano (in D)
K. 452   Quintet for Piano and Winds
K. 453   Concerto for Piano (in G)
K. 454   Sonata for Piano and Violin (in B flat)
K. 455   Ten Variations for Piano "Unser dummer Pöbel meint"
K. 456   Concerto for Piano (in B flat)
K. 457   Sonata for Piano (in C minor)
K. 458   Quartet (for Strings, in B flat)
K. 459   Concerto for Piano (in F)
K. 460   Eight Variations for Piano "Come un agnello"
K. 461   Five Minuets
K. 462   Six Contredanses
K. 463   Two Quadrilles
K. 464   Quartet (for Strings, in A)
K. 465   Quartet (for Strings, in C)
K. 466   Concerto for Piano (in D Minor)
K. 467   Concerto for Piano (in C)
K. 468   Freemason-Song "Die ihr einem neuen Grade"
K. 469   "Davidde penitente," Cantata
K. 470   Andante to a Violin Concerto
K. 471   Cantata "Die Maurerfreude"
K. 472   Song "Ihr Mädchen, flieht Damöten ja"
K. 473   Song "Wie sanft, wie ruhig fühl' ich hier"
K. 474   Song "Der reiche Thor, mit Gold geschmücket"
K. 475   Fantasia for Piano (in C minor)
K. 476   Song "Ein Veilchen auf der Wiese stand"
K. 477   Maurerische Trauermusik
K. 478   Quartet for Piano and Strings (in G minor)
K. 479   Quartet "Dite almeno, in che mancai"
K. 480   Terzetto "Mandina amabile"
K. 481   Sonata for Piano and Violin (in E flat)
K. 482   Concerto for Piano (in E flat)
K. 483   Song with Chorus "Zerfliesset heut, geliebte Brüder"
K. 484   Chorus "Ihr unsre neuen Leiter"
K. 485   Rondo for Piano (in D)
K. 486   "Der Schauspieldirektor," comedy with music
K. 487   Duo for Two Violins

K. 488 Concerto for Piano (in A)
K. 489 Duet for Soprano and Tenor "Spiegarti oh Dio non posso"
K. 490 Scena and Rondo for Soprano "Non piu, tutto ascoltai" "Non temer amato bene"
K. 491 Concerto for Piano (in C minor)
K. 492 *Le Nozze di Figaro,* opera buffa
K. 493 Quartet for Piano and Strings (in E flat)
K. 494 Little Rondo for Piano (in F)
K. 495 Concerto for Horn (in E flat)
K. 496 Trio for Piano, Violin, and Violoncello (in G)
K. 497 Piano Sonata for Four Hands (in F)
K. 498 Trio for Piano, Clarinet, and Viola (in E flat)
K. 499 Quartet (for Strings, in D)
K. 500 Twelve Variations for Piano (in B flat)
K. 501 Andante with Five Variations for Piano Duet (in G)
K. 502 Trio for Piano, Violin, and Violoncello (in B flat)
K. 503 Concerto for Piano (in C)
K. 504 Symphony (Prague, in D)
K. 505 Scena and Rondo for Soprano "Ch'io mi scordi di te" "Non temer, amato bene"
K. 506 Song "Wer unter eines Mädchens Hand"
K. 507 Canon "Heiterkeit und leichtes Blut"
K. 508 Canon "Auf das Wohl aller Freunde"
K. 509 Six German dances
K. 510 Nine Contredanses with Trio
K. 511 Rondo for Piano (in A minor)
K. 512 Recitative and Aria for Bass "Alcandro, lo confesso" "Non so, d'onde viene"
K. 513 Aria for Bass "Mentre ti lascio, o figlia"
K. 514 Rondo for Horn
K. 515 Quintet (for Strings, in C)
K. 516 Quintet (for Strings, in G)
K. 517 Song "Zu meiner Zeit"
K. 518 Song "Sobald Damoetas Chloen sieht"
K. 519 Song "Die Engel Gottes weinen"
K. 520 Song "Erzeugt von heisser Phantasie"
K. 521 Piano Sonata for four hands (in C)
K. 522 "Ein musicalischer Spass" (for 6 instruments)
K. 523 Song "Abend ist's"
K. 524 Song "Wenn die Lieb aus deinen"
K. 525 "Eine kleine Nachtmusik" (in G)
K. 526 Sonata for Piano and Violin (in A)
K. 527 *Don Giovanni,* opera buffa

K. 528   Scena for Soprano "Bella mia flamma" "Resta, o cara"
K. 529   Song "Es war einmal, ihr Leute"
K. 530   Song "Wo bist du, Bild"
K. 531   Song "Was spinnst du, fragte"
K. 532   Terzetto "Grazie agl'inganni tuoi"
K. 533   Allegro and Andante for Piano (in F)
K. 534   Contredanse ("Das Donnerwetter")
K. 535   Contredanse ("Die Bataille")
K. 536   Six German Dances
K. 537   Concerto for Piano (Coronation, in D)
K. 538   Aria for Soprano "Ah se in ciel, benigne Stelle"
K. 539   Song "Ich möchte wohl der Kaiser sein"
K. 540   Adagio for Piano (in B minor)
K. 541   Arietta for Bass "Un bacio di mano"
K. 542   Trio for Piano, Violin, and Violoncello (in E)
K. 543   Symphony (in E flat)
K. 544   Ein kleiner Marsch (in D)
K. 545   Sonata for Piano (in C)
K. 546   Adagio and Fugue (for Strings, in C minor)
K. 547   Sonata for Piano and Violin (in F)
K. 548   Trio for Piano, Violin, and Violoncello (in C)
K. 549   Canzonetta for Two Sopranos and Bass "Più non si trovano"
K. 550   Symphony (in G minor)
K. 551   Symphony (now known as the "Jupiter," in C)
K. 552   Song "Beim Auszug in das Feld"
K. 553   Canon "Allelujah"
K. 554   Canon "Ave Maria"
K. 555   Canon "Lacrimoso son io"
K. 556   Canon "G'rechtelt's eng"
K. 557   Canon "Nascoso"
K. 558   Canon "Gehn ma in 'n Prada, gehn 'ma in d'Hötz"
K. 559   Canon "Difficile lectu mihi Mars"
K. 560   Canon "O du eselhafter Martin"
K. 561   Canon "Bona nox, bist a rechta Ox"
K. 562   Canon "Caro, bell'idol mio"
K. 563   Divertimento (for String Trio, in E flat)
K. 564   Trio for Piano, Violin, and Violoncello (in G)
K. 565   Two Contredanses
K. 566   Instrumentation of Handel's "Acis und Galathea"
K. 567   Six German Dances
K. 568   Twelve Minuets
K. 569   Aria "Ohne Zwang, aus eignem Triebe"
K. 570   Sonata for Piano (in B flat)

K. 571	Six German Dances
K. 572	Instrumentation of Handel's "Messiah"
K. 573	Nine Variations for Piano (in D)
K. 574	Little Gigue for Piano (in G)
K. 575	Quartet for Strings (in D)
K. 576	Sonata for Piano (in D)
K. 577	Rondo for Soprano "Al desio, di chi t'adora"
K. 578	Aria for Soprano "Alma grande, e nobil core"
K. 579	Aria for Soprano "Un moto di gioia mi sento"
K. 580	Aria for Soprano "Schon lacht der holde Frühling"
K. 581	Quintet for Clarinet and Strings (in A)
K. 582	Aria for Soprano "Chi sà, chi sà, qual sia"
K. 583	Aria for Soprano "Vado, ma dove?—oh Dio!"
K. 584	Aria for Bass "Rivolgete a lui lo sguardo"
K. 585	Twelve Minuets
K. 586	Twelve German Dances
K. 587	Contredanse
K. 588	*Cosi fan tutte,* opera buffa
K. 589	Quartet (for Strings, in B flat)
K. 590	Quartet (for Strings, in F)
K. 591	Instrumentation of Händel's "Alexander's Feast"
K. 592	Instrumentation of Händel's "Ode to Saint Cecilia"
K. 593	Quintet (for Strings, in D)
K. 594	Adagio and Allegro (for a Mechanical Organ, in F)
K. 595	Concerto for Piano (in B)
K. 596	Song "Komm, lieber Mai"
K. 597	Song "Erwacht zu neuem Leben"
K. 598	Song "Wir Kinder, wir schmecken"
K. 599	Six Minuets
K. 600	Six German dances
K. 601	Four Minuets
K. 602	Four German (dances)
K. 603	Two Contredanses
K. 604	Two Minuets
K. 605	Three German (dances)
K. 606	Six "Ländler" for Orchestra
K. 607	Contredanse
K. 608	Fantasia (for a Mechanical Organ, in F minor)
K. 609	Five Contredanses
K. 610	Contredanse
K. 611	A German (dance)
K. 612	Aria for Bass "Per questa bella mano"
K. 613	Eight Variations for Piano "Ein Weib ist das herrlichste Ding"

K. 614   Quintet (for Strings, in E flat)
K. 615   Chorus "Viviamo felici in dolce contento"
K. 616   Andante (for a Small Mechanical Organ, in F)
K. 617   Adagio and Rondo (for Harmonica, Flute, Oboe, Viola, and Violoncello)
K. 618   Motet "Ave verum corpus"
K. 619   Cantata "Die ihr des Unermesslichen"
K. 620   *Die Zauberflöte*, German opera
K. 621   *La Clemenza di Tito*, opera seria
K. 622   Concerto for Clarinet (in A)
K. 623   Freemason-Cantata "Laut verkünde unsre Freude"
K. 624   Cadenzas to His Piano Concertos
K. 625   Comical Duet "Nun liebes Weibchen, zieh"
K. 626   Requiem

Bibliography

Anderson, Emily, ed. and trans. *The Letters of Beethoven.* 1961.

André, J. A. W. A. *Mozart's Thematischer Katalog.* 1828.

Angermüller, C. *Bürgerliche Musikkultur im 19. Jahrhundert.* 1981.

Bach, Maximilian. *Geschichte der Wiener Revolution im Jahre 1848.* 1898.

Bahr, Hermann. *Österreichischer Genius.* 1947.

Beer, Adolf. *Die Finanzen Österreich's im XIX. Jahrhundert.* 1877.

Behrman, Georg. *Matthias Claudius' Werke.* 1908.

———. *Matthias Claudius' Werke, chronologisch geordnet.* 1907.

Benedikt, Heinrich. *Die wirtschaftliche Entwicklung in der Franz Joseph Zeit.* 1958.

Berger, Ruth. "Köchel Listing" (in *Opera News*). 1956.

Bergmann, J. *Medaillen auf berühmte und ausgezeichnete Männer des österreichischen Kaiserstaates, vom XVI. bis zum XIX. Jahrhundert.* 1844.

———. *Erzherzog Friedrich von Österreich.* 1857.

Biba, Otto. "Ludwig Ritter von Köchel" (in *Österreichische Musikzeitschrift*). 1977.

———. "Ludwig Ritter von Köchel's Verdienste um die Mozartausgabe" (in *Bürgerliche Musikkultur im 19. Jahrhundert in Salzburg*). 1981.

———. "Das Katafalkwappen Ludwig Ritter von Köchels" (in *Wiener Figaro*). 1985.

Bradley, R. W. Herbert. *Brother Mozart and Some of His Masonic Friends.* 1913.

Brassey, Thomas. *Work and Wages.* 1872 and 1873.

Burton-Page, Piers. *Cataloguing Mozart* (reprint of broadcast lecture on BBC). 1991.

Castle, Eduard. *Lenau und die Familie Löwenthal.* 1906.

———. *Mesalliiert—Erzählung aus dem Nachlass von Sophie von Löwenthal-Kleyle.* 1906.

Claudius, Mathias ("Asmus"). *Sämtliche Werke.* 1775–1798.

Crankshaw, Edward. *The Fall of the House of Habsburg.* 1963.

Criste, Oskar. *Erzherzog Carl von Österreich.* 1912.

Deutsch, Otto Erich. "Aus Köchels Jugendtagen" (in *Festschrift Hans Engel*). 1964.

———. *Mozart: A Documentary Biography.* 1965.

Deutsch, Otto Erich, and Cecil B. Oldman. *Mozart-Drucke.* 1931.

Dobner, Walter. "Das Köchel-Haus in Stein" (in *Presse Schaufenster*). 1990.

Duller, Eduard. *Mozarts Feier.* 1837.

Duncker, Carl von. *Feldmarschall Erzh. Albrecht.* 1897.

Eigner, August. "Ludwig Köchel, zu seinem 50. Todestage" (in *Landeszeitung*). 1927.

Einstein, Alfred. *Mozart and Shakespeare's Tempest.* 1941.

———. *Mozart: His Character, His Work.* 1946.

Elvers, R. *Festschrift Albi Rosenthal.* 1984.

Engl, Johann Evangelist. *Das zweite Salzburger Musikfest.* 1879.

———. *Festschrift.* 1891.

———. *In Sachen Mozarts.* 1913.

Freisauff, Rudolf von. *Das erste Salzburger Musikfest.* 1877.

Friedländer, Max. *Mozarts Wiegenlied.* 1892 and 1897.

Fux, Johann Joseph. *Gradus ad Parnassum.* 1715.

Giegling, Franz. "Ludwig Ritter von Köchel. Zu seinem 100. Todestag am 3. Juni" (in *Neue Zürcher Zeitung*). 1977.

Gotter, J. F. W. *Gedichte.* 1787–88.

———. *Schauspiele.* 1795.

Grumbacher, Rudolf. "Einige Gedanken zu Briefen von Ludwig von Köchel an Dr. Josef Hauer" (in *Festschrift Albi Rosenthal*). 1984.

Haberkamp, Gertraut. *Die Erstdrucke der Werke von Wolfgang Amadeus Mozart.* 1986.

Hanslick, Eduard. *Aus meinem Leben.* 1894.

———. "Vom Salzburger Musikfest" (in *Neue Freie Presse*). 1877.

Hase, Helmuth von. *Der kleine Köchel.* 1965.

Hertenberger, H., and E. Wiltschek. *Erzherzog Karl, der Sieger von Aspern.* 1983.

Hildesheimer, Wolfgang. *Mozart.* 1977.

Hiller, Ferdinand. *Felix Mendelssohn-Bartholdy. Briefe und Erinnerungen.* 1874.

Hirsch, P. A. *Katalog einer Mozart Bibliothek.* 1906.

Holmes, Edward. *The Life of Mozart.* 1845.

Hummel, Walter. *W. A. Mozart's Söhne.* 1956.

———. *Die Internationale Stiftung Mozarteum.* 1931.

———. *Nannerl Mozarts Tagebuchblätter mit Eintragungen ihres Bruders Wolfgang Amadeus.* 1958.

Jacob, Heinrich Eduard. *Mozart oder Geist, Musik und Schicksal.* 1956.

Jahn, Otto. *W. A. Mozart.* 1856–9. 1867 and 1889.

Jindracek, Karl B. "Köchelverzeichnis Nr." (in *Wiener Figaro*). 1956.

Kandler, Adam. *Ludwig Ritter von Köchel.* 1947.

Karajan, Theodor Georg von. *J. Haydn in London 1791 and 1792.* 1861.

Kerschbaumer, Anton. *Gedenktafel für Dr. Ludwig Ritter von Köchel.* 1906.

King, Alec Hyatt. *Mozart in Retrospect.* 1955.

———. "Das neue Köchel Verzeichnis" (in *Die Musikforschung*). 1965.

Koch, Richard. *Bro. Mozart, Freimaurer und Illuminaten.* 1911.

Kranner, Eduard. *Antlitz einer alten Stadt—Krems, Ludwig von Köchel 1800–1877.* 1979.

Kuehnel, Harry. *Krems a.d. Donau.* 1962.

Lafite, Carl, and Hedwig Kraus. *Geschichte der Gesellschaft der Musikfreunde in Wien.* 1937.

Landon, H. C. Robbins *1791: Mozart's Last Year.* 1988.

Levi, Leone. *Wages and Earnings of the Working Classes.* 1867.

Longford, Elizabeth. *Victoria R. I.* 1964.

Lorenz, Franz. *In Sachen Mozarts.* 1851.

Lüdemann, W. von. *Leopold Schefers ausgewählte Werke.* 1857.

Maier, Anton. "Ludwig Köchel und das Kremser Gymnasium" (in *Kremser Zeitung*). 1927.

Mandyczewski, Eusebius. *Wien, Kaiserlich-königliche Gesellschaft der Musikfreunde.* 1912.

Mendelssohn-Bartholdy, Felix. *Briefe 1830–1847.* 1861–63.

Minkwitz, Friedrich. *Nikolaus Lenau und Sophie Löwenthal.* 1963.

Müller, E. H. von Asow. *W. A. Mozart. Verzeichnis aller meiner Werke.* 1943.

Müller, Karl Franz. *W. A. Mozart. Gesamtkatalog seiner Werke—Köchel Verzeichnis.* 1951.

Neilreich, August. *Nachträge zur Flora von Niederösterreich.* 1866.

Nemecek, Frantisek Petr (Niemtschek, Franz). *Leben des K.K. Kapellmeisters Wolfgang Gottlieb Mozarts, nach Originalquellen beschrieben.* 1798.

Niebler, Heinrich. "Begegnung mit einem österreichischen Naturforscher. Ludwig Ritter von Köchel 1800–1877" (in *Natur und Mensch*). 1980.

Nissen, Georg Nikolaus von. *Biographie W. A. Mozarts.* 1828.

Nohl, Ludwig. *Musiker Briefe.* 1867.

Nottebohm, G. *Mozartiana.* 1880.

Perger, Richard von, and Robert Hirschfeld. *Geschichte der K.K. Gesellschaft der Musikfreunde in Wien.* 1912.

Pfannhauser, Karl. *Kleine Köcheliana.* 1964.

Pfeiffer, Eduard. *Vergleichende Zusammenstellung der europäischen Staatsausgaben.* 1865.

Pirckmayer, Friedrich. *Zur Lebensgeschichte Mozarts.* 1876.

Pohl, C. F. *Die Gesellschaft der Musikfreunde des Österreichischen Kaiserstaates.* 1871.

Rath, R. John. *The Viennese Revolution of 1848.* 1957.

Rauscher, Heinrich. "Ludwig Alois Friedrich Ritter von Köchel" (in *Das Waldviertel*). 1956.

Rech, Géza. *Ludwig Alois Friedrich Ritter von Köchel.* 1971.

Rehm, Wolfgang. "Nochmals. Ritter von Köchels Verdienste um die 'Alte Mozart-Ausgabe'" (in *Festschrift Rudolf Stephan*). 1990.

Reich, Willi. "Köchels Canzonen zu Mozarts Geburtstag" (in *Österreichische Musikzeitschrift*). 1956.

Reijen, Paul van. "Die Literaturangaben im Köchel Verzeichnis" (in *Mitteilungen der Internationalen Stiftung Mozarteum*, Jg. 30), 1982.

Reusch, Karl Victor. Biographical sketch in the foreword of the second edition of the *Köchelverzeichnis.* 1905.

Riessberger, Helmut. "Von Köchel bis Einstein" (in *Wiener Zeitung*). 1984.

Sadie, Stanley. *Mozart Symphonies.* 1986.

Schiedermair, Ludwig Ferdinand. *Mozart, sein Leben und seine Werke.* 1922.

Schlösser, Rudolf. *Friedrich Wilhelm Gotter, sein Leben und seine Werke.* 1894.

Schmidt, Erna. "Grosse Niederösterreicher: Dr. Ludwig Ritter von Köchel" (in *Der Niederösterreicher*), 1991.

Schöny, Heinz. *Ludwig von Ritter, Ahnen und Sippe.* 1957.

———. "Ludwig Ritter von Köchel" (in *Österreichisches Wappenalmanach*). 1966.

Schrott, Ludwig. "Ein unbekannter Weltberühmter" (in *Zeitschrift für Musik*). 1950.

Schwartz, Boris. "Geiger um Mozart. Eine Marginalie zum Köchel Gedenktag" (in *Neue Zürcher Zeitung*). 1977.

Sittner, Hans. *Kienzl-Rosegger.* 1953.

Smekal, Richard. *Die schönsten Mozart Anekdoten.* 1921.

Smith, G. B. *Life of Her Majesty Queen Victoria.* 1897.

———. *Events of the Queen's Reign.* 1897.

Sonnleithner, Leopold von. "Dramatische und musikalische Literatur: Chronologisch-thematisches Verzeichnis sämmtlicher Tonwerke Amadeus Wolfgang Mozart's. Von Ludwig Ritter von Köchel" (in *Recensionen*). 1862.

Stifter, Adalbert. *Gedichte.* 1848.

Szabolcsi, Bence. *Zenetudományi Tanulmányok.* 1953.

Taylor, A. J. P. *The Habsburg Monarchy 1809–1918.* 1948.

Twdry, K. *Naturalienkabinet.* 1877.

Tyson, Alan. *Mozart Studies of the Autograph Scores.* 1987.

Valentin, Erich. "Hundert Jahre KV" (in *Acta Mozartiana*). 1962.

Waldersee, Paul Graf. *Die Gesamtausgabe der Werke Mozarts.* 1879.

Weinländer, Georg. *Zur Würdigung der von Köchelschen Mineraliensammlung.* 1878.

Wilson, R. *Life and Times of Queen Victoria.* 1887.

Winkler, Otto. "626 mal KV" (in *Wiener Figaro*). 1977.

Wurzbach, Constantin. *Feldmarschall Erzherzog von Carl.* 1885.

——. *Mozart Buch.* 1869.

Wyzewa, T. de, and G. de Saint-Foix. *W.-A. Mozart.* 1912 and 1946.

Zeissberg, Heinrich von. *Aus der Jugendzeit des Erzherzog Carl.* 1883.

——. *Erzherzog Carl von Österreich.* 1895.

Zerboni di Spinossi, August Wilhelm. *Der Orient.* 1868.

Zerboni, Joseph. *Aktenstücke zur Beurtheilung der Staatsverbrechen des süd-preussischen Kriegs- und Domainenraths Zerboni und seiner Freunde.* 1800.

Zöllner, Erich. *Geschichte Österreichs.* 1961.

ANONYMOUS SOURCE MATERIAL

Album aus Anlass der 1050-jährigen Feier der Gründung der Stadt Teschen (Cieszyn). 1860.

A Diary of Royal Movements and of Personal Events and Incidents in the Life and Reign of Her Most Gracious Majesty Queen Victoria. 1883.

Breitkopf & Härtel: A Short History. 1914.

Erinnerungsblätter an Wolfgang Amadeus Mozart's Säcularfest im September 1856. 1856.

Festschrift des Vereins für Landeskunde. 1964.

"Die Gedenktafel für Ludwig von Köchel" (in *Kremser Zeitung*). 1906.

Jahrbuch für Landeskunde. 1868.

"Die Kirchenmusik im Mozart Jahr" (in *Österreichische Musikzeitung*). 1956.

"Köchel Gedenkfeier" (in *Niederösterreichische Presse*). 1906.

"Lebenslauf des Ludwig Ritter von Köchels" (in *Kremser Zeitung*). 1906.

"Ludwig Ritter von Köchel" (in *Kremser Zeitung*), 1950.

"Ludwig Ritter von Köchel brachte Ordnung in Mozarts Musikwerke" (in *Niederösterreichische Lokalzeitung*). 1991.

"Ludwig von Köchels Charakterbild" (in *Kremser Zeitung*). 1906.

Mitteilungen der Gesellschaft für Salzburger Landeskunde. 1861 and 1878.

Mozarteum/Salzburg. Music Festival. 1914.

Salzburg/Mozarteum: Erster Jahresbericht. 1882.

ENCYCLOPEDIAS AND MUSICAL DICTIONARIES

Biographisches Lexikon, ed. Constantin Wurzbach. 1876.

Encyclopaedia Britannica. 1910–11 and 1994.

Everyman's Dictionary of Music, ed. Eric Blom. 1946.

Journal of the American Musicological Society. 1967.

Klassiker: Adalbert Stifter. 1852.

Die Musik in Geschichte und Gegenwart. 1949–51.

The New Grove Dictionary of Music and Musicians. 1980 and 2000.

Österreichisches Biographisches Lexikon. 1815–1950.

The Oxford Companion to Music, ed. Percy A. Scholes. 1938 and 1983.

Index

Adamberger, J. Valentin, 197
Adlgasser, Anton Cajetan, 201
Ahasuerus, King, (Xerxes I of
　Persia), 218
Aigner, Franz, 73
Aigner, Ludwig, 73
Airy, Sir George Biddell, 51
Albert, Prince, 49–51, 201
Albrecht, Archduke, 24, 36, 39–40,
　42, 44, 48, 59, 66, 68–69, 83, 89,
　132–133
Alt, Jakob, 16
Altman, Pater, 167
Ambros, August Wilhelm, 98–99,
　192, 210
André, Carl August, 187, 216
André, Gustav, 193
André, Jean Baptiste, 56, 187
André, Johann, 187
André, Johann Anton, 56, 187, 249
André, Julius, 98, 187
Anna Amalie, Duchess, 218

Bach, Johann Sebastian, 107,
　123–124, 166, 172–174, 191–192,
　215, 236
Bahr, Hermann, 127
Baltazzi-Scharschmid, Baronin
　Paula, 59, 83, 86

Baumann, Karl, 187
Baumgarten, pater Amand, 167
Baumgarten (Paumgarten),
　Comtesse de, 197
Baumgartner, Baron Andreas von,
　38, 127, 141
Beethoven, Karl, 161, 165
Beethoven, Ludwig van, 10, 26,
　63–64, 70, 89, 99, 102, 107, 119,
　123–124, 134, 142, 145, 159–165,
　177, 190, 192, 237, 257
Bell, Alexander Graham, 107
Benard, Johann, 232
Benz, Karl Friedrich, 107
Bergmann, Joseph, 38, 96
Berlioz, (Louis-) Hector, 64, 107
Berthold-Sonnenberg, Frau von,
　195 (see Mozart, Maria Anna)
Biba, Otto, 74, 102, 112, 144–145,
　188, 253
Biberschickr Franz, 80
Bihler, Johann, 38, 127, 141
Bingler, Johann, 38
Birk, Ernst, 75
Bitter, Carl Hermann, 192
Bizet, George, 107
Böhm, (theatrical director), 197
Bolfras, Baron von, 83
Borodin, Aleksandr, 107

Brahms, Johannes, 64, 69, 107, 125, 145, 237–238
Braille, Louis, 105
Braun, prof., 69
Breitkopf, Bernhard Christoph, 237
Brinsechi, H., 196
Brougham, Lord Henry, 106
Bruckner, Anton, 64, 107
Brunell, Isambard Kingdom, 51
Brunswick Count Franz, 63, 159, 258
Buccleugh, James Scott, Duke of Monmouth, 51
Bugeaud de la Piconnerie, Thomas-Robert, 48
Bürger, Gottfried August, 220
Burnacini, Ludwig, 170

Caldara, Antonio, 177
Cambridge, Duke of, 55
Cannabich, Rosa, 196
Carissima (or Carissimi), Giacomo, 178
Castelcicula, Prince, 50
Castle, Eduard, 31–32
Catania, Maria, 179
Caulfield, John, 56, 193
Cerrini, colonel von, 38, 40
Cesti, Cavaliere Marc' Antonio, 170
Cherubini, (Maria) Luigi, 64
Chopin, Fréderic, 107, 145, 190
Christlbauer, I, 83
Chrysander, Friedrich, 192
Claudia, Empress, 180
Claudius, Mathias, 217
Clementi, Muzio, 237
Colloredo von Waldsee and Mels, Count Hieronymus, 149
Colloredo-Mannsfeld, Prince Josef, 149
Cooper, Martin, 134
Cramer, Johann Baptist, 55, 194
Criste, Oskar, 38
Czoernig, Baroness Erny, 83

Daimler, Gottlieb, 107
Dalberg, Johann Friedrich Hugo, 227
Darwin, Charles, 107
Deiters, Hermann, 98
Dejean, H., 197
Deutsch, Otto Erich, 190, 192–193, 198, 201, 213–214, 229, 246
Devonshire, Duke of, 51
Deym, Josephine, 159
Dittersdorf, Carl Ditters von, 227
Donizetti, Gaetano, 64, 107
Draghi, Antonio, 170
du Mont, B. (captain), 48
Duffek, Carl, 77
Duport, Jean-Pierre, 163
Dussek (or Dušek), Franz (Frantisek) Xaver, 237
Dvořak, Antonin, 64, 107

Eberl, Anton, 227
Eichbuchler, Heinrich, 237
Einstein, Alfred, 185, 191, 200, 207, 212, 217, 220–221, 224, 226, 229, 243–253
Eleonore, Archduchess, 174
Ella, John, 55, 193
Eltz-Lodron, Countess Antonia, 39
Enderes, Karl, 150, 152
Endlicher, Stephan Ladislaus, 152
Engels, Baron Friedrich, 105
Engl, Johan Evangelist, 82, 84, 220
Englisch, Ernst, 81
Espagne, Franz, 238, 246
Esterházy, Prince Paul, 49
Eugen, Archduke, 85
Exeter, Lord, 50
Eybler, Joseph von, 64, 179, 230–231

Faber, Marion, 208
Faraday, Michael, 105
Fenzl, Eduard, 152
Ferdinand I, Emperor (of Austria), 39, 41, 43, 60, 104, 179

Ferdinand II (of Naples), 40
Ferdinand III, Emperor(of Austria),
	168, 176
Ferenz, (soprano singer), 233
Feuchtersleben, Ernst, Freiherr von,
	127
Firmian, Count Leopold
	Maximilian, 39, 195
Fischer von Erlach, 127
Fixlmillner, Alexander III, 16, 167
Fixlmillner, Erasmus Anton, 16
Fixlmillner, Maria Ursula, 16
Flammberg, Anna von, (see Count
	Walsegg), 231
Fleischmann, J. Friedrich A.,
	219–220, 222
Flies, Bernhard (or Carl Eduard),
	220–222
Franck, César, 107
Flury, 38
Franz II, Emperor (of Austria),
	34–35, 41, 104
Franz Joseph I, Emperor (of
	Austria), 24, 61, 104, 179
Frederick II (of Prussia), 164
Frescobaldi, Girolamo, 178
Freysauff von Neudegg, Felix, 38
Friedländer, Max, 192, 214,
	218–222
Friedrich, Archduke, 25, 36, 38, 42,
	44, 47–50, 53, 55, 68
Fries, Count Moritz Johann
	Christian, 163
Fuchs, Alois (or Aloys), 100, 174,
	187, 216–217, 225, 249
Fürstenberg, Landgrat Joseph Egon
	von, 25, 58
Fux, Eva Maria, 172
Fux, Johann, 168
Fux, Johann Joseph (or Josef), 5, 16,
	19, 63–64, 68, 99,102, 145, 159,
	166–177, 179, 236, 257–258
Fux, Matthäus, 172
Fux, Peter, 168

Gall, Ludwig, 216
Gallasch, Wilhelmine, 73, 77, 110
Gallina, Friedrich, 38
Gebler, Baron von, 197
Giegl, Maria Theresia, 16
Giegling, Franz, 102, 247
Glinka, Fëdor, 107
Goethe, Johann Wolfgang von, 18,
	127, 145–147
Goldschmidt, Otto, 239
Gombert (Gombertus), Nicolas, 180
Gotter, Friedrich Wilhelm, 147,
	218–220, 222
Grieg, Edvard, 64, 107
Grillet, 51
Grillparzer, Franz, 127, 159
Grünne, Count Karl, 24
Grünne, Countess Zoe, 26
Grünne-Pinchard, Count P. F. W.,
	23–24, 28–29, 33–34

Haberkamp, Gertraut, 184, 190, 214,
	238, 254
Habert, Johann Evangelist, 120
Haddington, Lord, 51
Haffner, Elisa, 196
Haffner, Sigmund, 196
Hafiz (Shams-ud-din-Muhammad),
	134
Hafner, Johann, 76
Haidecki, Alexander, 228
Hamilton, (autograph collector), 56,
	193
Händel, Georg Friedrich (George
	Frederic), 107, 123–124, 166,
	172–174, 191–192, 201, 212, 236
Hanslick, Eduard, 64, 69, 75, 109,
	192
Hansom, Joseph A., 106
Harasofsky (née Scharschmid),
	Theresia, 73, 83
Härtel, Gottfried Christoph, 237
Härtel, jur. Hermann, 239
Hase, Helmuth von, 249

Hasse, Johann Adolph, 177
Hauer, Josef, 120, 186–187, 192, 250
Hauser, Clara, 39
Hauslab, major Franz von, 38
Haydn, Joseph, 10, 107, 119, 138, 172, 186, 193, 206, 226, 237, 253
Haydn, Michael, 172, 198, 201, 243
Hebbel, Friedrich, 127
Helfert, Joseph Alexander, 214
Henkel, Emilie von, 73
Henkel, Heinrich, 187
Henri IV, King (of France), 170
Herbeck, Johann, 179
Herriot, Edouard, 192
Herzog, Anton, 231, 233–234
Hildebrandt, Johann Lukas, 127
Hildegard, Archduchess, 39
Hildesheimer, Wolfgang, 208
Hiller, Ferdinand, 70
Hirsch, Paul, 248
Hirschfeld, Robert, 64
Hoboken, Anthony von, 193
Hoffmeister, Karel, 232
Holmes, Edward, 185–186
Homer, 133, 142
Horace (Quintus Horatius Flaccus), 133, 142
Howard, Leslie, 144
Hübel, Elisabeth, 149
Hufnagel, E., 83,
Hügel, Karl von, 119
Hummel, Walter, 90

Isaak, Heinrich, 180

Jacob, Heinrich Eduard, 228
Jahn, Otto, 11, 62, 81–82, 97, 100–102, 109, 119, 160, 186, 188–189, 192–193, 203, 211, 216–217, 230, 240, 243, 246, 249, 251–252
Jähndl, (chorus master), 226
Jellinek (archivist), 61
Jersey, Lady, 50

Jersey, Lord, 50, 54
Joachim, Joseph, 124–125, 238
Johann Baptist, (brother of Archduke Karl), 39
Jones, colonel, 55
Joseph I, Emperor (of Austria), 63, 167, 170, 258
Joseph II, Emperor (of Austria), 34–35

KalchLerg, Josef, Freiherr von, 38
Kämpf, Sofie, 73
Kapsinger, I. B., 141
Karajan, Theodor Georg von, 98
Karl (Ludwig), Archduke, 23–24, 33–38, 41–42, 44–45, 47–48, 52–53, 55, 58–59, 61, 68, 83, 96, 104, 112, 120, 127, 132, 145, 152
Karl Ferdinand, Archduke, 36, 39–40, 42, 44, 68, 85
Karl VI, Emperor (of Austria), 63, 167, 171, 176, 179, 258
Károlyi, Count Ladislaus, 48
Kennedy, John F., 8
Kerschbaum, pater Maximilian, 121, 173
Kerschbaumer, Anton, 5, 83, 85, 98, 158
Kienzl, Wilhelm, 98
Kiesewetter, Ralph Georg, 192
King, Alec Hyatt, 94–95, 213, 245, 248, 253
King, Robert, 127
Kinsky, Prince Ferdinand Franz Josef, 161–163
Kirkpatrick, Ralph (Leonard), 193
Kleyle, Charlotte, 25, 27, 29–30
Kleyle, Franz Joachim, Ritter von, 24–25, 33, 37
Kleyle, Johanna, 25
Kleyle, Karl, 25
Kleyle, Rosalie, 25
Kleyle, Sophie, 24, 26–32, 92, 110–111, 126, 134

Koblitz, G. M., Ritter von, 69
Koch, Robert, 107
Koch, W. D. Joseph, 152
Köchel, Alexander Franz, 13
Köchel, Heinrich Gottlieb, 13
Köchel, Karoline Susanne Aloisia, 13
Köchl, Georg Gerhard, 15
Köchl, Jill, 81
Köchl, (later Köchel), Johann Friedrich Wenzeslaus Wilhelm ("Fritz"), 13, 20–22, 67, 71, 74, 110, 112, 130, 141
Köchl, Johann Georg (Georg Sebastian Fidelis), 13–15, 22–23, 87, 112
Köchl, Paul, 81
Köchl, Penelope, 81
Köchl, Victor, 81–82, 84, 110
Kögl, Michael, 15
Kögl, Valentin, 15
Kornhäusel, Josef, 36
Kotschy, Theodor, 119, 152, 257
Krüchten (writer on music), 233

Laager, Matthias, 15
Laimegger, Josef, 120–121
Landon, Howard Chandler Robbins, 229, 231, 234, 253
Landsberger (manufacturer), 246
Lange, Joseph, 35
Latrobe, Christian Ignatius, 226
Lebzeltern, major Wilhelm, Ritter von, 38, 48
Lechner, (pater) Gregor, 167
LeGros, Joseph, 224
Lenau, Nikolaus, 32–33
Lenz, Friedrich, 227
Leopold, Archduke, 159
Leopold I, Emperor (of Austria), 63, 167–169, 176, 258
Leopold II, Emperor (of Austria), 33–34
Leutgeb (clerk), 232. *See* Walsegg

Lincoln, Lord, 50
Lingölf, Franz, 41–42, 45
Linkel Josef, 164
Lister, Samuel, 107
Liszt, Franz (Ferenc), 88, 98, 107, 145
Liverpool, Lord, 50
Lobkovitz, Prince Franz Josef, 161–163
Lorenz, Franz, 5, 8–9, 73, 77, 101, 187, 190–191, 193, 217, 227, 236
Lorenz, Joseph Roman, 73, 77
Lorenz, Ludwig, 73
Lothringen, Prince Karl von, 177
Löwenthal, Max, 25, 32
Ludwig Joseph, Archduke, 53, 159
Lützow (Litzow), Countess Antonie, 196

Madersperger, Josef, 106
Malfatti, Johann Baptist, 162–163
Mandorfer, (pater) Alfons, 167
Mandyczenski, Eusebius, 64, 144–145
Marcus, Siegfried, 107
Maria Christine, Archduchess, 34
Maria Karolina, Archduchess, 36, 40
Maria Theresia, Archduchess, 36–38, 40, 48
Maria Theresia, Empress (of Austria), 33, 136, 173, 177, 180
Marianne von Lothringen, 177, 180
Marinovich, lieutenant commander, 48
Marlborough, Duke of, 54
Maroli, Gerd, 4, 79
Marshall, Charlotte, 81–82
Martial (Marcus Valerius Martialis), 133, 142
Martini, (padre) Giovanni Battista, 137, 196
Marx, Karl, 105
Mary, Queen of Scots, 52

Massenet, Jules, 64
Matiegka, Wenzel, 219
Mattheson, Johann, 167
Mayer, Ludwig, 73
Mayer, Philipp, 25, 28–30, 38, 58,
    144–146
Mayreckh, Oswald Jakob, 20
Mazzetti, Wilhelm von, 81, 86, 158
Mazzotti, Vincenzia, 180
Mecklenburg-Strelitz, Princess
    Sophie Charlotte, 195
Medici, Maria di, 170
Melly, Eduard, 5
Mendelssohn-Bartholdy, Felix, 50,
    64, 107, 123, 145, 190, 238
Messen, Count, 69
Messier, Charles, 94
Messmer, Anton, 214
Messner, Joseph, 217
Metastasio, Pietro, 172, 177, 224
Meyerbeer, Giacomo, 56
Mickwitz, Friedrich, 32
Mielichhofer, Mathias, 156
Mikschik, Eduard, 25
Mikschik, Emanuel, 25, 73
Mikschik, Wilhelm, 127, 141
Milder, Anna, 164
Millöcker, Karl, 121
Milm, David, 49
Minato, Niccolo, 170
Mitterhofer, Peter, 106
Mohammed (Muhammad), 133
Mohs, Friedrich, 127, 141, 154–156
Moll, Freiherr Karl Erenbert von,
    257
Monteverdi, Claudio, 170
Moser, Hermann, 173
Mozart, Franz Xaver Wolfgang, 96
Mozart, Karl Thomas, 69, 96, 229
Mozart, Konstanze (Constanze, nee
    Weber), 25, 92, 138, 186–188, 191,
    197, 217, 229
Mozart, Leopold, 4, 16, 87–88, 149,
    185–186, 195–196, 208, 249, 251

Mozart, Maria Anna ("Nannerl"),
    87–88, 186, 195, 208–209
Müllauer, F., 83, 86
Müller, August Eberhard, 227
Müller, Karl Franz, 251–252
Murray (general), 49
Musiol-Sollinger, 21
Musorgski, Modest, 107

Napier, Sir Robert, 52
Napoleon Bonaparte, 35, 54–55, 104
Nassau-Weilburg, Princess
    Henriette, 35–36
Neilreich, August, 21, 111, 149–152,
    258
Neumann, Franz, 16, 69
Niebler, Heinrich, 154
Niemeczek, Franz Xaver, 198
Nietzsche, Friedrich, 107
Nissen, Georg Nicolaus, 186–187,
    217, 219, 229, 241, 249
Nohl, Ludwig, 241
Northumberland, Duchess of, 51
Northumberland, Duke of, 51
Nottebohm, (Martin) Gustav, 109,
    211, 238, 243

Obermayr, (physicist), 233
Offenbach, Jacques, 107
Oldman, Cecil B., 213, 246
Ovid (Publius Ovidius Naso), 133,
    142

Pachta, Count Johann, 211
Paganini, Nicolo, 107
Palestrina, Giovanni Perluigi da,
    171–172, 180
Palmerston, Lord Henry Temple, 47
Pariati, Pietro, 171
Pasquini, Claudio, 172
Pasteur, Louis, 107
Paumgarten (Baumgarten)
    Comtesse de, 197
Peel, Sir Robert, 51

Perger, Richard von, 64
Peri, Jacopo, 170
Pertl, Eva Rosin (Barbara), 4
Pertl, Maria Anna, 4, 229
Pertl, Wolfgang Nikolaus, 4
Petit, Pierre, 80
Peyerl, J., 211
Pfusterschmied, Ritter I von, 230
Philidor, Anne Danicau, 224
Piret, Baron von, 69
Platen-Hallermünde, Graf August, 147
Plath, Wolfgang, 254–255
Plowden, C. W. C., 56, 193
Poe, Edgar Allan, 107
Pohl, C. Ferdinand, 64, 76, 98, 242
Pope, Alexander, 171
DesPrés, Josquin, 180
Prevost, Louis, 232
Prugkh, Arnoldus de, 179
Punto, Giovanni, 224
Pym, Sir Samuel, 49

Raabe, Peter, 247
Radetzky, Field marshal Johann Josef Wenzel, 43, 127, 141
Rainer, Archduchess Marie Caroline, 83, 155
Rainer, Archduke, 69
Rainer zu Harbach, Bruno von, 83
Ramm, Friedrich, 224
Rasumovsky, Count Andrey Kyrillovitch, 163–164
Rauscher, Heinrich, 127
Reichardt, Johann Friedrich, 147, 220
Reijen, Paul van, 213
Reinecke, Carl, 239
Reinhardt, Kilian, 179
Resch, Thomas, 21
Reusch, prof. Carl Victor, 59, 81, 84, 243
Reutter, Johann Adam Karl, 177
Riedel, Friedrich W., 167

Riessberger, Helmut, 212
Rietz, Julius, 239
Rimsky-Korsakov, Nikolai, 107
Rinuccini, Ottavio, 170
Ritter, Peter, 224
Rosenthal, Albi, 253
Rossini, Gioacchino, 64, 107
Rotter, Ludwig, 120
Rubini, Lucia, 179
Rudolf, Archduke, 63
Rudolf Franz, Archduke, 36, 119, 159–165, 257
Rudorff, Ernst, 239

Sachsen-Teschen, Albert von, 34, 36
Sacken, Baron Eduard von, 5
Sadie, Stanley, 202
Saint-Foix, Georges de, 250, 252–253
Salieri, Antonio, 35, 179, 229
Sauter, Anton, 153
Scarlatti, Alessandro, 166, 170
Scarlatti, (Giuseppe) Domenico, 166, 193
Schachtner, Andreas. 229
Schack, Benedict, 212
Schafhäutl, prof. Carl Emil von, 217
Schäffer, Gerhard, 6
Schäffer, Peter, 228–229
Schaller, Cäcilie, 16
Schallhammer, Anton, Ritter von, 153
Scharschmid, Fanny von, 76
Scharschmid von Adlertreu, Cajetan, 58
Scharschmid von Adlertreu, Franz, 8, 23–24, 31, 38–39, 58–59, 67–68, 70, 72, 75, 84, 92, 110–113, 128, 130, 141, 150
Scharschmid, Franz von, 76
Scharschmid, Johanna, 72, 111–112
Scharschmid, Marie von, 59, 75, 111, 128
Scharschmid, Freiherr Maximilian, 67, 72, 110, 112

Schefer, Leopold, 101
Schiedermair, Ludwig Ferdinand,
    246, 254
Schikaneder, Emanuel, 197
Schiller, Friedrich, 145, 147
Schläger, Hans, 123
Schlegel, August Wilhelm, 220
Schlemmer, Wenzel, 165
Schlichtegroll, Friedrich, 220
Schlichtinger, prof., 21
Schloissing, Baron von, 69
Schlösser, Rudolf, 218
Schmidt, (autograph collector), 56,
    193
Schneider, Friedrich, 227
Schnitzenbaum, Juliana Clara, 169,
    172
Schön, colonel Anton, Freiherr von,
    38
Schönstein, Baron Karl von, 25
Schopf, 60
Schroll, Kaspar Melchior, 156
Schröter, Johann, 212
Schrott, Ludwig, 102
Schubert, Franz, 25–26, 64, 76, 107,
    119, 127, 145, 147, 159, 186,
    192–193, 201, 219
Schumann, Robert, 107, 145, 238
Schuppanzigh, Ignaz, 164, 179
Schürer, Paul, 79, 158
Schwartz-Sennborn, Baron, 69
Schweiger, Joseph, Freiherr von
    Lerchenfeld, 159, 162
Sechter, Simon, 205
Sedlaczek, canon Wilhelm, 39
Seiller, Kaspar, Freiherr von, 159
Senn, Walter, 217
Shakespeare, William, 147, 219–220
Sievers, Gerd, 247
Sigismund (archbishop), 186
Sina, Ludwig, 164
Singer, Isaac, 106
Sittner, Hans, 98
Smetana, Bedřich, 108

Smith, Sir Charles, 48
Sohm, prof., 21
Sonnleithner, Leopold von, 63–64,
    98–101, 109, 119, 159, 168, 187,
    242
Sortschan, Johann, 232
Späth, Franz Xaver, 196
Spaun, Joseph, Freiherr von,
    118–119, 258
Speta, F., 153
Spitta, Philippl 192, 239
Sprenger, Paul, 73
Stadler, Anton, 179
Stadler, Johann, 179
Stadler, abbot Maximilian, 187, 205,
    230–231, 234, 249
Stain, Johann Franz Teophil, 4, 14,
    16
Stain (or Stein, Steiner), Maria
    Aloisia Maximiliana Susanna, 13
Stelzhamer, Franz, 127
Stephanie, Gottlieb, (the younger),
    35
Stephenson, George, 105
Sternberg, Countess, 233
Sterneck, Karl, Freiherr von, 122
Stiebar, Baron, 5
Stifter, Adalbert, 127
Stoll, Anton, 83
Stopford, Sir Robert, 47
Strauss, Johann, (father), 43
Strauss, Johann, (son), 64, 108
Stumpf, J. A., 56
Sullivan, Sir Arthur, 108
Süssmayr, Franz (Xaver), 205, 226,
    230–231, 233–234
Swieten, Baron Gottfried van, 201
Sydney, Lord, 50
Szirtes, George, 127

Tchaikovsky, Piotr, 108
Telford, Thomas, 54
Teltscher, Josef, 26
Thayer, Alexander Wheelock, 161

Thieriot, Ferdinand, 98
Thun-Hohenstein, Gräfin Philippine von, 126
Thun, Count, 198
Thun, Count Leo, 126
Trevithick, Richard, 105
Turner (bass singer), 233
Twdry, Konrad, 153
Tyson, Alan, 254

Vacani, Colonel Ritter von Fort Olivo, 38
Valentin, Erich, 102
Vay, Baroness Clemence, 36
Verdi, Giuseppe, 64, 108
Vergil (Publius Vergilius Maro), 133, 142
Victoire, Princess, 195, 209
Victoria, Queen (of British Empire), 49–51, 201
Vivaldi, Antonio, 166
Vogl, Johann Michael, 25

Wagenseil, Georg Christoph, 136, 173
Wagner, Richard, 56, 63–64, 69, 98, 108, 145, 237
Waitz, Georg, 218
Walcher, Ernestine, 73
Walcher, Ferdinand von, 26, 29–30, 73, 83
Walcher-Uysdal, Rudolf, Ritter von, 83, 86
Waldersee, Count Paul, 63, 90, 109, 192, 200, 225, 239–244, 247–248, 250–251
Walsegg, Count Franz von, 231–234
Walter, Bruno, 89
Waterman, Ruth, 144
Weber, Aloisia (or Aloysia), 35, 92, 215
Weber, Carl Maria von, 64, 108
Weinländer, Georg, 155, 157

Weinmann, Alexander, 247
Weiser, Ignaz, 201
Weiss, Franz, 164
Weissenbach, Alois, 165
Wellington, Duke Arthur Wellesley, 50, 54–55
Wendling, Johann Baptist, 224
Werba, Erik, 251
Werner, Abraham Gottlob, 155–156
Werner, Josef, 22
White, Richard, 144
Wichner, J., 83–84
Wieland, Johann Adam, 201
Wilhelm, Archduke, 36, 42, 44, 48, 68–69
Wilhelmine Amalia, Empress, 170
Whittman, Anton von, 23
Wontner, Sir Hugh, 50
Wortley-Montague, Lady Mary, 171
Wüllner, Franz, 239
Wurzbach, Constantin, 101
Wutky, Emanuel, 16
Wutky, Michael, 16
Wyon, William, 54
Wyzewa, Theodore de, 250, 252–253

Zaslaw, Neal, 248–249
Zeissberg, H. von, 34
Zeller, Karl, 121
Zerboni di Sposetti, Eduard von, 71, 110, 112
Zerboni di Sposetti, Franz Joseph von, 71–72, 110, 112
Zerboni di Sposetti, Joseph, 72
Zerboni di Sposetti, Julius von, 71, 72
Zerboni di Sposetti, Karl, 72
Zerboni di Sposetti, Max von, 71–72, 76, 110, 112
Zumsteeg, Johann Rudolf, 220
Zweig, Stefan, 56, 92

About the Author

Thomas Edmund Konrad was born in Vienna, Austria, in 1928. He fled to Hungary with his mother and sister while his father moved to England, after the Anschluss of Austria to Nazi Germany in 1938. His parents reunited after World War II in England, where Konrad also met his future wife, Jutka, a concentration camp survivor. They returned to Hungary only to flee again during the 1956 revolution, acquiring U.K. citizenship in England.

Konrad studied violin and piano as a boy. He has worked as a translator and writer, contributing to *London Musical Events, Musical Europe, Freies Leben,* and *Neuer Weg.* Today he serves as the London correspondent for *Neuer Pester Lloyd,* a Budapest publication. He also had a successful commercial career, retiring early as a company chairman in 1988. He and Jutka have three children and three grandchildren and greatly enjoy a happy family life.